THE MORATORIUM
of Anya

THE MORATORIUM
of Anya

A MEMOIR BY
SHELLEY GLASOW SCHADOWSKY

THE MORATORIUM OF ANYA
a goodlife guide
Published by goodlife guide, LLC
www.goodlifeguide.com

ISBN: 978-0-9833203-2-6
goodlife guide trade paperback / March 2011

Library of Congress Control Number: 2011921994

Library of Congress subject headings:
 1. Schadowsky, Shelley Glasow. 2. Intercountry adoption. 3. Adoptive parents—United States. 5. Adopted children—Ukraine. 4. Adopted children—Russian (Federation).

PUBLISHER'S NOTE: This book is a well-documented memoir based on true events. In order to protect the privacy of certain parties and their families, some names have been changed. All major characters, locations and situations remain authentic. In an effort to abbreviate, some journals, e-mails and events have been condensed or combined and, at times, elaborated upon. The author has made every attempt, through notes and memory, to remain candid and devoted to the honest story.

goodlife guide

www.goodlifeguide.com

For my daughters,
Anya and Katia.
This family and this book were made possible
through their unrelenting courage.

ACKNOWLEDGMENTS

To my husband, Charles, for your unending love and patience throughout all our journeys.

It is through the support of my mother and father that I persevere each day, in all my endeavors. My family has, and always will, remain by my side. I admire all of you for your wisdom and for the bravery to advise me to move in new directions. I love you, Mom, Dad, Greg, Becky, Julia, Ian and Grandma Glasow. Thank you for standing by our sides with encouragement throughout our adoption process.

A very special thank-you to Natasha, the "starfish thrower." You change lives every day. And I want to give special thanks to you for changing our lives. In addition, I want to thank your mother, Tatiana and Sasha and Masha for loving Anya.

For Vladimir, thank-you for keeping the faith.

I would also like to thank my editor, Carol La Valley, a wonderful storyteller, wise writer and dedicated friend, for reading the drafts of this memoir and continually encouraging me to finish my story over the years. My editor, Carole Emma Mathewson, polished this book into a masterpiece. Thank you for helping me find my point of view and making sure every comma had a place. You are a wonderful advisor, and I cherish your words. My editor, Jim Keyworth, for helping me to believe I "am" a writer.

CONTENTS

FOREWORD

*M*arch is certainly a time of passing and reflection for Anya and Katia. Three years of tearing down walls to build our family brought us to a humble toast on a Sunday night. March 15 passed once again—just another day, a festival, a dinner of extended family and friends.

The chiming of the glasses did little to reconcile the memories of our journey. I still felt a weighty chill down my spine, and I smiled, knowing that years and miles separated us from Ukraine. We became a family by adoption on March 15, 2006, in Poltava, Ukraine. Anya and Katia acclimated flawlessly at first sight, even recognized by some with a keen eye. Most strangers would never venture to guess we are a multi-cultural family. The four of us stand fair skinned, light haired and blue-eyed; although it is only through extraordinary courage, that we stand together here in America today.

I distinctly remember the meandering dreams from Katia's achy voice two weeks ago. "Ohhhh, I cannot wait for spring break."

"I'm bored," Katia emphatically boasts.

It is Monday, high noon, and her lip is firmly perched over and crinkled. Spring break fills the house with shrewd cackling and shrieks, cat-fights and giggles, but mostly the former. It would be a desperately long week. Jealousy overcomes me, while Charles kisses my forehead and leaves for the sanity of cubicles and office politics each morning. The radio hesitated to match pitch with the melody of sibling rivalry. I commiserate distinctly before returning to the confines of my dark home office to attempt working.

"Outside!" It was the most I could muster these days.

It is easy to admire the girls in their beauty and brilliance. From the exterior, they appear very similar, having originated from the same place having faced the same challenges of their respective past. Pride is easy to find in their eager spirit. Both are straight "A" students and are no longer in the English as a Second Language (ESL) program. What they have achieved, they earned on their own. Katia, continues to test in Advanced Placement (A.P.) courses, however, she chose to skip a grade instead—yet still tests for A.P. classes. She is determined to be a doctor—only to live in the big house, of course— nonetheless, determined. She placed third in the spelling bee amid all the native-speaking students. It seems to come so easy for Katia. Anya is equally determined. She works very hard to be the best at everything she does, usually with arms crossed in frustration at some point. Anya and Katia are very different, but both decidedly going somewhere—to the top, if they have anything to say about it.

Katia bubbles with energy and confidence, even as I sit watching the family work miracles on our winter-torn yard. Papa can always find Katia by his side. Not the same little girl she was a few years hindsight; just a little more of a burst of everything eccentric. She leaps from the patio door after changing her cool morning attire to her sun-ready threads.

"Don't worry, the Katia is baaaack!" She shouts from the patio while amicably stumbling and catching herself.

She is wearing three-inch wedged heels, pink-patterned flowing shorts and a matching camisole, while stylish Hollywood sunglasses of an enormous size cover her ice-blue eyes and rosy cheeks. Her hair is casually tossed up, arms out and hips swaggered for a short pose. She smiles relentlessly and stumbles off again to pull the best dandelions for her tortoise before Papa gets them with the unforgiving blades of the mower. Half Paris Hilton, half tortoise saint.

Big heart, but, if you ask me, dallying around the whole idea of "what can being a blonde really get me?" She is eleven, which is why I was surprised when she came home last month reaping the rewards of just being beautiful, blonde and ambitious Katia.

"Mama, Leonard bought Katia a yo-yo today!" Anya is quick to report the news first.

Katia beams brightly and flashes her yo-yo from her bright pink backpack.

"Katia, who is Leonard and why did he buy you a yo-yo?" I ask with my eyebrow perked.

"Leonard's her new boyfriend." Anya jibes and snickers.

"Well, at least he knows how to treat a woman!" Katia jousts back with vigor.

I am speechless except for a little smirk. He is only one of about ten boys to suffer a young crush on Katia, so far. Dinner can't arrive quickly enough.

"Katia, why don't you tell Papa about your yo-yo?" Anya and I glance with a grimace at one another, certain of Papa's interest in any new suitors.

Anya is 14. Certainly I could write a novel concerning the trials of suddenly becoming the mother of a teen. Nonetheless, we bond, we debate, we fight—and I win. My own mother says it's a viscous cycle, which she bestowed upon me. Anya is still so much of a puzzle to me, I enjoy the mystery of her endearing passions, all the while irked by her unpredictability. She has an untimely beauty and the blue eyes of crystals, appearing, on the outside, so much like her sister; although Anya is unwilling to ever be confused with a tomboy. Anya is careful to maintain the standards of Ukraine, where people dress as if they are society's elite, and never show defeat. Anya would never be caught in a Hurley T-shirt and sandals, unless comparably embellished with "bling." She walks with confidence in four-inch heals and doesn't look a day under eighteen. She is Daddy's little girl and worst nightmare. However, there is never mention of a suitor—nobody is suitable by Anya's standards. Trouble does have a way of finding her around school. It's the age of flirtation by rudeness and lack of responsibility before anyone would own up to their actual feelings. And, naturally, she is made fun of for her distinct Russian accent, to which she will cursorily retort with her sharp wit. I taught her that, I'm afraid.

I suppose everyone trivially tries to define the word normal when it comes to family. I look around at others and know we are nothing like them. I suppose I am old-fashioned. I learned how to parent Ukrainians from watching Ukrainians and listing to Ukrainian friends in a hierarchal society, and then, there is my mother.

The girls had come here with nothing. My husband and I have learned much and try to keep things real—level-headed, so to speak. My daughters don't have iPods, laptops or cell phones. They don't wear mini-skirts and painted-on jeans. They know respect when it looks them in the eye, and they know it is something you earn—without soap in your mouth and a good spanking. But, again, we did tear down walls to build our family. True happiness does not come without winning a war of many battles. The girls still like to remind me of the things their friends have, mostly acquired from their bitter battlegrounds of divorce. I have little to say to Katia. She breezed into our lives, but I still cry each time I read excerpts from her school journals.

"The best day of my life was the day I was adopted and got a family…." Her conclusions are, of course, witty and everything Katia. "… my family feeds me and buys me pink shoes."

Anya does not write in journals, she does wear her heart on her sleeve. I understand Anya, and her sheltered nature. It was not too long ago that Anya and I stood side-by-side against the world with guns leveled to secure her right to be in America. I had sacrificed everything for the love of a daughter I barely knew, resisted arrest and returned half-way across the world in our struggle to find ourselves, find each other, find home and finally become family. Anya's moratorium in Ukraine makes her story special.

THE NEST 1

*J*ronically, motherhood was never a badge I had planned to wear, much less traveling an extraordinary path to become one. I thought, if ever a mother, I would enter motherhood accidentally. With that said, I would also venture to guess that my adoption story does not begin like most, with miscarriages, in-vitro and spending years in and out of state-of-the-art hospitals for the latest in fertility treatments. Nor did I spend endless nights trying new yoga tricks in attempts for the latest conception technique, not that it wouldn't have been fun. Honestly, a baby was just not on the agenda. My husband, Charles, was humble in his opinion, being the eldest of ten and from a less fortunate family. Ten was a lot of mouths to feed, and food lead to process and elimination disposal, aka diaper duty for the eldest siblings. Charles had done his fair share of baby duty until his nearest B-line into the Army. He remained content with my hands-off policy, but like any man, he would have been honored to carry

5

on his name. Charles and I have been together since 1999 and were content with our family of two.

My destiny was always creative and spirited. I always thought I was meant to mother the earth. A mother, in any real sense of the word, to be honest, terrified me. I had a limited perspective of children and babies. Babies were simply "breakable." I went on to college as a professional student, enchanted by the mysteries of the world and all living creatures that inhabited it. I wanted to learn, travel and explore cultural differences and assert my opinion— when needed. Whether it was politics, animal rights or women's welfare, I felt a need to "be the cause," donating what little income I had to whatever poli-fur-peta-women shall rule the planet effort, when envelopes flooded the mailbox during the holidays. If I had ten dollars to give, I was certain, somebody needed it more than I. After I married Charles, I felt more fortunate, the causes around me somehow seemed more desperate, and donations corresponded with my paychecks—although certainly never as big as my imagination. Not surprisingly, I was drawn to marketing.

Charles and I helped, where help was needed. Our first attempt at really touching someone's life on a personal level was an attempt to host a foreign exchange student from Germany, Nadia. After our applications were accepted and the agency notified Nadia, we quickly learned, we lived in a narrow-minded, school district that practiced a strict, four-students-per-school lottery each year when it came to foreign exchange students.

Upon confronting the superintendent of the Gilbert Unified School District, he stated, "We aren't given enough funds for our own kids, let alone foreigners!"

I was appalled. "These funds are my tax dollars, too!" I argued reasonably.

They would not give in to their bias resistance. My contention grew as I thought back to my high school years and all the foreign exchange students I had befriended. They certainly were not a strain on the school, but an education in life that cannot be taught in any classroom or book. We were forced to dash Nadia's hopes and turn back on our approved application. Charles and I were saddened by the opportunities we were not allowed to provide Nadia in our close-minded world. My hope continued to fuel the fight for Nadia throughout the summer as the deadline passed.

Ironically, surprises came quickly in our family as we suddenly ended up with a foreign exchange student of a different kind, when Charles' sister arrived from Indiana. Any small town was foreign to me.

My first attempt at parenting began in my mid-twenties with an eager and albeit extroverted attempt to reform Charles' second youngest sister, Tiffiny, into an upstanding college grad, like myself, in an "I'm-all-that" diva mentality. Determined and eager to warp the young girl's mind, I convinced Tiffiny, my fifteen year-old sister-in-law, to come out from her humble situation in Indiana and venture toward college in Arizona. It was a hard sell for Charles to allow anyone from his past back in our lives after a few stints of visitors on the gravy train, fleeing in the night on a quest for nowhere with one last eight-ball and a few of Charles' prized belongings to live on. I convinced him Tiffiny was different. "She has potential to be anything." I was excited, with my optimistic blue eyes—something Charles never could dissuade. Tiffiny was a little harder to persuade, with her future cubed and quartered within the limits of her small town. I suppose for a young girl who had not seen outside her small town, perhaps the Phoenix metropolis could be daunting.

"C'mon, it's just a big ol' desert with opportunity," I pleaded.

Tiffiny arrived, looking freshly powdered, out of airport security, with stuffed animals in tow. It was 115 degrees in

7

Arizona. Charles and I both shook our heads and gazed with our mouths wide open, as we headed toward the nearest drug store for sun block.

"Do they make SPF 100?" Charles asked with a shrug.

At 17, Tiffiny had finally come to live with us. Her transition was not easy, coming from questionable circumstances, mostly brought on in part by their stepfather, which Charles had managed to escape with just a sliver of overlap en transit to the Army, yet enough to know never to return. So, childlike and emotionally stunted, Tiffiny carried herself like a 12-year-old in some solemn respects. Like no other girl of 17 who I had met, she had not driven a car, nor did she have the desire to do so. I was constantly flooded with surprise—ah, challenges.

Tiffiny flourished with us, although she was not as naive as we had feared she might be. She managed to turn her hardships into determination over time. Lies, deceit and neglect had smothered her years. Charles granted her closure in the truths of her past, allowing her to bridge the gaps of her troubled youth into a metamorphosis of a young lady. The years passed with lessons learned, diplomas earned, coasts traveled, a good job and a thriving college life at Le Cordon Bleu Scottsdale Culinary Institute. We were delighted to watch her radiance, and she spread her wings into a beautiful butterfly. And, somehow, she kicked the diva right out of my self-righteousness. I was now approaching my thirties with a teenager in tow.

The hot Arizona sun blanked me as I stretched across the porch swing reading. It was a perfect Saturday in April, with an ice tea and my *Marie Claire*. The freshly cut grass swirled in the air and tickled our noses as the beagles, Sierra and Bella, chased the gnats. Charles finished zigzagging across his lawn canvas. The day seemed pleasantly normal. I suppose, to me normal was boring with Tiffiny in check and self-absorbed in her own life now.

I flipped the pages from fashion trends to an article on Chechnyen women. *Marie Claire* had a distinct way of giving me a wake-up call. I read more, completely void of the larger scope of reality I was acutely aware of in my formidable college years. Tiffiny peeked her head from the patio door to say good-bye as she set out for work. As I continued to read, the fact occurred to me that our existence is randomly determined by our birthright. We are provided or denied opportunity based on our nationality, our skin color, sex, race, religion, and even whether we were born in an impoverished small town or big city slums. I watched Tiffiny disappear en route to work.

A 17-year-old Chechnyen girl had been raped, tortured and murdered for being nothing more than Chechnyen. I thought of Tiffiny back when she had been 17, pale-faced and scared.

Tiffiny's life with Charles and me was an inspiring time of growth for all of us. But, ultimately, her heart would call her home to the Midwest after graduation. We were torn to see her go, although I always knew Tiffiny was never my girl and I could not change her fundamental heartbreak from the Midwest. I did my best to help her learn, all the while finding my natural place as a big sister.

Tiffiny's absence left me restless. I had felt a sense of responsibility for so long. It seemed silly to feel such loss. I ached for something? I was 30, with empty-nest syndrome.

Time had passed, and I could not shake the face of the young Chechnyan girl. There was little hope for those in such a war-torn country. Nobody was going in, and nobody coming out alive. With a need to understand, I kept researching until I found a world of other girls, lost girls with hope, through international sponsorship and hosting programs in Russia and nearby eastern European countries—an opportunity for people like us to sponsor orphans

9

thousands of miles away with anything from food and clothing to college funds. Somewhere along my passionate "clicking" on the Internet, I found myself researching an application to host two Russian orphans, Sveta and Ana.

Charles, always supportive and ever enduring, came home to my pile of photos and my well-prepared proposal to host Sveta and Ana for the summer. Naturally, I knew he would be as excited as I had become after our lost hopes to host Nadia several years back. There was a silent understanding toward our drive to host Sveta and Ana during the summer. Both of us began talking about what life would be like with teenagers around again. I was terrified and excited to invite them into our lives. I had fallen for Sveta's beautiful brown eyes and long brunette hair. She was 15 and would "age-out" the following December.

Aging-out is a terribly sad process in which orphanages put children over the age of 16 onto the streets to find their way in Eastern Europe. There is no social welfare or support system. Ana on the other hand, was only eleven, with blonde hair and blue eyes, she had more time.

Casually, the what-ifs began, "What if they don't have a family? What if we fall in love with her or them? Would we, could we, adopt?" We asked ourselves.

Gulp. It was a little word with vast complications and huge meaning.

THE WEB 2

*L*ittle did we know of the demons that lurk on the Internet in the international adoption world. As we delved more deeply into the hosting agency, we found illegal practices, false promises of available children and FBI investigations. I was quick to act. I called my contact, Viola, immediately, inquiring about such accusations and the availability of Sveta and Ana for hosting, and maybe, well maybe, I said it—"adoption?" From that day forward, I never heard from Viola again, and I read later that they, too, had been shut down in an FBI crackdown for fraudulent adoption practices.

I quickly discovered the Internet was a glorious database for knowledge and finding adoption contacts. However, it is the wrong place to fertilize these particular dreams. It is all too easy and desperate to keep falling for those you could not save. Continuing to closely follow sponsorship and adoption organizations on the Internet news boards, watching as more agencies were shut down

11

by the FBI, my heart felt a loss for Sveta and Ana. They may or may not even exist. They may be modeling photos of Russian girls for marketing international adoption agencies. They may even have families, or some could have been adopted years before. These are the realities I started to question each day in our research. I became cautious to never let our hearts fall for a photo listing again. Yet, somehow, we consider ourselves lucky that we were only caught up in dreams and putting a room together for the girls, although I read about many others who had spent thousands of their adoption money on these agencies, only to watch the agencies flee, leaving families childless and financially devastated.

After mourning the false reality of Sveta and Ana, I continued to research the elusive world of international hosting and the possibility of adoption. There were hundreds of faces and stories of children who needed the world, and I wanted to give each of them just that. I discovered this was a confusing world of hopes, dreams and potentially ultimate despair if fallen into the wrong hands. There are state agencies, international agencies, licensed international agencies and religious agencies—where you must be devout and practicing, which we were not. In foreign countries, there are facilitators and translators, who can legally act as facilitators, not to mention the elusive ex-KGB agents who make things happen in dark alleys, at a cost. With so much who's who going on online, we decided against joining a church or the KGB. We would only align ourselves with a nonprofit or reputable humanitarian organization.

Charles and I deliberated in evening discussions each day about what I had found. The conversations became like the last drop of coffee on a caffeine binge, with never enough in our cup of knowledge. We knew then that our feelings had surpassed our need to provide an educational and loving experience for orphans. We needed to find them homes and families—our family, and a loving forever.

It was May 2, 2005, when the word "forever" shifted from word into actions. From that day forward, we knew our compass was pointing in the general direction of the former Soviet Union—with Charles' Slavic heritage and the memory of a Chechnyen girl from the story I had read. On May 16, 2005, we submitted our application to become adoptive parents with our small but reputable international and humanitarian agency.

Scott was our adoption coordinator. He called on a Sunday apologizing for the delay in his response. I wasn't sure what to think at first—we had just submitted our application the day before. He explained his overwhelming delight at seeing our request for two older daughters. He went so far as to clarify our paperwork was not submitted with an error. We had decided upon two daughters between the ages of eight and 15. It was an easy decision for us after nurturing Tiffiny, teenagers just seemed the natural choice and we knew nothing about babies.

"I have become numb to the repeated requests for infants and children under two," he explained.

I felt sympathetic toward those on the infertility track. I had friends running marathons there. I understood immediately what he meant as I had learned all too well the statistics for children who age-out of orphanages at age 16. It seemed to me Scott continued to ask me questions mostly out of curiosity, almost amazed at my very existence. Why did we have no preference in hair color or eye color? More importantly, how could I so easily accept minor medical conditions in the children we were to adopt?

Medical abnormalities were of little concern, having learned that most Eastern European medical conditions could easily be treated here in America, some simply with medication or outpatient surgery. They are conditions, treatments, malformations that are unheard of any longer in this country, simply because our society eradicated the prevalence through prevention, medication, treatment at birth and even during pregnancy, through DNA manipulation. Sadly, so many adoptive parents felt they should get what they pay for in a sense of pre-selection by adoption. Unfortunately, it's the children who were unable to choose their circumstances or their families.

Scott's shock was understandable, but my research had given me the knowledge to see past what many of the other pre-adoptive parents could not. I, too often, wondered why the online support groups were flooded with families calculating their risks of adopting a blue-eyed, blond-haired cherub, wanting a family resemblance. Many couples considered themselves unable to care for medical abnormalities—because they were, shockingly, another two-income family. Some days, I had wanted to respond, "Welcome to the club, capitalist America. We all work here. Why should your child be perfect?" Post upon post, requesting their adopted child must be at least 12, 18, 24 months younger than their three-year-old toddler, in order for him to rule the domain—in reference to the hottest new psychological book on parenting which they had read. I often wondered, if the orphans had been given the right to choose their destiny, would they choose such self-pretentious families. Family is about compromise. Does a family that is unable to conceive the moment they begin planning love their child any more or less than the child who arrives after years of obstacles? I would think not. I often wondered what such families would do if their adoption process were anything but perfect, took longer than three weeks or had, oh, a few setbacks?

I did not want to be that judgemental couple, and I began avoiding the who's who that inevitably broke out in name calling board banter. One thing was certain, we were not that couple, and we're also not adopting for "normal" reasons, I suppose, either, so I tempered my opinionated self not to judge. I had not walked in the shoes of a childless mother, desperate to hold a baby. I had not

14

spent fortunes on in vitro-fertilization and insemination procedures. I did have friends who had, and, admittedly, I never related or truly understood.

Regardless, I was excited to talk to Scott, too. I had suffered my own losses—first with our almost foreign exchange student, Nadia, and, of course, Sveta and Ana. And thus far it had been impossible to get any information out of most agencies until our $200 application fee had cleared the bank. Scott never seemed interested in the money. It was always about the kids when we talked. After our thorough conversations to gather our expectations, Scott was both eager and quick to suggest a sibling group he knew in Kazakhstan. The children he spoke of were 14 and 12—Natalia and Nina, respectively.

For the first time in the process, with the guidance of Scott and the reality of Natalia and Nina, I felt a newfound sense of hope. I anticipated photos from Scott and more information about the girls.

"Ding," I opened the e-mail in a state of disbelief. They were beautiful and they were real. I printed the photos and beamed with excitement when Charles arrived home. It was like my own personal ultrasound to hang on the fridge. After Charles and I spent the evening studying the elusive country of Kazakhstan, I propped the photos on my nightstand and fell asleep gazing at Natalia and Nina, amazed by their existence, with dusty, dark blonde hair and sultry blue eyes. They were looking into the camera with smiles. I couldn't help wondering if they were hopeful at that moment. Did they know someone was thinking of them now? It was a peaceful feeling when I awoke. I felt determined and started our long road paving with paperwork.

In the days that followed, breathing seemed a little harder as we waited for information from Scott and his contacts in Kazakhstan. I grew fearful at the mention of an elder brother to

Natalia and Nina. Scott's liaison says he was 16, and unadoptable, at his age. We were told someone from the agency would travel to the orphanage soon, and that we would learn more at that time. In the meantime, Scott e-mailed pictures from their orphanage in Petroprovlask. I cried.

The blue and white tiles were cracked and broken from the walls and floors and mold filled the squares where the textiles had been. The rusty painted pipes wrapped themselves around the room, I imagined the cold running water swirling through the rusted sinks where porcelain had been. There were no mirrors where their tiny faces should reflect. The bedrooms were lined with tiny beds made from planks of coated plywood and a single pillow, like a dollop of whipped cream at the top. The blankets were thin and torn, below an open window surrounded by peeled blue walls over damp concrete. I knew my expectations could never have painted this in my mind. I had never been to Eastern Europe, where Natalia and Nina called home.

Following the photos, I received a phone call from Scott. He shared with me that the girls spoke no English other than "hello" or "thank you"—words they had picked up from other adoptive families and, mostly, from missionaries visiting the orphanage. I was told most children learn English within four to six months after coming to America. I was amazed. He continued, explaining the girls were placed in the orphanage due to neglect and, more often than not in such cases, from extreme poverty. Abuse is rarely a cause in these countries. Although drugs and alcohol are epidemic, poverty is the root of despair, he told me sadly. I could love them, no matter their circumstance. I continued overlaying the photos with my former views on poverty. Sadly, I knew such images of frosty decay and mold, were indicative of a better life than where they had started. This was a heavy blow.

I dreamed night and day of bringing Natalia and Nina to America, hoping for a beautiful life here, sheltered from such surroundings.

Bad news traveled home as Scott brought word back from Petroprovlask. Our girls did have a brother. He was six, not 16. The children could not be separated, not that we would have considered such a measure; but three children were much too large an undertaking for us, nor could we be approved for so many children with the size of our modest home. A clerical error had once again smashed our dreams for the two daughters. I displayed their photo for another week, hoping it was a mistake.

I have learned not to build our what-ifs and dreams of tomorrow by planting roots on rocky foreign soil. The repeated heartbreak began to feel like its own breed of miscarriages, hidden behind the infamous Iron Curtain.

Even in the most honest of situations, people and agencies, there are no certainties in international adoption. My story is not all that dissimilar from hundreds of others. Some, sadly, had already adopted and later learned they had left siblings behind due to these all to common clerical errors. Clerical errors stem from a lack of finances to support basic technology. Most Eastern European regions don't have any methods other than hand-written forms to track thousands of children through courts and orphanages. Many siblings are separated, by age and errors, before they even enter the orphanages.

I ached, but once again I forced myself to move on. Scott began trying to find other girls for our family, but I was cold and closed off to hearing about them. It was then, after so many lost hopes, we decided to adopt from Ukraine. Ukraine practices a no-preselection policy. We would never see another photo or hear another child's story. Charles and I would travel blind to Ukraine and meet only available children, in person, upon our arrival. I felt certain this was the best way to shield my shattered heart. Scott hurt for us, too, and was understanding and supportive of our decision. Scott would help us proceed with their Ukraine program by the end of June.

As the mysteries of blind adoption began to entwine with my American life of marriage and job, I began to lean on the support of Internet adoption groups again to keep me believing.

While things were progressing, in the adoption world, time was spent mostly in waiting. Waiting is a daunting feeling of catch-and-release, with one's daily affirmations of hope and disappointment. News from Kyiv brought day after day of wasted tomorrows. When granted a task, we dutifully rushed to file paperwork and FedEx it to its destination of—delay. We then waited for the next step in the eternal itinerary of qualification events in what was to become our official adoption gauntlet—timeline.

A timeline, when possible, usually begins with a home study, consisting simply of a life novel, six references and, of course, another application and fee; then, waiting for the two home interviews. I dreaded the social service-type evaluation. I am unsure if it was because I had never been a mother, nor had I ever spent my life dreaming about being a mother. Was that required for motherhood? I wasn't a baby-obsessed, mini-van driver. Would they see through me? I reviewed in my head the application we had submitted the previous May, wondering if I had somehow answered the survey questions correctly.

What characteristics were we willing to accept from our child?

Bedwetting? "Yes."

History of Abuse? "Yes."

Rape, incest, bad grades, profanity, sleep walking? "Yes, Maybe, Yes, Yes, Yes."

However, I found myself stuck on question 21. Will you accept a child who starts fires? Hmm? "No."

Would we be condemned? After all, isn't it normal to have some limits?

The interviews were a lot less terrifying in reality. They were really a simple evaluation of our ability to provide for children and, more or less, the agency's chance to explore their curiosity of the multi-faceted parts of our life and lifestyle. We lay down some hefty fees to pass "Go." At this point, the financial expectations were still on a vast sliding scale. During that time, we also submitted our I-600a application to Bureau of Citizenship and Immigration Services, aka BCIS, with more hefty fees, and we waited. Eventually, BCIS would contact us via snail mail with an appointment date and time for fingerprinting to procure our background check and small fees; and try not to go to "Jail!" Assuming all is good, we then waited for our 171H from BCIS, meaning Immigration says it's okay to adopt foreigners through the steel gates of homeland security. We also waited for our home study summary. However, living in Arizona we had to wait for a judge to review and approve us for adoption, meaning return to "Go" and wait two months longer than in 48 other states.

Having become fluent in the abbreviatory terms, it felt almost like entering a new form of military sect. To sum it all up, we, my DH (Dear Husband) and I were officially PAPs (Pre-Adoptive Parents) who just filed a HS (Homestudy), waiting to file a I-600a with the BCIS (Bureau of Citizenship and Immigration Services) and receive a 171h, so our children could receive an A (Alien Resident) number at the USEMBKB (U.S. Embassy Kyiv Borispol) and enter the good ol' US of A.

With that accomplished, in a stoic effort to better ourselves for our future daughters, or maybe just to pass idle time, we found it best to enroll ourselves in Russian 101 at the local community college. How hard could that be? I quickly remember why I hated college so much in the first place as we scuttled into our acrylic

19

classroom with avocado walls. The professor was bulky and tall, and he shuffled through his books without speaking. I wondered if he was Russian, and if he had an accent? For those few minutes of his lingering silence, okay, I was intrigued.

It turned out he was not Russian or remotely culturally inspiring at all, having had only a stint of post-graduate studies in what used to be Leningrad, also known most recently as St. Petersburg. We continued to attend our language classes twice a week, for what we quickly realized were a half language course and, sadly, half-time warp for our professor, who was obviously unable to transcend his college years. His incessant talk about blonde Russian girls was terrifying, as I thought of our soon-to-be daughters. I negated to ever disclose our purpose for attending class due to my complete discomfort in his lustful degradation of the young Eastern European women we were trying to help.

I learned little except a few phrases, how to pronounce several women's names properly by nickname and patronymic—in a scary pedophile sort of way after too many lingering stories. In addition, we learned a few social taboos. There's a walking taboo that you may be considered crazy, or insane, for smiling at others on the street. And, watch for falling vodka bottles on sidewalks below apartment buildings. I seriously wondered if the events were in direct correlation to our professor.

Decidedly, we would not attend Russian 102; besides, we had hoped to travel by the end of following semester, therefore, justifying our decision to nix more of his stories.

In rapid succession, September arrived, when we received news of our homestudy approval, and the report and court documents followed by mail a few days later. It was a wonderful feeling of success. I was delighted to share the news with my online buddies who were embarking on the same adventure.

Having arrived home from Rhode Island after attending my brother's wedding, and following a quick trip to New York, we found our 171H two weeks later in the towering pile of mail from hold at the post office. However, news online from Ukraine left me in tears as I opened my golden ticket to the final step of submitting our request to adopt from Ukraine. Along with our request for permission to bring two of theirs home, Ukraine was not feeling so gracious. September 19, 2005, the National Adoption Center in Ukraine (NAC) would announce a "moratorium." In Eastern Europe, moratorium, was a complex word for a long, undefined period of waiting. During the moratorium, they would no longer accept dossiers from U.S. citizens, including many other countries, until further notice. The anxiety traveled fast through the circles of the adoption world that morning as I wept over my heap of unopened mail. Our agency remained optimistic and urged us to follow through with our dossier preparation and submission.

"Moratoriums are part of the process," Scott said, reassuring us. "They do this every year to catch up."

As we received the ever-evolving pile of current paperwork that would become our dossier, I diligently performed the tasks required, despite the moratorium. Form upon form would need to be completed, notarized and apostilled, a notarization, at the state level. Medical visits were to include HIV and syphilis tests. Contracts and agreements were executed to agencies, facilitators and governments agreeing upon fees and terms, and, naturally, holding no one responsible should Ukraine not provide any children for referral. Intimidating, yes; deterring, no!

By month's end, we notarized 22 forms, times two, for a duplicate set in the event we adopted two unrelated children or found ourselves in a region that required a separate dossier for each sibling. After notarization and forty-four apostilles later, I scanned every page for our records (well into the hundreds) into my travel laptop. It took two days to e-mail all of the scanned documents to Scott for proofing and translation to Ukrainian.

The agency found we had not included a state criminal clearance—only a city clearance with a notarized letter from the state, which cited it was against Arizona law to provide such information. This would not be acceptable to Ukrainian officials. I turned to an online friend in Arizona, who at the time was in Ukraine struggling with her adoption during the moratorium and changing laws. Her agency provided me with guidelines to submit for an FBI criminal clearance for all state levels that would be acceptable. So we found ourselves being fingerprinted again and paying a large fee for four original sets of prints to send off for processing in Virginia. I sent the prints via FedEx and waited. Amazingly, my letter pleading for a speedy return was answered. The FBI came through in 10 days instead of the usual three to six weeks.

Mid-October rolled into fall, we were finally ready, and mailed our two original dossiers to Ukraine for translation by our facilitators. I cautiously mark "Priceless Documents" all over the shipping form, explaining to the kid at the counter that there was no possible way he could replace the six months of government documents contained in the envelope. His blank stare, under his pierced eyebrows, convinced me to ship the packages over two separate days, "Overnight," and wait for Scott's confirmation of receipt before returning to the pack-and-ship "should we lose it, it's not our fault" store.

It was back to waiting, as the moratorium left everyone hopeless, hopeful and making accusations. The Internet support group became deceitful, with stress levels and emotional tidal waves flooding our Web haven. Tensions became high, and e-mails became a systematic genocide of religious, cultural, national fault and blame as to why we were being kept away from our future sons and daughters. The negativity became overwhelming. I chose to step back to a daily digest-and-sift-through-the-hate for some good news, any news, from the other side of the world. Certain of one thing, I have come to loathe the word "moratorium" and the eternal meaning of "whenever" which it concludes.

Late fall had brought a chill of loneliness, as my support group had all but fallen wayward to the pains of their own sorrows. There seemed to be no one left to point my spirits in the general direction of the sun. Again, finding myself left to my own resources, I returned to the original idealism that I felt about Petroprovlask, Kazakhstan. Though it was not meant for me to nurture and mother Natalia and Nina, did that mean I could not help orphans living in dire circumstances. I begin looking into Ukrainian charities, nonprofit and reputable, of course.

It was late October when, guarding my expectations, I discovered sponsorship again. I then became the proud sponsor of Aliona in Borzna region, Ukraine. Being a sponsor meant making a small monthly donation and sending a CARE package to my "angel." Included with sponsorship, the charity made a monthly trip to the orphanage to deliver packages and take photos of our angels, true to their titles. They were then asked to write a thank-you letter that was translated and e-mailed. Aliona was 14 years of age, and she had an amazing smile amidst her impoverished surroundings, not all that dissimilar to the photos ingrained in my memory of Petroprovlask. Borzna had the same quality of condemnation and despair, with rust and mold breeding in the walls and an outcry for donations toward coal, or they might suffer another winter without heat. I distinctly remembered the word "another." Aliona's story was heartwrencching, and occasionally my mind began to wander against the promises I had made to myself. I knew I could help beyond my $10 contribution and a monthly package of clothing and necessities, although these things were like diamonds and gold to Aliona.

I was forever changed when I read Aliona's first letter. I am accustomed to seeing American children throwing tantrums in stores if they cannot have the newest gadget marketed through their overly fixated, televised, sugar-infused minds. Needless to say, we in America have a different sense of reality when it comes to needs and wants, and differentiating the two. I suppose I expected a sullen girl with little expectations. I was prepared to cheer Aliona up and let her know there was an entire world out there for her to conquer, and that I was here to support and guide her to a better life, maybe?

Her first letter shocked me. Aliona was joyful, exciting and hopeful, and she inspired me! She taught me there was more on the other side of the world than I could yet see or imagine.

Aliona was constantly on my mind as I continued to support her and watch her grow, through photos and her letters. I was addicted. I spent hours writing to her in Russian and trying to check and recheck my translations from the little I had learned in my not-so-Russian 101 class. I loved the adrenaline of meeting Aliona's needs and sending her things across the world in time for the charity's monthly visits to the orphanage. If I could help her, how could I not help more?

Shortly after I started sponsoring Aliona, I also began sponsoring Maryana, who was a ten-year-old social orphan with a mother who visited and loved her but could not care for her. I built many incredible relationships with other sponsors and charity organizations. My new family was the release I needed as I waited for my own daughters. I began to wonder if the children I was to adopt could come from Borzna, as I cautiously fell in love with all the beautiful faces.

The word "blind" becomes questionable and a fuzzy gray boundary. Weary, I am lured into the possibilities that maybe my Aliona could be my daughter. Although Ukraine may be blind when it comes to adoption policies, there are loopholes and sponsorships and hosting qualify. I learned, you can "meet" your child in Ukraine through person or referral, which means if you or someone you know has traveled before you and refers a child to you by name, you can request that child and avoid the blind adoption process. However, there are no promises, and the Adoption Center will not "hold" children for anyone. I began to analyze my risk, as less than two percent of adoptions involve children over the age of eight. Sadly, I doubted that anyone would come for my Aliona.

I attached to Aliona differently. My heart was still frozen from all the other daughters that could have been. I realized I was no different than all the mothers who have bestowed their hearts on artificial fertilization, as I lined up and counted the names of my "almost" daughters in my life's Petri dish: Nadia, Sveta, Ana, Natalia and Nina. I made a point to resist making Aliona one of them.

In the meantime, people I had met sent me a few photos online through my new online support group for older Ukrainian children. I tried to remember my focus, to restrain myself and continue to resist filling the Petri dish again.

Time changed everything with Aliona as our friendship blossomed over the next few months. I could no longer not justify denying Aliona's only chance for a home. I realized in all my pain that, despite my series of previous online miscarriages, she had more to lose than I. I could break and I could pick up the pieces, Aliona had no one. I cracked and inquired about her adoption status. Every photo I saw of my angel had a heartbeat. The words from Aliona's letters spoke to me in a whisper as I lay sleepless across nine time zones in anticipation of hope.

It was from Aliona herself that I discovered she was unadoptable. She had an aunt who had custody of her and who lived with her eldest sister, a hairdresser with a child of her own.

Aliona's aunt could not afford to feed her, but visited her. She included with her letter a small note scribed in Russian.

"You have given my dear Aliona hope." She signed "With love."

Aliona lost her parents at the age of one and lived at Borzna thereafter. I then understood the life of a social orphan, or an orphan with a family who loves them but cannot support them. My sadness was somehow comforted with the knowledge that we had changed a life, a family. Again I set my mind at rest. Aliona would not be my daughter, either. I put my Petri dish in the garbage once and for all. It doesn't sting so much this time. I know Aliona will be my friend forever.

It was definitely a historical moment of celebration on November 23, 2005, as we received word from Ukraine that the Adoption Center would begin accepting dossiers, under certain criteria, to include children 10 years and older, meaning we were in! Our official letter of registration confirmed our excitement via e-mail on December 3, 2005.

We announced the good news to the entire family! I debated whether to write the online support groups, and chose to share my news with only selective online friends, recalling the unfriendly banter and competition from months before. At that point, with the two-percent odds in my favor for those adopting older children, I knew I'd mostly be gloating to all those who would wait, for what could be years, for their cherub babies. I had watched the group fight over who was most deserving of the next registration letter, by counting days and fertility treatments. I felt terrible for them, knowing some had waited years for a baby to call their own. Nevertheless, I could not foresee any congratulations in my favor from the majority—for what they would see as smooth sailing on my adoption timeline. I recognized that I was right as I read the outbursts on the absurdities of the new qualifications as they flooded in. The laws were irrational. However, we were happy that our future was moving forward.

CHAOS

The holidays were a delirious frenzy of preparation for our new children, who would arrive in the New Year. We celebrated our expectations, and the life we were to leave behind for a better tomorrow, with our growing family. My parents were eager to become first-time grandparents threefold, with my brother and sister in-law expecting our niece in early summer. Yes, rewind nine months to the honeymoon, they were blissfully happy with their news.

We began to set up the girls' room as we opened Christmas gifts for our daughters. Everything was perfect and moving at a gracious pace. We were ready, with our letter of registration in hand. I could touch it. Our adoption was finally tangible again. I could feel destiny pulling me toward my daughters. Although I remained blind, the more I tried to control motherhood, I failed. I learned that adoption imitates nature.

With our family expanding, we deliberated about upgrading our home and kept a keen eye on the market. Our Realtor approached us in late December with a find in our price range. Finally, something on my family's side of town. We loathed the hour-long drive on weekends for family time. It would certainly become more challenging with the children coming. Being Arizona, the market was hot, caliente! So we jumped. We were, and are, in love with our new home. It had never been lived in and was owned only by investors for two years. With our new house under contract, we were quick to prepare the old house for sale. Everyone expected it would sell fast in our gated golf community. Just as we found a sense of steady calm, life began stirring up again.

Work became increasingly busy, and, with the panic of my leave of absence for Ukraine on the horizon, tensions with my boss, Ray, came to an all-time high. Although in my nearly four-year tenure with the company as an art director, Ray and I had established a solid friendship and reciprocal respect for one another, something had changed in his supportiveness of our adoption. Awkwardness and uncertainty hovered as he invited a new team member to join my personally managed healthcare account. I ventured to empty my savings for our adoption and to triple my mortgage, despite Ray's empty reassurances as he declared my job more secure than anyone's.

I repeated his words like an affirmation as I drove from my home office on January 10, 2006, to meet Andrea, my new teammate. It was a typical Tuesday in morning traffic. As the metal entourage became a parking lot, I gazed around in the brilliance of the sun, somehow hoping to estimate how embarrassingly late I would be for my introductory meeting, when everything went white.

I heard nothing. Dazed, in a flurry of white and light, I finally stopped at the realization that I had been hit, several times. I spun around and tried to grasp why I was facing backward. Sound came back to me slowly, like the distance was nearing, when I heard a pounding sound from my driver's side window. I glanced up to see a man's face. He was shouting at me as I fought to understand, to make sense of something. I rolled down the window.

"Are you okay?" He asked.

I thought, *I don't know.* As I looked down, I saw blood everywhere and realized I could only see from one eye.

"I don't know," I cried in a shaky voice. "I don't think so."

He pleaded for me to open the door. "You are leaking oil, and her car is on fire!" He pointed.

I could not see.

I unlocked the door, managing only simple gestures. He forced his arm in the door and shoved the lever, pulling the mangled door toward him. He took my arm and propped me against his shoulder, carrying me across four lanes of gawking drivers to the side of the road. I looked at him in his white polo shirt and work-casual Khaki's covered in blood, my blood, before I tried to assess my wounds.

A stocky woman ran up to help. She spoke kindly and introduced herself as a representative of the governor's office and, fortunately for me, a former EMT. Since everyone was asking if I was all right, I thought it best to ask her. I was most worried about my eye. I knew it was bleeding. I hoped she would reassure me it was not my eye but the skin. Carefully she pulled my hair from the dried blood on my face to take a look.

"Your eye will be okay. You might need a stitch on your brow," she said, comforting me.

Blood had become trapped beneath my contact lenses, affecting my vision. I had examined my knee sufficiently to know it was not a bad cut, but it left the lower portion of my leg covered in red. I was too scared to look at my hand and kept it clenched in a

29

fist and close to my body each time someone reached to look. It had spurted blood for the better part of the trauma, which had covered what was left of me—my face, hair, chest and arms—in blood. Standing on the side of the road, I was a remake of Carrie.

"Please get my purse," I pleaded with the woman. "I will need my wallet and insurance cards."

I neglected to mention that I desperately wanted my cell phone. She obliged, although the concern for fire had not crossed my mind again. I could only think about calling Charles and my mother.

"Honey, I've been in an accident"

"Are you all right?"

"I don't know"

I began to cry. The woman took the phone and introduced herself. She explained that the accident was very bad but that I would be all right. Charles was slow to understand, expecting I had been in an all-too-common Arizona fender bender. She handed the phone back, as I composed myself.

"It wasn't my fault. I wasn't even moving!"

I did not know then that I had been hit from behind, at sixty-five miles per hour, by a woman who was working on an Excel spreadsheet on her laptop over the passenger seat. Her Chevy crew cab sandwiched me into a Tahoe belonging to the man in Khaki pants who pulled me from the car. I had bounced off his vehicle into the median, spun around and hit the woman in the crew cab again, head on.

Sirens echoed as the ambulance neared.

"Meet me at the hospital, north on Power Road." I told Charles and my mom.

My mom was already on her way to help prepare our house for sale by Thursday. She was half way across town when I gave her the hospital name to call for directions. I thought quickly of my meeting, since my clients were a nonprofit hospital network. I telephoned to tell them I was in an accident and would be going to the hospital. Very sympathetic, they understood I would not make the meeting as sirens rang piercingly in the background, still fighting through traffic to get to me.

The paramedics rushed to my side, perplexed that I was standing. I suppose I thought that if I sat down, I might not get up again. I wasn't exactly rational. They continued with a barrage of questions, strapped me to a board by the back and neck, and we were off. Talking among themselves, they decided to take me to Banner Desert, a hospital farther west, as I would need "better trauma facilities."

Better trauma facilities? I pleaded with the paramedic to let me call my husband or my mother as they were headed toward the wrong hospital. Finally, he called Charles on his cell, and Charles called Mom. I lay in the corridor for over an hour holding my arm in the air to keep the blood clotted in my hand. My mom had shown up earlier, intercepting the call in time, while Charles got caught turning around in the traffic caused by my accident. My mom tried to remain calm for as long as she could, but as time passed she began to cry. My mom is a strong woman, so I knew it must look pretty bad, and I lost it too. Charles showed up just as they wheeled me into a room after nearly an hour of waiting.

I received 17 stitches in my hand to sew my pinky finger back together with my ring finger. I spent the duration of my time in the hospital having my wedding ring sawed off. Charles had reciprocated counteroffers on our new home while they changed saw blades. "You are lucky to have survived," the policeman and the paramedics repeatedly stated. My Volkswagen was sandwiched and deployed all six airbags. However, the passenger compartments were amazingly intact, I found upon reviewing the photos Charles had taken on the impound lot.

As for me, yes, I am lucky, although I drive with a whole new relationship of defensiveness. I am now eternally obsessed with the realization that we have no control over our lives. My bruised body has healed and my limp has subsided. I fought in physical therapy with my neck and my hand. I had to learn to type again due to the lost range of motion from the severed muscles in my right hand, which was too painful. My focus was to point and peck on the left side of the keyboard while typing at my normal 70-words-per-minute with my right hand. Typing is a prominent part of my job in marketing and design. This has not been easy on my recent adoption-strained career.

During my recovery, Ray momentarily returned to the friendly boss I remembered. I had always felt fortunate to work at home, which made it easy to miss only one day of work. I believe that defines me as a workaholic! I had even sent out an ad to a publisher the afternoon of the accident, and Mom was furious. Ray is still obnoxiously quick to pat himself on the back concerning Andrea's new hire. I was certain life would go on, but I was left troubled and hurt by his unsupportive words.

"What if you had died?" He proudly pointed out.

I was getting by with each individual breath after the chaos of work, competing with Andrea, one-handed and no more support from Ray. The influx of house-hunters traipsing through my home and my home office was unbearable. I continued to spend my days in and out of physical therapy for my neck, back and hand.

I was completely caught off guard on February 8 when I received my letter of invitation from the National Adoption Center in Ukraine. The scanned letter arrived innocently enough with a simple "ding" in my In Box among the hundreds of work-related e-mails. We had worked toward this for over a year, but it hit me with turbulence. I ventured to guess someone had been trying to tell me something—the accident, our house selling, then having the buyer back out. I was still a veritable wreck, bruised and battered. I was terrified as the letter continued to stare me down. How could we start a family right now? I called Charles.

"When do we leave?"

"On February 23, we have to be in Kyiv!" I shrieked. "We can't possibly sign on our house on March first. What if this house sells; if it doesn't, how can we afford both homes and an adoption, and who knows if I will have a job when we get back!"

I called Scott and Dimitri immediately to learn our options. Scott was quick to congratulate me before he could sense my panic. I explained the explosion of chaos in our lives.

"I have no idea how we can pull this together in two weeks!"

Scott calmed me and urged me to call Dimitri, our Ukrainian liaison. "Maybe rescheduling is a possibility."

Dimitri was quick to respond to my tornado of a voice message.

"This is your only chance, and you risk not being invited back at all!" He was forward in his response.

Dimitri explained that all dossier submissions that met the qualifications, which weren't many, were given the same date. He made himself very clear that there would be no more appointments before the Adoption Center changed over to The Ministry of Children's Health and Welfare in May. Nothing would be done, if not sometime later due to the transition of government entities on adoption. So this was it—we would go now, and we would go to Ukraine. Everything else around us would just have to find its place.

Our family was as nervous and elated as Charles and I were. We notified our employers that afternoon.

Charles works for a large corporation and was, therefore, covered by FMLA, the Family Medical Leave Act the federal government provides as a law to protect employees of companies over a count of fifty. My company was comprised of 20, give or take. Charles' manager had been through this before with another employee twice, so nothing much was made of it—just more paperwork on his end. Ray congratulated me, however, I felt a shrug of disdain under his breath. No matter, I would not let him ruin this moment. Fortunately, my clients rallied with support and excitement, to follow along with my family and friends and share in our online journal. I was comforted by their advice and support as they cheered me off, on my way to Ukraine.

"Shelley is adopting foreign children and has no idea what she is getting into. The company feels she is in way over her head and won't be able to perform her job responsibilities with two children, that don't even speak English." It was unclear who had made the comment.

The rumors sparked a massive blow-out at work in my final days, but I'd hoped to be treated with the same rights as any other expectant mother. I wrestled with my fury over the discrimination of my future Ukrainian daughters. How could anyone discriminate against the orphans for whom I had dreamed and struggled so hard to provide a family?

The following day, Ray called me into his office to talk about this on "our level." After all, we were friends, right? I closed the door, and he was quick to remind me of the glowing personal reference he wrote for my adoption months before. He reassured me again that my job was perfectly secure. The empty feeling in my gut said otherwise.

The remainder of the week was exhaustive and, regrettably, was spent working until the middle of the nights—taking sixteen-hour days to get most of my larger projects done before I left. I hurriedly archived the database of client files since their inception in 1999 so that I would have them to work on in Ukraine. I spent endless hours arranging an Internet connection for satellite phones in Kyiv and the various regions, since I had no idea where in Ukraine I would end up, or how desolate it might be. I needed to be completely accessible for work and simply could not afford to lose the confidence of my clients, which I had spent years building and months salvaging due to the recent conflicts with Ray. And I became increasingly aware of the incompetence of Andrea. I was too engrossed in my tasks to fully understand the extent to which I was sacrificing my own priorities.

In a parallel universe, Charles and I managed, with the help of our Realtor, mortgage consultant and title agency, to close on our new house, take out a second mortgage on the old house, and withdraw funds for the adoption from our second mortgage—all in a week's time. Most fortunately, we were able to negotiate and sign a contract to sell the old house the day before we left. I knew I was in nervous-breakdown territory by then, but I fought back the tears of anxiety and forged my listless, bruised body ahead with the anticipated dream of our sweet girls. I believed they needed us despite all of this.

Our packing list still needed to be tended to. There was a historical 30-below winter freeze in Ukraine. The store racks in Arizona were strewn with bikinis, as springtime had already arrived here. A very expensive shopping trip at REI for long underwear, hats and scarves was squeezed into our overwrought agenda. In our free time, we spent our lunch hours and commutes visiting every bank in the Phoenix metro area to find whatever we could of $15,000 worth of crisp, new one-hundred dollar bills, which, of course, don't exist. We had to settle for ones without "call me" and sexy phone numbers. We sifted hurriedly with the tellers, settling, as acceptable, for the bills with simple creases down the middle.

For weeks, I had been preparing clothes for the girls, knowing they would leave everything behind in coming with us to America, just as they had come into this world—naked. The agency had

35

prepared us for that. Everything in the orphanages are communal property, and they were to leave with nothing but a family. Since we knew nothing about who our new daughters would be, I guessed from the sizes of our sponsored angels, Aliona and Maryana. Ages 10 and 13, both were about size ten, a result of their malnourished and stunted growth. It was much cheaper to buy clothes in Arizona at discount stores than spend nearly $90 overseas for a pair of jeans that had been imported. We also prepared a few stuffed toys and language books in their suitcase to bring home with them, along with a few small gifts of perfume and leather gloves for their caregivers, at the agency's recommendation.

On the eve of our departure, I was fortunate to not give myself time to fret my good-byes. I had just begun packing at nine after dropping off my final work files at a co-worker's nearby home. We packed light, following the lists prepared by those who had traveled before us; four pairs of jeans, six warm tops, six undershirts and long underwear. We packed about 15 pairs of socks and 25 pairs of underwear, so that we could get by with doing laundry only once in the three weeks, and survive if we couldn't.

It was past midnight, and less than three hours before we would embark on the journey of our lifetime. We looked over our bags and rearranged a few necessaries, and un-necessaries such as pediatric medications, prescriptions, hand sanitizer, Ziploc bags and dried food for "what-ifs." Finishing, we zipped up our high-tech gadgets for the long haul across the ocean. Although this was not an unfamiliar flight for us, the rewards would be much greater than ever before.

THE JOURNEY 4

*J*t was February 21 when we headed for the airport, at three in the moonlit morning, for a pressing six o'clock flight. We would say good-bye to our house—forever—and the pets, our other children, for what we were told would be a three-week trip.

Exhaustion colored our normally sun-kissed faces as my mother arrived at the door. With her unique ability to radiate encouragement, she lit up the house with her 3 a.m. smile. I know she was nervous for us. However, mother is never one to front anything but strength and devotion. She seemed filled with energy. I assume it was in comparison to our weary bodies, as she helped load our three suitcases and two carry-ons into her white Honda CRV. We napped until the lights of the airport crept upon us. I walked from the curbside, borrowing my mom's confidence and love, as she held back her tearful good-bye. It was what I had needed from her at that moment, and, without words, she knew. And so, I was able to hold my tears as I walked away from my mother, my unwavering strength and my best friend. I knew she would be by my side and the voice in my heart, regardless of the distance and miles between us.

As we settled into the plane and let the miles take us away from the week's chaos, we were finally able to rest and begin looking toward our future. We talked about our dreams and what it would be like to walk into a room and meet our daughters for the first time. We lingered in and out of consciousness. Our first leg was short, as we landed in Chicago for a four-hour layover. We decide to nourish our tired bodies and start our online journal back home, simply to catch up with everyone whom we hadn't been able to keep in touch with recently and say good-bye.

21 February 2006, Journey to Kyiv

As many of you know, the past few weeks leading to our adoption journey have been chaos, mixed with stress and excitement too. To recap, the past six weeks Charles and I have waded through so many things, to include my car accident on the 10th of January. I am doing well, although I had to stop physical therapy yesterday, and the short plane ride has already proved a reminder. I am thankful that I could make this journey to meet our daughters so unexpectedly. I hope to continue working on my recovery, but, despite everything, I am delighted to be doing so much better than expected. On a happier note, we found and bought a beautiful home for our new and expanding family. It is closer to our family in north Phoenix, and we are so excited to raise our girls with Mom, Dad, Greg and Becky and, coming soon, little Julia Grace! Our closing date was scheduled for March 1. Our lender and our Realtor worked miracles to get us signed early. We sold our current house, only to have the buyer back out five days later, which was unfortunate. Luckily, we sold the house again two days before we left and managed to sign most of the necessary paperwork yesterday! We will have a whole week in which to move after we return home with our girls. So much for nesting! Thanks to my family, and especially Mom, as she will spend the next few weeks of our absence packing and moving us while we are adopting our girls in Ukraine, so they will be able to come "home!"

I am writing from the familiarity of Chicago O'Hare, Charle's hometown is about an hour from here, in LaPorte, Indiana. Our next layover is Frankfurt, and, our final destination—Ukraine.

I have relied on and learned so much from so many people during this journey, and to all of you who are joining us, I wish to thank you for your support! I would especially like to thank you, Mom, Dad, Greg, Becky and Grandma, for your unending love and encouragement!

We love you!

S & C

Frankfurt dawns on us, still restless and fading. Although we have made this journey a handful of times, I have always grown weary by the timelessness of an overseas flight. I was relieved at the emptiness of the plane on this, the longest leg of our journey. Unlike the five-hour trip to Chicago, we were able to stretch our cramped limbs across the middle row, which we were quick to claim as our in-flight sleeping quarters. The voices were subdued in the near empty plane as we buckled up for arrival. The faces of soldiers were all too familiar, mixed with the deep undertones of the German language. We are fortunate to understand German, however, our Russian is "nyet" so good. As for Ukrainian, we have none to speak of, however, Ukraine is mostly Russian speaking. For now, we enjoy being in the familiar and take pause of the changing voices and faces as we find our departure gate, which feels very secluded from the familiarity of the Frankfurt airport.

Our plane is small, most likely a former commercial U.S. plane. The unfamiliar Aerosvit logo for the Ukrainian airline is intimidating. I quickly put my manners in check and remind myself to keep an open mind. I watch closely the unique and unfamiliar faces surrounding me. The women are dressed for travel similar to the expectations of generations ago. Make-up paints drapery around the windows of blue eyes, and coats lined with fur mingle with their locks of blonde hair. The men with them seem much older, however, travel is a luxury for most in Ukraine. None of this surprises me. My ears have become keenly susceptible to the voices speaking English, which are like lighthouses in a storm when you're in a foreign country. I quickly notice a college couple dressed casually, much as we are dressed, speaking English. I watch them as they practice their Russian flash cards. They are much better than we with the words.

I am in awe of the flight attendants who speak Russian, English and German. As they move about the cabin, they immediately speak English to us. I suppose it is obvious we're Americans by our casual attire. Although presumptive, the Germans are dressed in suits and business attire and the Ukrainians are dressed to the nines in fur and jewels. I admire the reverse economic agenda, I was always taught to dress for the position you desire, and I suppose it makes sense, looking at the state of America.

As our flights change, the people change. The view outside has turned to white from the snow—nothing like Phoenix. The food is different, bitter with the essence of vinegar and cold sour dough. We are far from home.

It was almost two o'clock on the hour when we arrived in Kyiv. Butterflies swarmed in my stomach, and they had nothing to do with the icy landing. I began to worry about how we would navigate through the rigid foreign land as we trailed away from the safety of the flight attendants' voices and into the chilly afternoon air. We waited for a bus to take us to the terminal of Kyiv Borispol airport. The people hustled impolitely onto the buses as they arrived, leaving women and children in the cold to wait for the next bus. I realized a lack of social etiquette in our new surroundings. The language sounded angry and abrupt as I tried not to stare into the eye of the crowds of knuckly looking men. Everyone reached for their cell phones. Seemingly, I was made aware by the phones, we are not too dissimilar. I was pushed into a tall, blonde woman in a tan suede coat with fur lining. She was stunning—beautiful with thick blonde hair and the deepest blue eyes I had ever seen, I had a hard time looking away, wondering, Will my daughters be this stunning? American supermodels would shy from her presence.

We arrived at the terminal as locals knowingly pushed their way into the airport. We looked around at the few buildings and doors and decidedly followed the crowd toward the military garbed guards. We searched for "Fast Jack," whom we were told was a slightly man who would elusively get us through customs in a sort of "V.I.P. lane." We were to provide a pre-sealed envelope containing 80 U.S. dollars. After some time of dallying around, we felt our lost tourist routine was beginning to look obvious, and, ignorantly, we moved toward the passport line. As we cleared one line and found our luggage already waiting but still no "Fast Jack" to be found, we were completely at a loss as to what to do next. It was not like other European destinations, with five or more language-friendly signs, one being English. Nothing was legible. We watched others who were obviously unseasoned travelers. I walked toward the crowd at a wall of forms and skimmed them carefully until my eyes became fixed on letters that translated correctly to my brain. The form was in English and read "Customs and Immigration Declarations."

I recalled the endless customs conversations from my online support group, and we gathered ourselves through the next few steps. We completed our individual forms, knowing we had to divide the money on hand between us to less than ten thousand in cash, per person. Charles anxiously shuffled five thousand dollars into my leather coat pocket, hoping no one would see and rob us when we stepped outside. Charles is cautious like that. We approached the counter as the attendant cocked her head, taking notice of our U.S. passports. She spoke abruptly in broken English. Given the absence of any signs hinting at recognition of my native language, this was a pleasant surprise. She reviewed my customs form thoroughly.

"Are you together?" She asked, peering at Charles in the next line.

"Yes."

"Why you carry large sum currency?"

I felt nervous, although I knew it was best to keep things honest and simple.

"We are here to adopt two children."

Without hesitating, she stamped my form and instructed me to safeguard it for my return through customs. With eye movement, she ushered me onward. I waited a few more seconds for Charles to engage in the same conversation in the next line and to join me. We headed for the doors and into the unknown; and we waited for someone to find us, which didn't take long as we were immediately greeted with a large bouquet of yellow roses and a sign bearing our name, "Schadovsky." The letter "w" does not exist there.

Our facilitator, Vladimir, and driver, Vassily, were quick to take our luggage, without a word, while our translator, Nathalie, kissed our cheeks and made quick introductions en route to a white van with a luscious red velvet interior. I recognized their faces from an Internet photo. Everything still seemed surreal as we boarded the van with our adoption team.

Nathalie explained that it would be necessary for us to wait an hour for another couple, coming from Utah. There was no time to take us into Kyiv and return for them. One hour became three as rain and sleet covered the already frozen ground. Vladimir had remained in the airport telephoning Nathalie with flight updates. We retired into a comatose state as Nathalie talked at length about Kyiv and its history. We awoke our collective consciousness long enough to ask a few questions about the adoption process. I was most curious as to how our team would handle two adoptions at once. I felt restless about it, since she eluded any firm answer.

"Everything will be fine," she assured me.

Nathalie was young and frail in appearance, although bursting with energy and personality. She was not like other Ukrainians I had seen thus far. With her short dark hair and a narrow face, her frame was half that of mine, and almost childlike. She was wonderful to talk to and just as curious about America as we were about Ukraine. Nathalie talked about her four-year-old son at home, ten hours from here by train. I could imagine it would be terribly hard for her to be apart from him for months at a time.

Vladimir returned with the couple from Utah, as Vassily jumped out in the rain to load their luggage. The mother introduced herself as Linda, as she shuffled into the van with her husband Daryl and a bouquet of pink roses. They were to adopt two boys from the Sumi region, whom they had hosted during the summer. They were very much at ease, having met Nathalie and Vladimir on their hosting trip in the states. We were just putting the puzzle together. We were the outsiders and very much in the dark. Vladimir and Vassily finished arranging the piles of luggage and got into the front of the vehicle. We were finally on our way to Kyiv.

Vladimir was a kind man, if I could put my finger on it, and I make no mistake about such matters. Although he spoke little English, I was sure he knew more than he let on. His appearance was a bit disheveled, and he had the eyes of a man who bore too much stress. He spoke in a manner indicating he had had one too many espressos to compensate for overwrought nerves; yet, he was very much a gentleman. Quickly, He sat with Vassily in the front of the van, to escape the rain.

Vassily was an older man with stringy white hair and deep creases where wrinkles should have been. It was obvious that he spoke no English at all. His language deficiency could have been a challenge. However, in place of words, he was quick to present himself in a chivalrous manner.

Nathalie pointed out the sights as we made our way into Kyiv, and we talked to, and became acquainted with, our American comrades. They were the ages of my parents and had five grown children, including a daughter nearly my age. They were an interesting couple. It became apparent, in our short conversations, that they were Mormon. We made efforts to keep our conversations light. We were delighted to hear that they, too, were adopting older children. As our nerves knotted over our blind adoption, they were empathetic.

Sunset poured over the city in a drizzle, and the chill of Kyiv's cityscape was reminiscent of the Cold War. We had left the lush forest brush for soviet-era architecture. The buildings had personalities of their own, which spoke of depression and hardship, as the paint held on in small patches to chipped and broken concrete. The colorless, gray- washed buildings became lifeless. I wondered, which one would shelter us for the night. I was certainly not about to insult my native host by asking, and I was simply too tired to be high maintenance.

Prior to checking in for the night, we had executively agreed to make a quick stop at a market for bottled water, snacks for the morning and local currency. Daryl and Linda strongly agreed on the bottled water idea. We parked at a gray dormitory-looking building, not resembling a grocery store. Inside, it was bright with electric lights advertising the various kiosks at the end of the cashier's lanes and somewhat separate from the store.

Nathalie explained that we must put our money through a small hole in a chartreuse wooden kiosk. Curiously, we bend down to look inside. It did not appear to be an ATM. She explained that a person in the booth would give us change in Ukrainian currency of hryvna's. I didn't see a person, and I thought perhaps it was an oompah loompah? We decided only to exchange a small sum into the faceless little hole. We were successful in receiving change in varying sizes and colors, with and without foil stamps. As we moved into the grocery, my hope was that it was not toy money!

Charles and I wandered from the yogurt and dairy section, hoping for something more— safe, you know, unliving, with something like preservatives. I enjoy using my limited Cyrillic encryption ability to translate words of similarity. Beef, chicken, vegetables— they all sound similar and are dried, hydrogenalyzed soup packets. I was satisfied. Vladimir rushed down the aisle panic-stricken, as though he had lost a toddler. He stayed with us, saying nothing, as I strolled around, amused with my newfound brain decoder— amazing!

We joined the others in produce, where techno music was playing quite loudly over the speakers. I looked at Charles while listening to the lyrics: "I want to sex you on the beach, I want to sex you up and down." It was surreal. And I watched the babushkas as they fingered the melons and bagged potatoes against the sex themed background music. Everyone appeared to move about as if it were silent. It was clear they didn't understand

45

the words. We glanced at the Mormons, whose faces were as perplexed as ours. We all had a good laugh.

As the van slowed before a concrete brick building with paint nearly worn away, I accepted our new home for now. Incessant chatter and shuffling began in the van upon our arrival. Vladimir explained to Nathalie that there were two rooms, one of more luxury and ten U.S. dollars more per night, for a total of fifty dollars. Our friends and we would have to choose which room to take. We were to be in Kyiv only a few days before traveling to our respective regions. We were all limited in the amount of money we were allowed to take into the country, therefore, we were on very strict budgets. Charles and I agreed to take the luxury room, with its added expense, only because I was in lingering pain as a result of three days without physical therapy. Linda and Daryl, though older than we, were avid hikers, and clearly fit.

"We don't mind the extra cost!" I volunteered.

Vladimir, in a chivalrous manner unloaded the luggage and sent Linda and Daryl to the luxury room. Somehow, despite my desperate cry in volunteering for the room, we, the junior couple, ended up in the small room. I say "small" as in matchbox size.

Our room was pink and consisted of a foyer that opened directly into the bathroom, which was a lovely shade of pistachio accented by cracked tiles and mold. The kitchen was similar in size to a closet. In the bedroom, we found a roll-out couch, unlike anything I had ever seen. I stood listless and battered, my hand in a leather Mens XXL glove with the pinky and ring fingers cut off and a mummified bandage protruding. I was bruised, and I looked around wearily with my black eye. I lacked the energy to be animated for the sake of cultural diversity. Vladimir apologized. He obviously translated my sad expression. He pardoned himself.

"Is no luxury. We find nice place tomorrow," he said, as he repeatedly nodded.

I recognized, without noticing any influx in his English, that this was a question. I finally replied, "Da, yes."

I had prepared my expectations for traveling to Ukraine. The journey was about finding our daughters. As I sat in the room, I felt them. What must their surroundings look like? Was my thought, as I remembered photos of Aliona's orphanage in Borzna and those of the orphanage in Petroprovlask. The rooms were not at all dissimilar in style. But certainly we had much more in amenities. I felt some comfort with the empathy of Aliona, my friend, as I accepted my Pepto Bismol washed walls, skewed tiles and mini-couch. We turned in for the night and left the TV on, with its static, to cover the outside noise. I was restless, and I tossed across the two-by-four that framed the sofa directly below our shoulders, as our necks dropped onto the emptiness of the unstuffed pillows. *My physical therapist will curse me upon my return. I am here against his recommendation.*

Vladimir arrived promptly at ten o'clock, as promised. He was insistent upon our listening for his voice before opening the carved inner wooden door, and looking through the peephole of the outer steel door before prying open the two bolt locks to let him in.

"You okay?"

"Yes."

He pointed around the apartment. "Okay?"

I was puzzled as he repeated himself. I realized he was hoping we might change our minds about switching rooms after sleeping on the two-by-four wooden plank. I walked over to the bed and pressed against the two-by-four crossing the bed, with its one-inch-thick mattress.

"Nyet, okay!" I pleasantly replied.

I pointed at my neck and tried to explain my car accident and months of therapy by punching my fists together with a crashing sound. He stared, with a puzzled expression. I was beginning to wonder how he translated my black eye and bandages as he looked curiously at Charles. He was confused but understood, "nyet."

"We get new room," he said. "I come back." He closed the doors, while waving a series of lock and key motions at us.

We waited, having no idea what was next. I headed to the kitchen to make packaged soup that we had purchased at the store. It was almost noon. A large gray slug stared at me from the pan, quickly curing our appetites. I was happy to hear the tarnished cell phone ring, which Vassily had shuffled out of his pocket late the night before, and switched SIMM cards in.

"Allo?" Charles was delighted to hear Nathalie's voice.

"Hello."

"Allo, Charles, good morning! For today's schedule, Vladimir will take Linda and Daryl to their appointment at the Adoption Center this morning, and your appointment will be at 2:30 this afternoon. Okay?" Nathalie was very concise.

"Yes."

"Vladimir will return in 30 minutes, after he drops off Daryl and Linda, and he will take you to a nicer apartment. Okay? Good-bye."

I was happy with the news but confused as to why Vladimir was not staying for their appointment. Vladimir arrived again promptly on schedule and grabbed our awaiting luggage by the door. We drove for 10 or more minutes, as I attempted to take in more of the city by daylight. But I found myself holding on for dear life in the Indy-car race we had involuntarily joined. I reached for the seatbelts, vividly recalling the horrendous car accident I was in so recently, only to find they had been stripped out and used to harness stereo wires.

We arrived in a few short minutes. The exterior looked the same as all the other apartments. Again, we entered through a vinyl padded steel door, and then a wooden door, to another pink apartment. However, I found the windows to be expansive and the view beautiful. I walked in and took notice of the cleaning ladies finishing their tasks. I continued to survey and noticed a living room and one full, actual, bedroom, with a king- size bed and a door. We paid $70 per night.

"Okay?" Vladimir asked.

"Horoshow e bolshiya"—Good and big—I happily replied.

Pleased with his find, he smiled and headed for the door miming his key gesture again. I found it gentlemanly but silly, as though we had not been in a big foreign city before. Vladimir would return at about two o'clock to take us to our appointment at the Adoption Center. We were terrified and curious about how Daryl and Linda fared.

Left to our own devices, we were drawn in and out of our jack-in-the-box discussions of "what-ifs" as the clock loudly pulled us closer to the moment that would take our adoption out of its blindness. Anxiety filled the room as Charles began his normal routine of nervously pacing. The floor did not seem to mind, with the tracks of other worried souls worn through the wood grains from generations before us. The telephone rang early, piercing the silence.

"Are you ready?" Nathalie asked. "We will go to lunch now, if is good for you."

I hadn't thought about food since my run-in with the slug, nor had I ventured to check the pots and pans in our new apartment.

"Sure," I replied.

She asked me to repeat myself.

"Yes, Yes! That will be nice."

"Vladimir will arrive for you in five minutes. Good-bye."

I then learned that the only way to reply to a direct question is with a firm yes, "da," and no, "nyet," and that it is impossible to hang up the phone faster than Nathalie, with the click of her clamshell.

Kyiv is a bustling city, where everyone is in motion and you just might get trampled by stiletto boots if you don't keep up the pace. I had learned social etiquette from my eschewed professor—that Russians find smiling at strangers in passing on the street is rude, and simply crazy. As we walked down the main boulevard in Kyiv to meet our party, I took notice of the faces and realized the curious, albeit shocked, reaction to my smile. So I am American. I continue my rudeness in light of the day's occasion. I am happy— smiling.

The café was light and trendy, with brilliant vibrancy. The food was greasy but appetizing in its cafeteria-style assortment. I viewed my slug-free food before committing. Nathalie and Vladimir talked among themselves, and we prodded Daryl and Linda for every detail concerning the Adoption Center.

"Were they nice, intimidating?"

Linda calmed us, "Everything went smoothly. Our appointment was 30 minutes late. We were invited in, they confirmed our boy's information and everyone was very polite."

"I can't image what it will be like for you, with a blind adoption, but I am sure you will do well with seven- to 14-year-olds." She tried her best to consoled us and admitted to listening in on the other families in the room.

Smiling, Vladimir chimed in, "I write 10."

"Okay, 10- to 14-year-olds!" I smiled, having given our agency the permission weeks before. It was necessary to submit our paperwork under the new requirements of the moratorium.

"We will begin walking while Vladimir drops Daryl and Linda at their room." Nathalie nodded to confirm the schedule with everyone as she stood and wrapped herself in her bright orange suede coat dolloped with a white scarf.

We all followed her lead in the common routine of layering ourselves for the cold. Our walk was short, but I was not acclimated to the bitterness of the below freezing temperatures. My double-breasted wool coat I had purchased years before in Colorado was holding up well. I began to mummify myself. Wrapping my scarf upward, it nearly reached my knit cap. Vladimir's car spun up onto the sidewalk in front of us. I took note of the efficiency, although I don't think that would fly back home.

Vladimir pulled to a stop in the middle of the road and ushered us out. It seemed apparent he planned to meet us inside? We were pushed with the backward motion of Nathalie's arms as she cordially insisted on crossing the street ahead of us. Charles was confused with his new role, but let her have her way—she then pushed us back with her five-foot-nothing frame.

"I am responsible for your safety," she sternly affirmed.

LET FATE DECIDE 5

he National Adoption Center building before us, dark gray with intimidation, had a simple iron gate that stood open. We proceeded past the guards into another drab concrete building where we were immediately halted in the foyer. I scanned the room, and easily recognized the Americans and differentiated their accompanying facilitators, and translators, in huddled teams.

"The psychiatrists are still on break. We must wait here." Nathalie translated the guard's abrupt shouting.

I asked Nathalie if there might be a moment to use the restroom. She asked why I had not done so at the restaurant. I soon discovered the reason for her question, as I approached the open stall and saw the often-talked-about porcelain footsteps and corresponding hole in the concrete ground. The facilities were filthy—covered with urine and feces. Looking down at my black boots, I knew we would have to part ways upon my return to the

States. I removed tissues from my pocket to touch the stall door and latch, discarded them into the hole and prayed for balance. Thirty or 40 tissues later, I emerged without having touched anything. I found it best not to touch the sinks or door, and kindly nodded my head while an employee opened the door for me. I doused myself with hand sanitizer from my pocket as we returned to wait in the foyer, I caught a strange look from Charles.

"Remember my road trip through Italy, when my mom and I chose to use the open road instead of the restroom?" I asked.

"Yeah." He smirked. I saw sympathy in his eyes, despite the slight chuckle in his voice.

The guard announced something I didn't understand, and the crowd forged upward. We climbed dozens of flights of stairs. I was winded as we reached the Adoption Center. I wedged my way onto a seat to catch my breath. Nathalie explained it could be a wait. Vladimir appeared among the crowd, talking to get the daily gossip on adoption progress. It was obvious the moratorium had caused quite a disturbance among the facilitators. It was only 15 or 20 minutes before our mispronounced name was called, "Schadovsky?" Nathalie held my hand, and mine was crushing Charles in a synchronized chain of anxiety. We made our way down the long corridor past four doors and sat in front of the last door at the end.

Nathalie popped her head in. "It will just be a moment."

The room occupied by the psychiatrists was small and held three desks. All the psychiatrists were women. We were seated in the corner by a window and were introduced to Olga. She was very businesslike, with sultry red hair that intrigued me. She was prompt in beginning her psychiatric evaluation. For comprehensive purposes, she confirmed our names and our occupations. With that completed, she moved on to the children, and I assumed we passed the evaluation. Nathalie translated.

"How many children are you looking for?"

"Two girls"

"Only girls?"

"Yes, please."

"What ages?"

"Seven to 12. But 13 or 14 would be okay, too." I added.

Olga flipped through our paperwork, nodded and walked to a wall of bookshelves. The wooden shelves were slanted and in need of repair. She retrieved two binders, which were five inches thick, black and notoriously infamous among the Internet support groups. Our children would be conceived from one of the binders. I felt nauseous.

Nathalie pried open the book and explained that our appointment was limited to an hour, so it would be best for us to flip through every page quickly and pull out each file matching our qualifications. We would review them later for our decision. The translator, seated to the right, overheard our request and asked Nathalie to pull out any sibling boys in the same age range for his couple, and they would do the same for us. She translated his request and we smiled at the couple, knowing exactly how they felt.

Nathalie warned us that we would need to read the statistics, as the photos held no real identifying information. Photos were often photocopies of photocopies, later faxed there to be filed in binders. Some photos were large, although, most were mug shots approximately one inch in size, and almost all children had had their heads nearly shaved for lice treatment upon entering the orphanages, and were concurrently photographed and registered for adoption. This also meant that some photos were from infancy, and were rather old. Therefore, we could not allow a photograph to guide our hearts.

The binders were horrifying, and I tried to pull my emotions from my body. Hundreds of homeless children were flashing before my eyes, and there was no time to mourn them, or feel anything. The pressure was intensely sickening. As the clock ticked above us, Olga kept her eye closely upon it. We quickly learned various words: sex, "stat"; boy, "cholovic"; and girl, "jinocha." With each girl's file, we scanned the birth date. If in range, we would follow the trail of paper clips attaching sibling profiles. "One, two—okay!" "Three, four—pass." And so it continued as we set several profiles aside and handed some to the adjacent couple. There were many more boys than girls and very few siblings of less than four. There were endless families of six and seven children or more. *I thought, How could this happen? Why would a mother keep giving birth if she could not provide for her children?* I reigned myself in again. This was not the time to question or make judgment.

Olga alarmed us with a 15-minute warning. My heart dropped to the pit of my stomach. We had looked through four books, and not even looked—I mean, really looked, at a single profile. I tried to hold back tears from a panic onset. Nathalie closed the binder and reached for our pile. We uneasily settled on a few after Nathalie narrowed out some major medical conditions. We handed three sibling sets to Olga. She said she would call the orphanages and verify availability and health before we submitted our referral and request to travel. We had yet to "look" at them.

"You may look at another binder while you wait," Olga said as she waved her hand toward the bookshelf.

Nathalie rushed to the bookshelves and removed two sibling binders. We quickly flipped through the first and pulled out three more profiles, setting them aside. Olga was still on the phone as we delved into the sixth binder. A most beautiful girl appeared. The photo was small—about an inch—and was a smudged, black, blotchy photocopy, but her large almond-shaped eyes leapt from the page. She was precious, and she was 11. A yellow Post-it with foreign scribbles was centered over her file. I continued and thought nothing other than, *Interesting, they have Post-its here, too.*

We followed the paper clip to the next page, with a photo of a younger child, whose hair was shaved bald for lice treatments. "Jinocha"—a girl—it read. The photo was a black silhouette. She must have the same almond eyes that leapt from the previous page with such sweetness—I could only imagine. For the first moment, our appointment was going as I had hoped. With emotion, I handed the file to Charles.

"Place this one on top." I said with a hint of breathlessness, keeping a watchful eye on the file as I continued through the binder.

Olga had narrowed out two of the previous three options through phone calls and asked if we would like to take a referral on the third. I asked Nathalie to tell her we found another set of girls in the new binders. Olga carelessly grabbed our new stack and quickly discarded two of the four profiles. The yellow Post-it crossed her view, and she rattled something to Nathalie and set it down. I reached out my hand to stop the precious file from falling to the discard pile.

"Could she please take a closer look? Nathalie, what is wrong with these girls?" I pleaded. "They are the ones!"

"They had two younger siblings who were adopted last year to Italy. The note indicates the family will come back for them." Nathalie read and reciprocated with Olga.

"But they haven't come back! They can't hold children, can they?" I argued.

Nathalie knew where I was going and pried Olga to take another look. Olga shook her head and tried to convince us to go with a less complicated profile. I planted myself firmly as Olga and Nathalie reviewed the three available files. I was certain we did not travel across the world for our children to waiver now for "less complicated." Charles recognized the look in my eye, knowing full well I was steadfast for a challenge against Olga.

I picked up the profile again as Olga made a call to records inquiring about the adoption of the younger siblings. I looked at the eldest girl's name—beautiful! One of my favorites, "Anastasia." I turned the page to look at her sister's name. My eyes swelled with tears as I translated, "Katerina," slowly in Cyrillic. I was speechless as I pointed the names to Charles. His Russian is worse than mine.

I managed a whisper—"Anya and Katia!" We both knew at that moment that they were our daughters.

Olga returned and said they couldn't find any record of the younger children's adoption. The Post-it was beginning to piss me off, with its elusive scribbles and no real information. Olga tried to telephone the orphanage, as Nathalie carefully and expediently did her scour of the documents for health and legal problems. She said it checked out. Olga said the orphanage did not answer, adding that we must leave for her next appointment. However, we could return in 30 minutes with our decision.

Nathalie grabbed her thorough notes, as the profiles may not leave the room, and she rushed us into the foyer to meet Vladimir. We hurried down a flight of stairs where we could talk away from the lingering crowd. Nathalie talked in a marathon of words I didn't understand, while Vladimir nodded and asked several questions. Our heads bounced back and forth between the two, reminiscent of a tennis match. Nathalie stopped and clenched my arm.

"Vladimir needed to hear from you that you are attached to these two girls."

'Yes! Da! Da!" I exclaimed.

Vladimir smiled, "Da, da, da," proceeding in his attempts to get through to the orphanage by telephone.

It was necessary to establish that the siblings were adopted, as we were approved by U.S. Immigration to adopt only two children. In addition, families cannot be separated in Ukraine, not that such a measure would ever be considered.

"The best way to confirm the girls' status is to call the orphanage themselves, as records here are in shambles." Nathalie explained.

I was desperate for a response. I believe in fate, and I knew those were our daughters. I confided in Nathalie the meaning of Anya and Katia and our story.

"Charles and I were gifted our airline tickets by my parents to help with our adoption expenses. However, we had to provide names for the girls' airline tickets. We could change them later, but we needed to get them home. We chose our two favorite Russian names — Anya and Katia. I felt feverish as I said the names aloud. Charles pulled the airline tickets from the travel wallet in his leather coat.

"Anya Schadowsky"

"Katia Schadowsky"

"It is a miracle, Da!" Nathalie was speechless and wept at the sight of our daughters' tickets. She immediately translated our story to Vladimir.

"We had not even read their names until after we started arguing over the Post-it, when Olga left to check the records." I added.

We were all convinced.

Disappointed, but not dissuaded, our attempts to get through to the orphanage were to no avail. We returned to Olga, and Nathalie pleaded our case. Olga had Nathalie explain that if we requested this referral and traveled to their region, we were at risk. The girls could have siblings, and although the Adoption Center cannot hold children, the girls, at their ages, could refuse us if they believed the Italian family would come back to reunite them with their siblings. Ultimately, it was their decision. Our risk meant we would have to request another appointment, which could take two to three weeks. Certainly, we were concerned about the risk, but we knew in our hearts these were our daughters, and we did not hesitate to accept the referral.

Olga appreciated our resilience in the end and gave Vladimir until 10:00 in the morning to get through to the orphanage and get back to her. At ten o'clock, he could indicate whether we requested the referral or a second choice. She laid the two other acceptable files on her desk, swayed her hand above them and nodded. We were given a mere moment to choose. We knew Anya and Katia were our daughters, and we put little thought into a second choice. We realized our fortune and left, elated at our choice and relieved to be released from blindness of our adoption.

"This never happens; in all my years, they have never allowed such a favor!" Nathalie expressed in disbelief as Vladimir nodded, a shocked expression covering his face.

The whole group was energetic for a night out on the town to celebrate our successes. Daryl and Linda would join us shortly as Vladimir sped off to pick them up. The Potato House was a popular venue, Nathalie had exclaimed. It was round and looked very trendy from the outside, so I was excited too. The restaurant was radiant with bright lights and electric blue tables. The curved entrance mirrored the expansive bar inside. We walked to the back through a hallway of tables and ordered fast-food style, with a backlit menu above. It occurred to me we were dining on Southwest fare. *Should be interesting,* I thought. I ordered a burrito, simple and light on my nerve-racked stomach. The cashier, dressed in a red and white cowboy uniform, complete with a red cowboy hat and boots, asked Nathalie if I wanted cucumbers and potatoes on my burrito.

I was confused, and politely replied, "No thank you," directly to the cashier.

"Nyet, spaceeba."

While waiting for our food to arrive, Nathalie and I headed to the restrooms, which were definably good and met my expectations, to clean up for dinner. We successfully found a table to host our larger party. The stools were covered with hide similar to the top of an old Indian drum. It was a definite clash with the blue neon lighting and brushed aluminum, but I enjoyed analyzing the interpretation of the Southwest there in Ukraine. Daryl, Linda and Vladimir finally appeared through the growing crowd of patrons, just as our food arrived. We all had a good laugh over my burrito, which was a plate of tortillas and cups of shredded carrots, cubed goat cheese and chopped parsley, with a side of the cucumber I had declined and a green pesto sour cream sauce, not to be confused with guacamole—but possibly an attempted imitation.

I was jealous of the ribs Charles ordered, although he was kind enough to shred the meat of a couple of his ribs to add to my goat cheese and sour cream tortillas. Daryl and Linda were pleased to arrive late and view the menu in person prior to ordering their ribs. We had a good laugh at the Southwest cuisine, as Nathalie tried hopelessly to translate the complete cultural confusion on my plate.

We discussed our appointment as our new friends had been asking Nathalie on the phone all afternoon how it was going. In politeness, she felt it was best for us to tell them. Linda also felt the contagious chills from our story of Anya and Katia.

"It is meant to be!" She assured us.

"Da, da!" Vladimir said with a smile. It had been a long and successful day, and he was pleased.

Unable to sleep, Charles and I talked throughout the night. We tried retrieving the smudged photocopies of the girls in our minds repeatedly, like an old movie projector with tattered film, trying not to forget Anya's beautiful almond-shaped eyes. Anya's eyes were powerful with confidence and striking enough to steal your heart in a glance. We had yet to see a photo or anything of Katia but a silhouette. We imagined aimlessly, *What would they be like, where do they live?* We wondered most, *where did they come from and what brought us to them—homeless.*

We were never more in love with each other and with life as we lay there together. Words can't explain. I felt motherhood and I felt close to them, being there in Kyiv, as I lay staring at the ceiling. It was four past ten in the morning when the telephone finally rang. We were half conscious, eagerly awaiting this moment. I pressed the talk button as Nathalie spoke.

"Shelley, Allo?"

"Yes, hello!"

"I have good news for you! You will travel to Poltava to meet your daughters tomorrow!"

"Yes, they are available?" Charles read the pure happiness on my face.

"Yes! The girls' siblings were adopted in November to a family in Israel, not Italy," Nathalie explained. However, the girls harbor no knowledge of the family or expectations of them returning to adopt them. The director of the orphanage would be delighted for you to visit the girls and become a family."

"We can't wait! When?" I exclaimed, welled up with tears, trying to whisper to Charles as he tugged on my pajamas with his head smashed against the telephone.

"The girls have spent a summer and a Christmas in Italy with families, on hosting programs, however no family has expressed any intention to adopt them there either," Nathalie continued.

This was wonderful news, however my heart felt heavy concerning all the families who had left them abandoned; and more so, all the families that could have been had it not been for that stupid little Post-it that caused them to be "too complicated!" I knew it was fate. Maybe the Post-it was there to deter those who were not worthy enough to stand up for them! Content in our stance, my mind began dreaming of my daughters in Poltava, Ukraine.

Vladimir spent the day at the Adoption Center trying to secure our request to travel to the orphanage. It was a Friday and apparently a pre-holiday to Monday's holiday. Everyone had been leaving early. It is Europe, after all. Our paperwork relied on a waiting game for Vladimir to get someone's attention crossing the parking lot. Nathalie kept informing us of his attempts. I felt bad that he had succumbed to stalking the psychiatrists, but I was told that is how things are done there.

Nathalie braved the Metro, so we were able to meet Daryl and Linda in Independence Square at an Internet café she found in the center of Kyiv. Finally, contact with the outside world! We met our friends as they were just finishing their virtual exploration. We collectively decide on lunch first so that Daryl and Linda could return home while we enjoyed the Internet café, I was certain I would be there for awhile.

A short tour of Independence Square left all of us poised at the base of the Maydan Nezalejnosti monument. A globe with iron birds set atop a towering column. Nathalie explained that the globe represents Kyiv, the capitol. Bronze lines ran down the statue and out onto the cobblestone walk connecting plaques at different lengths around the circumference. Each plaque, we were told, represents the distance to Ukraine's regional centers. We followed the bronze lines and were excited to find Poltava, which is 304 km. Sumi, right next to us, is at 307 km. I was unsure at the time what that meant, or what it meant for our double adoption. However, I felt confident in Vladimir.

We enjoyed lunch at a restaurant in the underground mall below the square. We found the décor elegant and the food delicious Italian, although, I was eager to get back to the Internet café. Nothing is real until I have shared the news with Mom. I couldn't wait to hear her voice after e-mailing our cell phone number to her.

24 February 2006, Getting Our Feet Wet in Kyiv

So much has happened, I am not sure where to begin. I am happy to say that we are excited and moving forward, but I will start by moving backward.

We arrived in Kyiv after twenty-four hours of flights and layovers, and we were exhausted. Our adoption team was cheerful to meet us after making it through customs with ease. Everyone is very polite and professional, and we feel safe here. We have made friends with another couple from Utah who are adopting from the Sumi Region. Our second apartment in Kyiv is very nice, with wonderful views of the city.

N, our translator is a sweet girl and very energetic. V, our facilitator is all hard work and does everything to the highest standard. N described him well today when she said, "He is like the fairytale when the king says go to town and get me this, but I don't know what "this" is, that I want yet. V is that man who will do this." He is brilliant and kind.

Our appointment was yesterday at the NAC. Everyone was very serious and, at times, intimidating. The language here, influences that a lot too, everyone sounds angry. The psychologist asked little of us, mostly what we were looking for in our children. N helped us wade through binders with hundreds of abandoned children. It was heartbreaking—life altering staring into all the faces. Our appointment was only an hour, and we had time only to select files that met our criteria of two girls, and we were pretty open about ages. Most of the files were large sibling groups, and many boys. I felt sick. It is not an experience I can put into words.

When our appointment was over, we were left with only three files—two the psychologist, Olga, found acceptable and one with a Post-it. Olga discarded the Post-it file as "complicated" and dissuaded us. It wasn't until later that we learned the names of the beautiful sisters, Anastasia, "Anya" and Katerina, "Katia." We both knew it was meant to be. These are our favorite Russian names, which we chose to book their flights home. Olga continued to prod us with the other files and finally asked us to select one as an alternate referral. Nonetheless, anyone who knows me should know that my path in life is always the most challenging, so I was not deterred. We risked having to request another appointment in two to three weeks, but Charles and I knew these were our daughters.

We did receive a phone call at ten this morning from N that she had good news! We leave tomorrow for the region of Poltava, about an hour west of Kyiv for our girls. V found out from the orphanage that the Post-it was about two younger siblings who have already been adopted, and there are no intentions of the family returning for our girls. It is very sad, but I believe that our determination and compassion have led us to Anastasia and Katerina.

I don't want to write too much now, until I know our referral has been accepted by the orphanage director and the girls. I will keep you posted.

With love,

S & C

Vladimir and Natalie retreated to our place last night for a nightcap and to present us with news of a new translator. Conveniently, she is a facilitator, too. Her name is also Natalya or Nathalie. However, to refrain from the myriad of confusion, we may call her by her nickname, Natasha. Vladimir spoke highly of Natasha from his previous encounters with her at the NAC, and although he had never had to split the team up like this, he was confident of her highly prestigious reputation. Vladimir is steady to reassure us he will still handle both adoptions on his return to Kyiv. Surprisingly, as a translator, Nathalie was with few words while we said our good-byes. I hurriedly put together the modest gift I had brought for her upon our parting. I had not planned to part so early. Nathalie was in tears and was sad to let us go.

"I will still see you tomorrow. We are driving together with Vassily. We will take you to Poltava on our way to Sumi. It is not good-bye for now." She choked back, hesitating to say a final good-bye.

I knew that a good-bye on the cold roadside was not an appropriate ending for everything she had done for us. We were terribly sad that evening as we wondered about our new Nathalie. Would she be so spirited and kind?

NEW BEGINNINGS 6

*W*e awoke early the following morning, fresh with anticipation of the life that awaited us on the road ahead to Poltava. The group was scheduled to arrive early for our five-hour journey. I felt for Linda and Daryl, who had to carry on for an additional three hours north to Sumi. I knew we were slightly out of their way, but it helped both of us to split travel costs.

The rhythm of Vladimir's patterned knock sounded down the outer door along with the shallow call of his voice. Natasha, with striking blonde hair pulled taunt in a lengthy ponytail, stood tall beside him. Her face was stern and brimming with intellect. It was obvious she would not be quirky and finding ways to lighten the intensity around us and the harshness of Ukraine. However, she looked more than capable of getting the job done in a "don't-cross-my-path" sort of way. She spoke minimally except to greet us that morning as Vladimir rushed our suitcases to the van.

"Must go!" He ushered.

Our journey was an interesting vibe of cultures mingling in the red velvet van. We talked mostly among ourselves, the Americans nestled in the back. The fast unrecognizable clatter of voices in the front was mixed with cell phones ringing, clamshells snapping and intermittent conversation. The Nathalies took time getting to know one another, while the men hosted their own conversation. Charles and I decided to watch a movie on the ibook to break up the monotony of the drive. I was most impatient, not one for road trips. Daryl and Linda helped choose the movie and watched from the seat behind. Occasionally our Nathalie, Natasha, as we began to call her when confusion set in, would talk to us between phone calls, politely excusing her interruption of *Maid in Manhattan*.

The scenery on the drive was comparable to that of Mexico — only it was bitterly cold and the old men walking along the road were draped in rabbit fur hats and matching coats, in contrast to straw and ponchos — although the labored faces were similar in this same small world. We stopped in a quaint village nestled below a large windmill. Nathalie told us of a beautiful noir love story that was filmed around the towering windmill where we stood. I appreciated the different view of the decaying village of dried fish stalls.

The market smelled of the starry-eyed fish as we peered around for something identifiably edible. It's moments like these when you think back to your little house in suburban America, wondering, how did I end up here, in the middle of Ukraine, of all places, debating, amidst my hunger pains, whether to go ahead and give fried grasshoppers a try? Miraculously, a bag of Pringles appeared in the slight of my eye, the logo in English, however, the flavors I translated to "paprika" and "chicken." The other flavors were all different — unique, but the preservatives I would normally stray from felt somehow safe, reminding me of home.

The cryptic alphabet on the wooden sign deciphered itself as a welcome sign to Poltava. Moments later, Natasha flipped her phone closed with a quick snap and turned to ask with a whip of her long blonde ponytail, "You will meet your girls in one hour, yes?" Her face gleamed with excitement as a result of the arrangement she had just made for us.

"Yes, of course," we replied in shock, not expecting to meet until Monday. I had hoped for some hours to use the restroom, to splash my face with battery acid, or something, and regroup, but "nyet—no time!"

Butterflies stirred in my stomach, as Charles gripped my hand, "This is it!" He said with a smile.

"Ah Huh." Gulp.

I was terrified. *What would they think of us? Would we be suitable parents. More importantly, would they accept us?*

We stopped as we entered town. Vladimir and Natasha quickly looked at a couple of apartments for our stay before nightfall, and returned to the van disappointed. Oddly, we dropped the Realtor in the middle of the street, for a takci, and headed down the road, stopping at another building.

"Where did she go?" I asked.

"Nyet." Vladimir replied.

"We have other options. We are at orphanage now!" Natasha explained simply.

My heart had now dropped into my stomach, to swim with the butterflies. I was nauseous. We pulled farther into the drive. The orphanage was unbelievably nice, with a fountain in front. I was very surprised at the view. It was nothing like Borzna or Petroprovlask. We waited in the van, watching children come in and out of the large wooden doors, wondering if one of them was one of ours. Vladimir and Natasha shuffled into the orphanage with the orphanage lawyer, to arrange an "unofficial" visit with the girls in the director's absence. Fifteen minutes dragged by before their return. They explained that we could only see Anastasia, the eldest of the girls. The younger groups, or groupa's as they call them, are in lock-down on weekends. Natasha invited our friends from Utah along too, to enhance the tourist appearance. I welcomed their company and Linda's motherly support in my state of anxiety.

Natasha clarified the situation. "Anastasia will not know who you are. The groupa is being told you are American tourists visiting the orphanage. You may talk with them about their studies and observe as you like."

"Okay, let's meet our girl." I took a deep breath and grasped Charles as we walked toward the large wooden doors.

"The smell of urine may be hard to take," Natasha warned crassly as we entered the orphanage. "There are just so many kids living here."

The hallways were a maze of broken tiles. Passing through a long corridor of windows draped with drawings, we all halted in admiration. They were beautiful, and all penned by the children. I was amazed at the talent, as we all stood for a moment admiring the art. After five long flights of stairs, my heart was pounding. Adding to my overwrought nerves, I was now winded.

The children were arranged in a classroom at the end of the hall, just to meet us. Natasha began to speak to us in English, as they would not understand. Before Natasha got the words out, I recognized our Anastasia looking at us. She was nervous, too, and she was beautiful!

"Anastasia is…."

I cut Natasha off. "I know, I know, I recognize those eyes, her brilliant almond eyes. They are so blue. She is, beautiful!"

I felt Charles' heartbeat through our hands. "She couldn't be more perfect."

"Yes." His eyes glistened. He was speechless.

"What is this?" Daryl asked in silliness, pointing to a poster on the wall, knowing full well it was the Ukrainian anthem.

"Can you sing for us?" Natasha translated his request.

The children giggled, while Irena, the orphanage lawyer, led them in song. We all stood, nearly brought to tears. We had tried so hard not to stare at our Anastasia—it was physically exhausting. Irena initiated the class in talks of their studies and their annual trips to Sicily.

Anastasia, as the group leader, guided us through the rooms, showing us her quarters, with her bed. The rooms were minimal and contained no personal belongings. She carried her room keys and locked the doors behind her. We followed her to the boys' room. I admired her as she explained everything in exquisite detail to Natasha, and we hung onto her words in translation.

Natasha beamed at us. "She is so smart!"

I wanted to hug her as I lingered, holding her hand to say— good-bye—"Poka!"

"Would it be okay if we came back and spent more time with all of you this week?" We asked.

"Yes!" The kids chanted as we left.

"Spaceeba, strasveetya"—thank you, and goodbye.

I kept my head turned down the hall, enchanted by her eyes. We returned to the main entrance as Vladimir and Natasha talked hurriedly among themselves with Irena. They took turns whispering and Natasha repeatedly turned to us.

"What you think? She is beautiful, yes?"

"Da, Da, Yes! She is perfect!"

"You will meet Katerina Monday, and, if you like the girls."

"If?" Of course, we like the girls!"

"You would then need to accept the referral, and we will submit your papers to the Adoption Center. We will then need permissions to the region...." Natasha droned on, but we were too excited to listen to details at the moment.

"Da, da?" Vladimir remained nervous, as we had yet to meet Katerina.

"Unless Katerina displays psychotic episodes, with sharp objects and fire-starting tendencies, we love the girls! We will not leave without our daughters!" I explained in perfect detail to relieve his nervous tension.

Natasha and Vladimir were delighted, however, it was unparallel to our new found happiness! We returned to the van, reveling in our bliss. Silently, we committed to memory Anastasia's sweet voice and beautiful smile. Night set upon us as we pulled away in search of our "other apartment options." Irena was in tow, and she guided Vassily through the winding icy back roads of Poltava. I secretly hoped they didn't intend to drop her in the street, too. After a thorough review, Natasha informed us the apartment was quite suitable, should we approve, inviting us in. The two-story house was guarded by a towering iron gate. Inside were two housemaids who politely nodded as Natasha translated the rules of the house—the first being to remove our snow clad shoes at the door—now! We toured the more-than-suitable 4-bedroom, 2-bathroom house, we could conveniently share with Natasha. This would become our temporary home in Poltava, Ukraine.

Natasha explained that it would be necessary to negotiate the price, as they usually request $80 per night. However, given our long-term stay she was certain $50 would be more than acceptable. After agreeing to the equivalent, 250 hryvnas, or $48 per night, everyone nodded as we tried to assemble for our last supper. The team stood in an endless argument as to how many days, and on what day payment would be made. Restless and starving, I used my cut-to-the-chase business attitude from back home. Everyone tossed their heads at my forwardness. I reached for our large

American travel wallet in Charles' coat and handed the lady of the house a handful of cash along with one week's rent.

I asked Natasha to translate. "Please tell her she will receive the same sum each Saturday."

Nighttime had blanketed the sky as we set out seeking dinner in our new city. Irena was disappointed when her favorite restaurant was short of tables for the night. We found ourselves dining on Indian cuisine at a dimly lit venue. Though our bodies were tired and listless, the atmosphere was nice. We recapped the days' emotional events. The grease of the meal left our stomachs feeling heavy as we said our quick good-byes to Nathalie, Vladimir, Daryl, Linda and Vassily in the moonlight on the icy streets of Poltava. We parted ways in our "takci," as the car's yellow sign read, slightly cryptic in Cyrillic. Natasha, Charles and I are headed home. We were empathetic for the rest of the group as they forged on for three more hours in the icy cold to Sumi. Wishing their journey well, we snuggled into bed for the night. How I longed to share the news with Mom back home about her first granddaughter.

Daybreak came and left while we hid from the activity of our new world. We were happy in that moment to regroup with everything unfolding before our eyes in a foreign land. We mourned the loss of everyone we had come to know and trust. We began to gripe about initiating a new day, with the even more foreign blonde keeping silence in her room next door. It was 2:00 in the afternoon before our new roommate ventured out for a very late brunch.

"I have not quite been myself." Natasha explained, "The completion of my last adoption ended at 4:00 in the airport the morning of our acquaintance."

She was pleasantly more talkative that day, after a long sleep. In our more approachable conversation, we learned of her native

73

region, Zhytomyr, and her family back home. She livened up with interesting stories of past adoptions, obviously keeping respectful anonymity. Natasha was polite and prided herself on social etiquette, which was ever apparent throughout the day. Our conversation ended with places she had traveled. I realized that she was much like me, concerning her adventurous nature, determination and strong will. We managed to find common ground and some laughs over lunch.

Natasha's English was more challenging to understand, as we stumbled through our first day together, frequently saying, "What," "Pardon," and "excuse me." She lightheartedly explained that she was educated in the Queen's English, which we had already discerned. Unlike Nathalie's laid back American way of speaking. I was impressed by her fluent English, German, Russian and Ukrainian. To judge her in speaking my native language more elegantly than my own western slang would be absurd.

"It will only take a couple of days for me to identify your individual dialects." She said.

"Sure?" I didn't realize I had a dialect.

Brunch was short, with the same greasy food. I was enthusiastic to rush through another less pleasurable and greasy dining experience for my quick fix at the Internet café. Afterward we would head out to stock up on groceries for the house and buy cookies, in anticipation for meeting Katerina the following day.

26 February 2006, Waiting for Katerina
We met Anastasia today — she is miraculous! Our visit was unofficial, since it was a weekend, without the director. Meeting her meant she didn't know who we were or our intentions. We visited as tourists. Anastasia is so amazing and smart. She is beautiful, with blue eyes and blonde hair, like me. The entire class sang the Ukrainian anthem for us. It was amazing! Well, I will brag and say

that Anastasia is the leader of the class, and she showed us around her wing of the orphanage. She takes so much pride in herself. It was wonderful watching her today. We could not take our eyes from her and were nearly brought to tears leaving after our short visit. We are so anxious to meet our Katerina tomorrow, and hope for no delays. We will know more on how the process will go from here.

We arrived in Poltava yesterday with the whole team and our friends from Utah. D and L carried on to Sumi region last night for their boys, with N. Since there are two families, we have been assigned to another translator. Her name is also N and, conveniently, she is also a facilitator. V will work from Kyiv on both of our adoptions. I am told this is how he always works. We met N early this morning. She is stunning, smart and quite assertive. I am confident she will do well at the job. We are sad to see our first N go, and V for now.

We have finally rested and got to know N a little better over lunch. We discussed the process and timeline, and N is pleased with our progress. We are staying in the city of Poltava in the region of Poltava, similar to a capital city of one of our states. Poltava is not rural and has much of the same amenities of Kyiv. Irena, the orphanage lawyer, referred us to a two-story house last nigh, with two bathrooms, two living rooms, four bedrooms and a kitchen. We are sharing it with N, making everything convenient, affordable and well within our budget. The food is very affordable here, too. The food in Ukraine is interesting, very greasy and it's killing me, although, Charles loves it. We've had some interesting dining experiences already, including a burrito with blocks of goat cheese, parsley, carrots, cucumbers and a green pesto, sour cream sauce. Did I mention the fried grasshoppers?

We are doing well, and, to our surprise, it is not too cold—not much worse than I remember Colorado being. N says it has warmed up here quite a bit in recent weeks. This is good, but I think it is still *around ten degrees. N can only tell us Celsius, so I am not sure. Tonight, we will go out to buy cookies, or something nice, for the girls' groupas. N recommends we hold off on one-to-one gifts for now. However, we will have to compete with the soccer ball that D left for them. He had brought several for their orphanage in Sumi. D is very good with the boys, as they have only one girl and four boys—soon to be six! Well, we're off to go shopping. I love to shop!*

Lots of love,

S & C

P.S. Proof of Life

I have conquered the ability to upload photos from across the world, with some difficulty. First, here is our proof of life, along with some historical photos of Kyiv.

Gazing, we stepped from the takci, along the encircled entrance to the Poltava Regional Boarding School for Orphans. Our nerves were still frayed as we waited to meet our dear Katerina and be formally introduced to our daughters as their parents-in-waiting. Wooden planks carried us to the cracked concrete steps of the school. Through the towering wooden doors lay a child's old shirt to wipe the snow and soot from our shoes. Slipping across the tiles a few doors down to the administration office, we were pleasantly greeted by another Natasha, of course. She is the secretary to the director. The director was delayed in her travels until this afternoon, she explained to Natasha.

Quietly smiling at us, "Allo," she shyly said.

Shortly after her arrival at the school, Irena, the lawyer, invited us to join her in the basement to view the children's records. We were intrigued by the invitation to calm the curiosity currently burning in our minds. We deeply wanted to know every secret of the girls' past. We crouched down into the dark corridor. Everything became black. I could not see the steps.

"Alessander! Alessander?" Irene shouted.

"Da. Da?" a tall, lanky man murmured appearing from the darkness.

Hovered below the stunted ceiling, they began speaking, while we were lured farther into the depths of the basement. He took us through a chain link gate, rattling his keys at an enforcing lock, dangling from chains. We squeezed though stockpiles of gigantic canned tomatoes as high as the ceiling. Stopping in a room lighted by lamplight, and surrounded by file cabinets, we continued to listen to more cryptic conversations between Irena, Alessander and Natasha.

Fumbling through metal cabinets, seeking to find what we were certain would be the girls' most dreadful buried pasts and our uncertain futures, Irena and Natasha were quick to become friendly acquaintances as they weeded through the folders. Charles and I sat in old school chairs looking up with an occasional glance, seeking understandable words entangled within our minds from our Russian 101 class. It was all we could do to make any sense of the conversation going on between them. After what seemed like lifetimes of void, Natasha began to translate the elusive file contents.

"This is good," she began, as she read through Anastasia's file.

"Good?" I couldn't imagine any situation orphaning a child as "good."

"Her mother's rights have been terminated and she has no father, meaning the father is unknown," she explained. "This presents no problems for the adoption. A very ideal situation." Natasha asserted in confidence.

She looked at my face covered in sadness and quickly took to empathetic reproach. She continued through the folder as she and

Irena established a death certificate for the mother. This time she approached the finding in a more sensitive manner, explaining the expedition of our case, with no mother to contest or sign outdated notaries. With Katerina, the situation is similar—father unknown and mother's rights terminated, and later deceased.

"We have no way of knowing if the girls have the same father. These things are simply— unknown?" Natasha stated questionably, prying as to whether it might be a problem for us.

Encompassed by much curiosity, Natasha and Irena explained the circumstance surrounding the separation of their younger siblings. Irena was certain in her recollection of the adoption, concluding the decade or so that she had overseen, and I discovered more after prodding. Natasha helped to interpret Irena's knowledgeable but broken English.

"There have only been 12 or 13 adoptions from the school." Irena clarified.

"The girls were in Italy with Irena over the holidays, when she received a call about the adoption of Maryana and Mikola. The girls were told what was taking place and asked to write letters stating that they understood their brother and sister were to be adopted to Israel and they may never see them again." Natasha translated as Irena gestured emphatically.

Irena added, "I translated this information myself, so they know."

"They were happy for the babies and not sad to write the letters. They were in a happy place at that time in their lives—in Italy." Natasha continued in Irena's attempt to console us.

I sensed regret for the separation, however, everyone in the room, including us knew fate had stepped in. It was nearly impossible for four siblings to be adopted. I silently battled with my anger over the illegal separation. At the same time I was consoled knowing we, too, would not be here had it not been for the unfortunate series of events. We eagerly moved past the solitude of the moment in the dreary basement, while Natasha and Irena gathered the files and ushered us out the door. We were told we would then visit City Hall.

City Hall is similar to government buildings in the States, with the undocumented code of international interior design standards—like mold on bread. The building was drab, of concrete with sea-foam green paint crumbling from the walls. Walking up cracked stairs, I was taken aback at the lady we were there to see. She was painted with makeup and blue eye shadow—painted. Natasha and Irena were confident in their file presentation upon arrival, while Charles and I were still dwelling on the girls' past.

We were politely seated in the office, as we sat back for another episode of Ukrainian lost in translation. I found myself not so lost as a point-and-shout match occurred between the ladies concerning Anastasia's documents. I was at a loss for words, literally. I knew it was not good when the city inspector stubbornly repeated, "nyet, nyet, nyet," verbally and physically abusing our "good" files with her fists.

"Anastasia was born in Russia," Natasha calmly attempted to explain, as the inspector continued tossing things about. "There will be some more paperwork and a few more steps. Everything will be okay."

I have learned in my journey this far that I do not like the word "nyet," and I will soon tire of hearing, "everything will be okay," in a perky cheerleader sort of way. We concluded our meeting and returned to the school. Charles remained equally disturbed as the ladies bantered nonstop on the return takci ride.

Upon our return, Natasha, the director's assistant was profoundly apologetic for the director's continued delayed absence. After some time in the metal school chairs appropriately suitable for a principal's office, Irena granted us the good news that she would allow us another "unofficial" visit that day with Katerina, in lieu of the director's delay.

The day would be similar to Saturday. We will appear as American tourists and deliver our cookies to the entire groupa. We were ecstatic to just move forward in review of the day's events and, most importantly, to finally meet our Katerina. The children were seated in their class, with their best behavior and persnickety posture. Firmly clasping my hand, and with a tear in her eye, the teacher gave me a wink.

"Thank you for the wonderful thing you do. Katusha is precious. I am so pleased!" Natasha translated her tearful appreciation. Katia was one of her favorites.

Katerina was instructed to come to the front of the class and pass the cookies to the students. She was adorable, vibrant and giggly, while trying so hard to hold her demeanor. She most politely returned to us with the remaining cookies and handed one to each of us. At first, I declined, with my unnatural dislike for chocolate, however, Katerina remained steadfast and refused for the class or herself to indulge until we had enjoyed our serving. I bit into the double-fudge-coated cookie for my dear Katia and gulped. I admired her courage as she stood firm in her social morals. She was miraculous, a fiery and precious jewel. Irena instructed her to guide us back to the administration office. She confidently took stance and tightly grasped my left hand, drawing blood from my stitches. In that moment, I knew I would never let go. She was perfect, just like her sister. Painfully, clutching my bandaged hand— Katia paid no mind. She guided us, with an adoringly silly smile and wobble while continually looked up at me in our walk through the corridor. Her smile bonded us. It was as though she knew we were there to adopt her. Her giggles echoed as we turned into the administration office. I listened to her skip back down the hall.

27 February 2006, Back in the USSR with Cookies

We are moving forward and backward at the same time. Unfortunately, back to the USSR, Russia that is, in a time of outdated paperwork. Our "good" adoption has unfortunately found a knot. Just this morning, we learned that Anastasia was born in Russia, and not Ukraine. To shorten the story, our facilitator and maybe we, although we are without visas, must travel to Russia at least once for a little piece of legislative paper about the father, or lack thereof. The U.S. Embassy also requires a second and final trip for a birth certificate after the court date.

Fortunately, the region of Russia in which Anastasia was born borders with Ukraine and is not too far. We hope that N can do this with a power of attorney. But nobody seems to know what to do in this case yet, not even V, there has not yet been a case similar to this since the fallout of the Soviet Union and therefore, no legal precedence. We are very discouraged after today's events, as everything started out so well when we began in the basement archives. I knew immediately something was wrong when the city inspector began shouting, "nyet, nyet, nyet" and pounding the papers in her folder.

We must now find a means to fix the errors to bring the girls home. Many people are apologetic and trying to help with this "impossible" error. Legally, there is no way Anastasia's mother could have had her rights terminated in court without the birth certificate. There is no way Anastasia could have entered the orphanage without the certificate, and there is certainly no way she could hold the Ukrainian passport she has, and which she used twice to travel to Italy, without her birth certificate! However, they did, she is and she does. Some are even arguing she is not a Ukrainian citizen, which is absurd, as her mother somehow became one, therefore Anastasia would become Ukrainian. Anastasia's Ukrainian passport is proof of her citizenship, not to mention the fact that she is an orphan and a

81

ward of Ukraine. In the meantime, N will prepare papers for the judge tomorrow so that he may better determine how to proceed with our adoption, and we should know more then.

Unfortunately, the orphanage director did not return in time from her business trip, so we were not able to have our formal visit with either of the girls and declare our intentions, or submit our referral.

On a happier note, in another "unofficial" visit we were able to meet Katerina today in the director's absence. She is adorable, with big blue eyes, so perfect, too, just like her sister. We again came in as "American guests" touring the orphanage. We brought cookies for her groupa. Katerina shared the cookies with everyone and escorted us down the hall. She held my hand tightly and was full of smiles. She is fiery and gangly at the same time, but just so happy and spirited. Katia certainly doesn't carry the responsibility, pride and seriousness of her sister.

Tomorrow we will arrive early again!

Love,

S & C

OFFICIAL BONDS 7

*W*e left the school that afternoon better for knowing the girls with just a glimpse of their hardships. There was no turning back on the love we have encountered or the sacrifice we are willing to endure to ensure that they become "our daughters." Charles and I are increasingly more serious in the realities surrounding our now multi-country adoption, where we have learned there are no rules. Natasha wanted to reassure us that "everything would be fine," however every sentence ended in just that or, "well, we'll see?" She retired to her montage of phone calls, seemingly translucent of our talks, dreaming about our future with the girls in the room next door. We rested in the happiness of the following day's introductions.

Natasha was happy to advise us concerning the presentation of our personal gifts to the girls the following day. "Tomorrow, it will be the right time, when you will meet your daughters as a family!"

Wrapped in our winter best, we greeted Natasha at the door, where she was quick to compliment us on our timely schedule. I could not think of another reason to be on time. *Are other American couples fashionably late to meet their children for the first time?* I wondered. Promptly at 9:00, we met our takci outside the door. The director arrived within minutes of us, shedding her winter drapery.

"Strasveetya!" She exclaimed with a deep voice and a gold-tooth smile.

"Strasveetya!" I was quick and confident in my reply.

Charles was much more shy in speaking the language, with his delayed grin and lack of response. He followed my lead with a gentlemanly nod. We were quickly gestured into her office behind two sets of doors, cranking lock and key. She was happy to meet us, nodding approvingly while looking us up and down. She reviewed the girls' files and concluded by smiling amicably at us.

"You make good choice—such wonderful girls!" Natasha translated.

We smiled in acknowledgment. Irena and Natasha continued to fill the director in on the legal conflicts with Anastasia's Russian birth. She was pleased that we had not refused her because of the difficulties. Admittedly, I was confused by the admiration, I was certain I had found my daughters, and I simply couldn't walk away over a birthplace.

The director gestured Irena to retrieve the girls, while we sat in a line of school chairs similar to those in the principal's office. At the height of our anticipation, Natasha continued to make friendly conversation about the school, as Irena returned with sweet Anastasia. She stood poised in front of the director's desk in silence. After a few minutes of stillness, the darling Katerina was escorted in by her teacher. She stood next to her sister, albeit, a little more restless and persnickety. They were dressed in pressed blue plaid uniforms with their hair meticulously placed in enormously large organza bows. I realized the two girls were together for the first in an undeterminable length of time, while living in opposite wings of the school. They began to giggle in sync as they reached for one another's hand. They were trying to keep their best demeanor in front of the director—emphasis on "trying."

The director's tone was sternly formal with the girls, so that they might be steady and listen carefully to each word. The girls stood upright, shoulders straight, and were not too fidget at the first bellow of her voice. They failed in their attempt at secrecy, peeking at us continuously out of sincere curiosity. Meanwhile, Charles and I sat on the side of the room clutching our hands and smiling to veil our shaken nerves, wondering what exactly was being said, how they felt and, most importantly, how they might respond to accepting us as their family. The director motioned her arm toward us and both girls smiled submissively and bowed their heads shyly. They began talking, and we hung onto their voices, waiting desperately for translation.

Natasha smiled profusely as we lingered on each breath for words. "The girls say you are beautiful and would love to be part of your family in America."

Suddenly, the agony is replaced with sheer exhilaration, and the room is filled with oxygen. In that one moment, an instant bond is made between the four of us without spoken words. It was something more primal, as the girls detached from their shyness in approaching just me. They reached for my long locks of blonde hair and giggled just a little louder synonymously. They touched my face, and Katerina leaned in to hug me.

"Mama." She whispered, without hesitation, as though she has been waiting for me to arrive.

Anastasia was curious and looked for permission to use the word, before reaching for a smile and whispering, "Mama," with a shy affirmation.

"They are not used to men." Natasha explained to Charles as they shied away from him.

He was okay with that as he watched his girls in our elementary bonding. Everyone admired our ritual as they began to resume business affairs and confirm the approval of our adoption and referral. Natasha and Irena had to prepare and file the documents for the adoption center, while we were sent to another room with the girls to get to know each other. We were left to discover one another, without words or translation—just the four of us.

The girls were eager to perform their talents for us as we sat on a scratchy gray, sunken couch. At first, it appeared almost as though they were trying to prove their value. I sensed a fear to earn our love, so we would not change our minds. I was sympathetic for an orphan's way of life. I was entranced by their enthusiasm and bright spirits. They are truly unique, and we watched in admiration as their two different personalities unfolded before our eyes. Together, they played fútbol and volleyball with balloons. They moved along to dancing playfully, reading and a game of chess with their new "papa." We spent most of the day with few words, except our limited Russian and Italian vocabularies. With a passion for Italy, the girls explained their vacations there with incredible crayon drawings.

Abruptly, a stern gray-haired woman interrupted our playful bliss to escort the girls to their respective lunchrooms. The girls hesitated in leaving, and we began counting the moments until their return. After only a few minutes, the girls ran back to the room, one after another, gulping their food in one swallow. We were happy to see them again so quickly. The girls eagerly invited us to tour their home.

After several days devoted to visiting the school, it had lost its pungent odor and had become a part of our day-to-day life. Even so, we had seen very little of the school, and I ached to see the grounds and breathe fresh air. The girls were not allowed to leave the premises unescorted. The first day of sunshine since our arrival in Ukraine called to me as we passed each dusty window. I longed to venture outdoors.

We walked upon tiles in complete disarray, mismatched in varying red and white patterns. The eldest children minded their chores of mopping the halls. Anastasia and Katerina had only dreamed of such responsibilities. It was clearly an honor for the elders to wander unescorted with their mops and brooms. Their presence shouted "freedom" from within the confined walls. The classrooms were small and the desks and shelving in many of the rooms were desperately in need of repair. However, I had seen much worse. We learned much about Anastasia and Katerina in their favorite niches and hallways. Anastasia was just as intrigued by the hall of drawings as I was. She has a true artful eye. Taking a step back with a squint, I recognized the motion from my own childhood. She is an artist.

"I will make Mama proud with my pictures!" She later told Natasha.

It was getting late as we watched the snowy playground of submerged tires and a few steel monkey bars cover with dusk through the corridor windows, as we headed back to our room to wait for Natasha. By the time Natasha and Irena returned, the girls had warmed up to Papa and were comfortable at our sides. Natasha is good at easing them in our good-byes, although Katerina shed a tear in the fear we may never return. Natasha, the director's assistant, escorted Katerina back to her wing on the other side of the orphanage. Anastasia is strong but holds me tightly as she walked us to the front entrance. Something was built that day beyond the

Ukrainian borders—that can never be broken. Anastasia held her arm out to us from the door as the takci pulled away.

We revisited Irena's overbooked restaurant from recollection and finally found a culinary sanctuary, Xytopok. The sign, which appears in Cyrillic, is pronounced "Who-toe-roke." A lively place, it is filled with friendly faces and lighter entrees, Xytopok quickly became our daily home for food, relaxation and conversation. We settled in with Natasha to discuss the status of legal progress along with the girls' development from our end. The evenings were lovely, and, within a few visits, a table was kept waiting for the long-term American visitors. Charles was adventurous in letting Natasha choose native delicacies, while I found something more— tame. I continued to eat variations of vegetable broth, "greekskie salat," "puree," or mashed potatoes with butter and parsley and, occasionally, beef dumplings boiled in soda water.

Our routine was comfortable as we nestled into accepting Poltava as our new home and waited to bring our daughters to America.

After our early evening meal, I was happy to retire to the Internet café located in building seven on Lenina Boulevard. I eagerly awaited replies of encouragement from family and friends and uploaded my daily journal and photos before beginning work from thousands of miles away. There were pleas from the printers and clients for corrections. I heard nothing from my "suitable" replacement, Andrea, back home—just a slew of complaints from clients. Charles sat patiently beside me waiting for bedtime.

28 February 2006, A Family is Born
Today we arrived early at the orphanage with Teddy bears from home, ready to meet our girls—officially. The director reviewed Anastasia's paperwork problems. She smiled graciously, saying what an amazing child Anastasia is, that we were very lucky. We smiled

*in return. Of course, "unofficially" we had already figured that out.
The girls were asked a series of questions and whether they would
like to be a part of our family in "Amerikanskee." Anastasia nodded
yes and smiled brilliantly. Anastasia told N that her mama was
beautiful and hid her face. Katerina was a ball of excitement. She
walked over and stood in front of me and stared. N says, she would
like to know what to call you, "Mama and Papa or Mommy and
Daddy. How do you say in America?" They called us Mama and
Papa, since that is all they can remember. So, "Mama" I am!*

*We spent the entire day alone with the girls as N and the
lawyer prepared papers in the archive room of the basement. With
the language barrier, it was challenging, but we listened to them
read, and we played on the laptop and took photos. However the
girls mostly played and Katerina—yes, our eight-year-old— kicked
Papa's butt at chess! We had fun and toured the orphanage, which is
nice in comparison to some I've seen in photos, but still makes the
heart ache. The sun was out today. I had wanted to take the girls
outside, but it is not permissible, at their ages. We left the girls
smiling, reassuring that we would be back, although Anastasia asked
N a couple of times, "Why us, and will they change their minds and
leave?" It is a very sad reality of abandonment, but we will not
leave, only for today—and, soon, never.*

*N did meet with the judge today and learned more than we
already knew. She will draft a document tomorrow that we must
sign for the judge to send to Russian Parliament.*

Love,

S & C

Greetings at the orphanage the following morning were met
with a mix of uncertainty and melodrama, as Katerina latched onto
Natasha rather than Mama. I watched closely, with a curiously
striking loss for words. Natasha let out a subtle laugh and leaned

over. "Moiya malenkiya, Katusha," I understood nothing but the sentiment as I settled back, arms crossed, for the anticipated translation of my daughter's newfound crisis that could turn her against Mama already. At last, Natasha turned, holding back profound laughter, while Katerina retreated to my side with her arms around her Mama, where they belong.

"Katia was told stories last night by another girl in her class, Alla. Alla told her she should not go to America because it is dangerous and all the...." Natasha gulped and caught her breath again. "... All the rivers in America are on fire! Katia told me immediately this morning that she does not think she should go with you. I reassured her that was not true and that America is very safe." Natasha glanced at Katerina with a reassuring smile.

"Americanskee horoshow!"—America is good. I smiled, grasping Katia's hand.

"It is normal for the children to be jealous and discourage others in their newfound families during this time." Natasha said.

Albeit, I was new at this, however, I quickly snapped into maternal mode and looked around for this Alla girl! Regaining my composure, I realized I had a new protective instinct that I have never recognized before. I clutched my little Katusha and brushed her hair with my hand, giving her a small kiss on the forehead. For the time, she was okay. I realized I would need to protect her from the Allas of the world, from herself and from the inevitable "rivers of fire."

After instilling calm after the morning melodrama, we were elated by Irena's news that the girls would join us for lunch at Xytopok. I was not sure they grasped the concept of leaving the grounds for the afternoon. The rest of us spent the morning in delightful preparation. The girls were assembled at the front door dressed in their entirely mismatching, but adorable, winter wear. Katerina looked like a polar bear, with a powder- blue coat stuffed outrageously making her arms prop up, like the little boy in A Christmas Story. We were packed into two takcis, when Anastasia revealed her affliction with motion sickness. Every few minutes, I asked, "Tvoi horoshow," meaning, "You good?" Eventually, we taught her the English translations for "Are you okay?"—"Yes" and "No." We discovered later, through translation, that for the most part she suffered nausea from the fumes of diesel petrol, and that she had not suffered of nausea during long road trips in Italy on the open highway.

Xytopok welcomed us with eager faces as they came to realize we were there for an adoption. The waitresses were wonderful with the children, as Natasha and Irena helped us settle in and order our food before returning to the inspector's office. They would join us upon completing their business. The girls were bright eyed, as they sat before their plentiful meals. Anastasia was noticeably picky and cared little for the food on her plate. It was Katerina for whom I became concerned, as she inhaled her food with reckless abandon. I feared a case of "orphanage syndrome" that I had read so much about. Often when the children arrive home, they are unable to satisfy the hungers they suffered for so long, eating to the point of vomiting.

I was terrified as I witnessed her recklessly devouring half a chicken from the bone, along with potatoes, and bread by the fistful. Katerina refused to pace herself or even utilize the silverware at her side. I was unable to find the words to slow her. I frantically motioned with my hand above her plate, indicating slowness. She was clueless concerning my gestures, and I finally pulled the plate from under her for a moment. Clearly not grasping my intentions, Katerina reached for her juice with the same reckless abandon, crushing the frail, thin glass in her tiny hands.

"No!" I cried out, "Nyet, Nyet!" trying to find words that don't come naturally to me.

She was stunned and scared. I tried to ease her. "Okay, Katasha." Both Charles and I grabbed for her arms and wrists. We felt fortunate she was not bleeding. She was speechless and did not let go as we picked the glass from her tiny, frail hands. I tried to ease her with a calming smile. She noticed our smiles and proceeded with a faint giggle, which bellowed into laughter. She began to bounce about as the waiter cleaned the mess. We tried to explain to her that it was "okay." But, at the same time, it was not funny.

"Nyet horoshow." — Not good — I pleaded.

We were unable to communicate anything, as silence consumed the four of us. Natasha and Irena returned an afternoon too short, as we mimed ice cream to the waitress, to restore a sense of good memories of the day. The girls had all but returned to their lively demeanor before Natasha was able to translate our concern over the episode that engrossed our first outing. My heart shattered with the same magnitude of the thin glass as Katerina burst into tears. I had no idea what Natasha said. I only needed for her to understand how badly she could have been hurt, and that it wasn't funny. My heart was broken as we were forced to endure, over boundaries, our first moment of bonding. Anastasia was equally hurt, for she had lived a life as the eldest child and assumed the role as disciplinarian before entering the orphanage two short years before, thus forcing herself to accept the blame — although there was none, to speak of.

I felt for Anastasia and the changing roles she would have to face in the months ahead. I did know, most importantly, that she had raised three children by the age of nine and that she deserved a childhood of her own. I would fight for that, knowing the battle would be mostly against her inner demons.

1 March 2006, Getting to Know You

Today was another long day in regard to the legal process, mostly for N. We were lucky to spend our time with the girls. At the end of the day, we had discovered only that, N and Irena will travel to Kremenchuk in Rostov Region of Russia tomorrow, by car, about seven hours. N needs original documents explaining why the father's name was left blank, per Russian legislation, since it is not legal in Ukraine. In Ukraine, if a father is unknown he is simply stated as Ivan Ivanovich, or John Doe, as we would say in America. However, it must say something. We all find this step somewhat unnecessary. Luckily, the judge is proceeding with the preparation of our decree on the basis that she will provide the paper by our court date, hopefully on Monday. Then we will hope to have the 10-day waiting period waived. We are optimistic in that the judge has not said "nyet." This is very good, "ochen priatna." If on schedule, we would have only a few days more while N travels back to Russia a second time to get the birth certificate, which cannot in any way be done before the final court decision. We are appreciative for N because it could take us up to a month to obtain a Russian visa to travel ourselves.

Anyway, on to happier news about our girls, not in any order of favorites, but by age!

Sweet Anastasia is 11 years old and was born on my grandma's birthday in December of 1994. She is very beautiful and resembles her new papa. Everyone says it is definitely the Slavic roots! She has been very reserved around Papa, since the girls have little access to men, but she is warming up to me quickly. Nonetheless, she still has very shy moments. Despite her nature, she is very confident when she is around the "scholya," or school, and with her groupa. She is very assertive and a fast learner. She is also very protective of her sister. She does not like to eat much, as we learned today when we were able to take them to lunch. She did not care for potatoes, chicken, *bread, beets or carrots. She ate the oranges and bananas off her ice cream but did not care for the sweetness of the ice cream. I think it was too sweet. Her favorite color is silver, we have discovered. She has taken an interest in my laptop and in learning through my Russian/English picture book, always turning to the animal page. She has a book of drawings that is filled with flowers and animals. She loves giraffes and pretty dresses for Ukrainian girls. As a result of her two trips to Italy, she likes to speak Italian. Fortunately, we find that helpful in communicating. Anastasia always tries to be helpful to others and her sister, but still she remains guarded, which is a normal trait for the eldest child. She is a sweetheart and absolutely beautiful, but she does not think so! Her life may have given her a bit of low self-esteem, although I am sure, with a loving family like ours, she will shine in no time!*

Our dearest Katerina is eight, having been born in September 1997. Our little Katia is a ball of energy. She bounces around as though she has had nowhere to go in her short lifetime. I believe she will give the beagles, Sierra and Bella, a good run! She is extremely loving and is full of hugs. She will hold our hands and sit on our laps. If she is not being held, she is close by. It was both terrifying and amusing this morning when we first came to the orphanage, as she ran up to N and told her she couldn't go to America because the rivers were on fire. N laughed and explained that she would be safe and happy with us in America. There are many jealous children who tried to misinform her so that she would not leave. She agreed with N and said she would go if N said so! She ran up and hugged us, with a big smile on her face. She keeps asking us when will we leave and why do we wait to go to America. I smile at N and repeat the question, knowing she is working very hard to make this happen for us. Katia is fearless and simply runs out on a limb. My cautious nature is constantly on edge. Her favorite color is pink, and she loves to speak Italian, with a full dramatic flare. She eats everything! At lunch she ate as much as Charles, I think, and twice as much as I. Yesterday, as I ate trail mix, she kept returning for more, although Anya picks out only the M&Ms. I thought she would make herself sick eating so much, and two glasses of juice, too! She is a handful, but so much fun and loving it.

The days have been a little long while N is away doing business. By late afternoon, the communication barriers are tiring. I think it is a bit much for the girls, too. We had a challenging lunch, as N and the lawyer went to the notary during half of our meal. Katia was bouncing around and laughing, and we could not communicate well enough to calm her down, and she crushed her juice glass in her hand, nearly cutting herself. We could not get her to let go, and it was scary. It's hard to explain to a child in another language that it's okay and it's not funny. When N returned, Anastasia translated that she thought we were mad at her and at Katia. I explained what had happened and N interpreted my concerns to Katia. She began to cry. This was very hard, as we need to bond and establish boundaries at the same time. They were both happy by the time the ice cream came. Now, I just need to communicate "slow down and chew" to Katia before she makes herself sick. She eats just like Papa!

Love,

S & C

NAVIGATING CYRILLIC 8

*P*oltava dawned on us again in a fascinating new light as we wakened without the guidance of Natasha. Only a few scribbles on a handful of Post-it notes left a trace of her and our ability to navigate the lucid city. It was cold and snowing again as we shuffled down the stairs and discovered the most unfriendly of our two housemaids.

"Takci pojalsta?"—Taxi, please—we asked politely.

"Cemb"—Seven—she coyly replied, indicating a seven-minute wait.

She quickly moved off to sleep on the kitchen sofa, where they had resided since our arrival. The housemaids had remained relatively elusive during our stay, only venturing away from the kitchen television to talk to Natasha a few times. Luda is pleasant and eager to please us, and learn English, too! I found it most unfortunate that her schedule rotation had given her a day off. The takci arrived as we watched from the window and saw the tires spin around the corner and push through the snow down our street.

"Dobry Den."—Good day—I said politely, greeting the driver.

Charles handed him our first Post-it note. The note was clearly labeled "Internat," meaning orphanage, with specific directions to our daughters. Our drive had become familiar, and I began taking visual notes of buildings, the market, signs and the beautiful, regal concrete lion statue that lead us past the medical schools and around the corner to the internat, housed, innocently enough, next to a chemical testing plant.

"Vocemb." The driver spoke, asking for eight hryvnas, or $1.60.

"Spaceeba e da sveedanya!"—Thank you, and good-bye—I muttered.

We were safely there, strangely unsupervised and virtually speechless. A drenched T-shirt on the floor at the entry hailed us as we searched for the assistant, Natasha.

"Allo!" She greeted us with her pleasant phone voice.

"Dobry den, Natasha."—Good day, Natasha.

Keen on the point-and-play method of communication, she practiced her English whenever possible, even when irrelevant. I found it cute, and smiled to reward her effort. She pointed us to their museum, or "musee," after obtaining a key from the director's office. Charles and I were intrigued by the montage wallpaper of newspaper clippings covering the school's recognitions, trips to Italy and personal achievements, dating back to what must be the 1950s. Although the words were cryptic, a picture is worth a thousand words. The musee volunteer, an elderly hunched man with white strands and a mouth filled with gold crowns, interrupted our viewing of his collection. He recognized the fact that we are foreign and eagerly opened a tattered book, extending a fountain pen toward me. He nodded in reference to a few pages. I recognized the Roman alphabet, scribbled Italian and other languages before my eyes realigned at the sight of my native English. He smiled at my recognition as I read an entry, discovering the tome to be a guest book dating back to the 1960s, from the best I could tell. I flipped through the pages. Finding our permanent place at the end, I dipped my pen in ink and made my entry just as the girls arrived.

Our most sincere gratitude to our hosts and wonderful family to our children. There are not enough words of appreciation for the love you have bestowed upon Anastasia and Katerina and the welcome you have so kindly granted us. May your futures be filled with plenty and may the children be strong with courage. Poltava will forever be in our hearts!

Sincerely,

The Schadowsky Family

2 March 2006

Arizona, USA

Anastasia and Katia watched my every word swirl in cursive as the ink soaked the page with my insignia. They were amazed at everything we did, taking each moment to discover their new parents.

The day awaited a new adventure for the girls within the shiny little ibook. They were happy to see the computer as I pulled it from my bag, expecting to look through the assortment of family photos we had reviewed many times before. On that day, we attempted to break barriers as we pulled out an assortment of DVDs. The girls were confused but liked the animals collaging the cover of *The Lion King*. The computer ignited with music and filled the screen with animated characters. They were drawn into something most divine.

Charles and I watched them as they enjoyed *The Lion King*. We were enlightened by the innocence of every new moment they experienced, and which we were able to share. With each sound of laughter and the gaze in their eyes, we began to realize the miracles of our actions.

Although the girls didn't understand the words, they followed the movie in complete comprehension, with emotions of sorrow and joy. After watching the movie, they were excited, for the first time, to understand the English language. We preplanned the English/Russian picture book, as we started with the animal section. Anastasia was quick to point and declare, "Simba." It was the same enthusiasm with which she called out "Simba" earlier to a visiting caregiver. The success of the day was wonderful, and we left the girls for their afternoon lessons.

Our next Post-it from Natasha directed the takci driver to Xytopok for an early dinner. We arrived at the door without our normal table, desperately searching the faces for a glimpse of familiarity. We quickly realized there had been a shift change, and no one was recognizable. We pried open our menus and quickly tried to remember Natasha's translations of our order among the dyslexic characters dancing on the pages. The waitress patiently attempted to help us several times before a man called to us from behind.

"May I be of assistance?" I recognized his accent was not American English, and certainly not British.

I was stunned. "Yes, please!"

He helped us with our standard order and interpreted Ukrainian flawlessly before introducing himself as a German businessman. He was kind and immediately struck up a conversation with us. He and his companions were in town to invest and build in the impoverished areas of Poltava.

"That's wonderful! We are here for an adoption and will be here for about a month."

He was surprised at our lengthy stay and congratulated us on the girls and once again on his departure. The waitress was kind and handed us business cards and a souvenir postcard as we departed with our next Post-it for the Internet café.

Upon our arrival at the corner of Lenina and "freedom," I convinced Charles to stray from our agenda and stroll up the snowy road to do some much-needed gift shopping, in light of our now doubled adoption team. I was able to successfully purchase hairspray, a nice pen for Vladimir and a leather-bound notebook for Natasha, two coloring books and two sets of colored pencils, simply by pointing and saying "pojalsta," which, ironically, means both "give me" and "please." I left each store with a pleasant "thank you"— "spaceeba."

It was dusk when Charles reminded me I had spent most of the hryvnas we had on hand, and he would like to find his way back to the Internet café. We were greeted by our familiar and exuberant salesman. He was gangly and appeared to tower in the underground venue. He was quick to kick out the kids playing video games, and, I venture to guess, not paying. He always made the best terminal available for us. As we crouched down into the entrance, he threw his arms up to ceiling in a jovial manner as he welcomed us.

"Previyet!"— Hi— he shouted

Natasha had sent a text message to us—her fourth such message—indicating her way-past-due arrival in Russia due to a blizzard, which had delayed their travels. "Doing fine. We will stay here for the night and conduct business in the morning. Returning home tomorrow. How are you?"

Charles wrote back, fumbling with the ancient and not-so-blackberry-esque phone "We R good, 3 hours w girls. Ate dinner. Now at Internet."

"Very good. Please text when you are home safely."

I finished my e-mails for the day and paid one to two hryvnas, or about 30 cents. "Spaceeba, takci pojalsta?" I asked our animated friend.

Naturally, our final Post-it destination brought us safely home, although we were somehow charged fifteen hryvnas, or $5, instead of the usual $2 for the ride home. We chalked it up to having "American" written on our foreheads, along with my savvy, but choppy, attempts at "strasveetya" from the backseat, and the snow-smudged Post-it from my seemingly mute husband. We let him have his fun with a night of ripping off the tourists for an extra $3, as we tucked into our down comforters for the night and sent a text message to Natasha.

"Home safe."

2 March 2006, Alone on Safari in Ukraine

Today we spent only a few hours with the girls. We have come to realize this is the best for all of us. There is too much strain with language barriers now that N is in Russia. N left us a handful of Post-its to give to takci drivers and get around town. We did really well. I am using my Russian and Charles is pretending to be mute. We felt confident enough to get a takci to the orphanage, the Internet cafe and walk around the shops. We bought thank-you gifts for Natasha and Irena and some things for the girls—via a point-and-"da" method of Ukrainian shopping. V and the other N have been calling all day in N's absence to make sure we are okay. I think they would kill us if they knew we strayed from our Post-its to go shopping.

We watched "The Lion King" on the laptop with the girls, and they really enjoyed it. The girls love animals. I was a little concerned about Mufasa's death. Fortunately, the girls did not seem affected. They were reassured when he reappeared in the clouds and happily called out, "Papa." They got the meaning of the movie, although they do not understand English. We watched the movie with a treat of bananas, which the girls requested. Fruit is quite a delicacy here, and even better than cookies, candy or ice cream. Who knew? I think that is great. Of course, little Katia had two, compared to Anya's one, I am not sure yet if it is the shyness. We are certain she does love bananas.

Anyway, after the movie Papa was happy to pull out their Russian/English picture book, and he started with the animal page and, more respectively, Simba. The girls were very much into learning today. The movie was helpful. We are so grateful for their knowledge of Italian. This means they know and understand the Roman alphabet, making it much easier to teach them. You must understand how confusing Cyrillic is when a "p" is an "r" and an "n" is a "p" and a "y" is a "u" and a "b" is a "v," and then, of course, there are several characters that look more like the Greek alphabet. It is almost comparable to training yourself to be dyslexic. The girls are very bright and will learn quickly since they know the Roman alphabet, from time spent in Italy, and must only build their vocabulary. Language structure comes with education, naturally.

N has been text messaging us during her long drive to Russia. Her six-hour trip became more like 13 hours. However, they arrived about an hour ago. They had planned to do this in one day, but we had a blizzard yesterday and the roads kept them to speeds of around 40 kilometers per hour, with little visibility. N says she will fly from Kyiv next time to get the birth certificate. We are very grateful to her and will never know how to say thank you. It is strange here how much work and effort people put into their jobs, and it is never a

103

problem—more so, it seems expected of them, whereas, in America, a lawyer would laugh if you asked him to drive to Russia, or next door, for that matter, at no additional charge. We are only paying for petrol and the driver's expenses, which are sadly low. The only way to show appreciation is with gifts. They do not accept tips here—well, unless they are involved in politics.

Well, tomorrow we will do the same and see the girls from noon until 3:00 in the afternoon. Perhaps we will take another movie. Also, we bought them some coloring books and paper. Anastasia told N she hopes to impress us with her drawing—which she already has!

Love,

S & C

We awakened late in the morning, with the knowledge that we had only a few hours with the girls, which had become our life at the time—our routine. It dawned on me, as I recollected the vastness of daily blogs I had read, and I recalled the term "groundhog days." I was quick to point that out to Charles, as he numbingly nodded in agreement. We have little time to spend with our girls—all this time just waiting. I have been conflicted with the irony of the fact that we are cheated out of so much time in America—always wanting to turn back the clock—when it is in plentitude here. After a certain amount of time here we began to feel like caged souls. I missed the energy that moves me back home. In Ukraine, we were in a place where the sun does not come out to kiss our faces. Our moods resembled the groundhog as the snow drearily smirked at us. We felt the need to crawl into a hole until spring, or into bed for the time. Our clothes were able to walk over to the bedside and dress us themselves. We were pleasantly motivated as the clock neared noon, when, after layering our winter garb, we headed out for our cherished moments with the girls.

"Takci pojalsta!"

The spirit of excitement that radiated from the girls as they entered the room brought meaning to each day. My breath was taken away with their happiness and ability to take in each moment with hope. Anastasia and Katia were full of hugs and held onto to us in a sense of forever, as they were sent to find us in the musee.

Anastasia took off my scarf. "Da?" she coyly asked.

She wrapped it around herself like a saché around a ball gown for a princess. I was mesmerized as I watched her dance around the room, holding my Italian knit scarf to her nose, giggling and breathing the scent of Mommy's perfume. Katia was quick to mimic her with my suede hat, although, at eight, she was not so coordinated, tripping about with my hat over her eyes and her button nose peeking out, amid spurts of laughter. They are perfectly amusing. Restlessness set in, Anastasia had already curiously poked through my bag for the shiny ibook, undoubtedly searching for another enchanting movie. We were happy to please with a feature of *Finding Nemo*.

The girls settled into their seats, both trying to cram the chairs as close as possible between us, nestling into our arms before immersing themselves in the movie. Again, I watched them instead of the movie. Their every expression and smile was so new and tantalizing to me. I felt the need to memorize every movement in recognition of each of their smiles, laughs and pouts that I have missed throughout their lives. I caught Charles doing the same. The girls must have thought that we in America are strange, but, for the time, they were engrossed in the movie. Our silence was interrupted by the loud chiming of the cell phone.

I became curious as Charles fiddled with the buttons. "Natasha had sent a text. She had left Rustov and they were on their return trip. Everything had gone fine, and she asked how we were."

Charles replied, "We r w girls and good. Safe trip!" We were eager for her return. There will never be enough words to thank them.

After the movie, the girls were excited for another lesson from our Russian/English picture book. We were ready to start with the underwater section, finding "Nemo" first, of course. We had also taken with us drawing pads and colored pencils, which we found on our shopping spree off Lenina the previous evening. The freedom of it all felt so Fifth Avenue!

Both girls were delighted to draw. However. Anastasia, the artist, blushed at the opportunity to show off her talent—very unlike her mother, who shelters her work until the unveiling. The girls had never owned a drawing pad and pencil set of their own, although Anastasia had dreamed of it. Admiringly, she flipped through the crisp, white pages, pressing her hand across the texture as though it were linen from a most exquisite palace. With hesitance, she began to draw Nemo for "Babushka" and "Deydushka," their new grandparents, to accompany a photo home. As in most areas, Katia followed her sister's lead, but did not pay as much attention to her book as Anya did. With her rainbow pencils, Katia replicated the motions and curves on the page so that her Nemo would be as impressive for her new family as her sister's. I smiled at Katia's adoration of Anastasia and the bond between the two that has suffered time and will endure beyond lifetimes.

The girls finished their drawings with a blue sea across the bottom soaking the borderless pages. With pride, Anastasia wrote "Nemo" in English on the top of her canvas. Katia followed. I encourage both girls to sign their respective canvas, like all great artists. Katia smiled graciously and spelled "Katia". Anastasia shocked us with a shrug of her shoulders.

"Nyet! Nyet!" She shouted and crossed her arms.

Inquisitively, I pointed at the drawing. "Anastasia?" Asking again.

Stubbornly, she held her ground. "Nyeeeeeeeet!"

I reach for her pencil and pointed to her masterpiece with its missing signature, "Ah-na-sta-see-ya." She quickly drew her hands to her face and began to cry.

I was saddened and shockingly confused at what had upset my sweet Anastasia so violently. After torturing myself beyond patience, I began to evaluate the possibilities in my head and came to the conclusion that she apparently did not know the spelling in English, although it is the same Roman spelling in Italian. I should never have assumed she would know the similarity. As our day drew to an end, I felt the need to resolve the problem, and I made one more attempt to reach for her pencil. She turned toward me with an angry expression. I wrote "Anastasia" on a small receipt from my bag. She softened at the familiar Italian sight, not being too dissimilar from her native Cyrillic. She smiled and touched the pencil to her ocean masterpiece, signing "Anastasia" for the first time in her new language. She looked back at me with an expression of pride.

As the day wound to an end at Xytopok, Charles and I reviewed the day's accomplishments. We were satisfied by the bonds we were establishing with our new family. Aliona, our waitress who translated with the kind German man and helped place our order the previous night, was happy to see us again. She pulled out a piece of paper and read the itemized menu she had kept from the night before, and she smiled proudly.

"Da?" She nodded as if to ask if we wanted the same order.

"Da, Da!" I smiled appreciatively.

Charles and I began to worry, as night was far upon us, yet we had heard no word from Natasha. We had become accustomed to her courteous and prompt text messages. Charles anxiously reached for the phone as it chimed during dinner, relieved momentarily, to discover our fourth call from Nathalie in two days. Vladimir was on three-way, unconfident with his English, but desperate for a comforting reply concerning our safe disposition. They were worried about the American tourists left alone to their own devices in the humble suburbs of Poltava. We tried to break in with our worries concerning Natasha, as we enjoyed a humorous conversation about our dainty female bodyguards who fret at breaking a nail or misplacing a blonde lock of hair, yet jump in front of traffic to hail a takci on our behalf in four feet of snow. How I wished she would call.

3 March 2006, Groundhog days

Well, I think we can safely say that for now Charles and I have a firm grip on our appropriately phrased "groundhog day." We waken each day in our routine and live out of suitcases, with the same five outfits to choose from. We take a shower and pack our computer bag, however, it is an "oversized purse," per his complaints, when Charles is carrying it. We head out in our takci to the orphanage, where we try out our Ukrainian greetings, and the secretary does the same with her English while escorting us to the musee and retrieving our darling girls. The best part is that each day when the girls come through the door they are even happier to see us than on the previous day. They are full of hugs, although it still takes them awhile to warm up to Charles each new day. Then we dig through our "purse" for tricks of things to do or treats to eat—anything to break the monotony of the language barrier. Ultimately, time will wear and Mama and Papa have to leave, and we let them know we'll return on "Ponedelnik," "Piatnitsa" or "Sabotta," naming a day of the week. They have come to understand the routine well, and they even ask the ladies to call for a takci for us. While we wait, they are full of hugs and kisses and sad to see us leave. But they always know we will return. For the first time in their lives, they believe in tomorrows.

N was able to finish the paperwork in Russia by 10:00 this morning and is still en route to Poltava. In her absence, we decided to watch another cartoon. We chose "Finding Nemo," for the happy ending and the story line—to search for the love of a child. Again, they were completely into the movie and were sad when they were called away for lunch. We explained to the secretary yesterday when they missed their lunch. We did not know the time, and no one came to get them. She took Katia to eat something, but Anastasia would not eat. I recognize that this is going to be a challenge with her. Today the director demanded they eat with their groupas. I certainly agreed! They were pleased to learn of the pause button when we continued watching the movie where we left off. After the movie, we tried to talk a bit about ocean vocabulary, and then we pulled out drawing books and colored pencils, which we purchased last night. The girls were very excited to draw Nemo for Babushka and Deyedushka, aka Grandma and Grandpa.

Anastasia had her first emotional tantrum when signing her name. I tried to comfort and help her, but to no avail. I decided to write her name for her and explained it was very much the same except the "C's" would be "S's" and the "H" would be an "N." She seemed relieved to find how easy it was, and she lightened up and began drawing again. I think it was difficult because her name is longer, and we are changing her nickname—a whole other drama.

In Ukraine and Russia, the naming is quite complicated, as we learned in school. Each person's common name is actually the person's nickname. A person is very rarely called by his or her given first name, but you know what a person's first name is by his nickname. Then, the middle name is the father's first name, however, there are different endings for males and females—single and married. Surnames are rarely used except in formality.

With that said, some first names have several nicknames, Anastasia being one of them. The nicknames are Ana, Anya, and Nastiya. Unfortunately, our Anastasia has the nickname name of Nastiya, and we have chosen to change that to Anya, as she would be teased in the States. She does not understand this, since she does not understand our language or our culture. N has explained her full American name, and she knows, but does not yet acknowledge it. For now, we continue to call her by her full name. Anastasia, which is, pronounced Ah-na-sta-see-ya— not like the Americans say it, Ann-a-stay-ja. This is very hard since Katia is still being called her nickname since there is only one for Katerina, and we are forced to ignore "Nastiya" and to put it behind us. To sum everything up, as a child, she has always been called Nastiya. We are now switching back and forth between Ah-nah-stah-see-yah and Ann-a-stay-jah, as a result of our own bad habits, and she is not accustomed to either; and now we are slowly trying to introduce Anya, for short. N thinks it is funny how their American birth certificates indicate their nicknames and first names. N says it is reads similar to "buttery butter" to say Katia Katerina and Anya Anastasia, but we like it— to keep their heritage instead of just slapping an American middle name like Molly in there for fun.

We miss everyone and hope all is well. Take care!

S & C

NAZDARÓVYE! **9**

$\mathcal{I}$ was restless throughout the night as I watched for the hallway light to radiate across our bedroom floor, through our door, which was missing its panel of glass since our arrival. It was 5:00 in the morning when I heard the sounds of Natasha's six-inch suede boots climb the painted wooden stairs with a fluttering of clicks. Several doors opened and closed, and then silence. I was finally able to rest, although riddled with guilt at the endlessness of her journey to Russia for our Anastasia. I was anxious to pry for details upon her awakening. I had nudged Charles to confirm her arrival.

"Is she home?" He asked.

"Yes, I heard her come in. She is finally home safely." He nodded and again fell asleep.

It was late afternoon before the hum of Natasha's sweet voice echoed through the corridor, following an elevating music level as her door opened. I bolted through the glassless doorframe hoping to catch her.

"Good morning!" she said, acknowledging my urgent entrance.

"Hello, how are you? We were so worried about … Russia!" I had tripped through my words, talking so fast "We tried calling and texting you all day and night and heard nothing. I think it must have been our phone?"

"No, my phone battery died sometime yesterday, shortly after my last message to you. I apologize for causing you worry. I am just fine. Will you both be wanting dinner shortly? Since it's Saturday, it'll be too late to visit the girls."

"Dinner would be nice. We'll get ready."

Strangely, Natasha was beaming with energy as we headed out for dinner. She stood in the living room in her best black pants, an elegant black blouse draped below the neckline—much more elegant than her casual professional attire. I felt it best not to disturb her mood as we waited for the takci. The car arrived as she threw her floor- length fur coat around her. She had affectionately named it Bear—"Mishka." With grace, she elegantly pulled her leather gloves over her petite hands, one finger at a time, and strutted to the door.

Both Charles and I were confused as we drove to Xytopok, not a dressy or special place. Nonetheless, we followed her lead. Natasha hung her Mishka and sat down, immediately toiling with her dinnerware. It was not long before she began moving to the music. She had a way of shuffling her head and shoulders to the beat of music—Ukrainian and American music, which they played a frequently. It appeared as though she let the stress of the world bounce from one shoulder to another with the rhythm of the music. In appearance, she was much more like the 20-something crowd.

"We will celebrate with spirits this evening!" she said with a most unusual gesture.

"What's the occasion?" Dumbfounded, I had finally broken the silence. After all, I had never seen Natasha drink alcohol. Was Russia that bad?

"Today is my 31st birthday!" She exclaimed.

"Your birthday? I feel horrible—you've been driving all night!" I said in shock.

"I am just so happy to be here safe and not driving anymore—Nazdaróvye!" She toasted with a laugh.

I was surprised to find that she was the same age as I. She seemed so twenty, so energetic. "Well, then, we must celebrate. Happy birthday!" We toasted.

Natasha regaled us concerning her 21-hour drive home in one of the worst blizzards of the season. She explained some of the climate patterns to us. They had needed to travel through Lughansk, southeast of Poltava, to the Russian border. Lughansk was widely known for its harsh winters and had made records that year, in deaths alone, as a result of the temperatures of 30 and 40 degrees below zero. Charles and I listened with what I imagine were expressions of pale-faced shock.

The wine had obviously begun to affect Natasha's five-foot-nothing frame as she giggled like a schoolgirl, relating the nightmarish tales of their journey. She spoke of towering hills of ice, with cars rolling backward and colliding into one another in masses, and dodging them, like bullets, in fear for their lives. Although she had a firm "no smoking" policy with her drivers, she let it slide, and smoke billowed through the tiny Rada, as the driver perspired in his frantic attempts at dodging the other Radas. She pointed to her brown calf-length suede boots that were covered in oil, soot and mud—with holes nearly worn into the sides.

"Irena and I had to get out and push the car from snow banks four or five times," she said, with a burst of laughter.

I couldn't speak. I was in awe of her six-inch heels. She had preferred them in the snow and ice for leverage—like ice picks. I did not think that was what she had in mind! Witnessing a side of Natasha we had not seen before, I suspected the wine had affected her, as she revealed her most embarrassing moments to Charles and I.

"Irena and I had to pee on the side of the road by the car!" she said, explaining in a whisper that they could not walk from the road or the driver's eye because the snow banks were taller than they.

We were speechless, wallowing in guilt with the knowledge that Natasha, our Ukrainian princess, did all that for our dear Anastasia and us. I was beside myself as I watched our prim and proper Natasha in a drunken state, making light of her Russian nightmare.

During our six-hour meal, we learned much more about Natasha. She was a great deal softer than revealed through her tough exterior. She spoke more of her family—much of her brother, who lived in Portugal at the time. Sadly, she explained that her brother had been a very successful and reputable businessman in Zhytomyr until his business partner had involved himself in illegal transactions and borrowed money from him, never to return. Her brother remained an honorable friend and never reported him to the authorities. Instead, he retreated to another country and banished himself from his then tarnished reputation. I sympathized for her loss.

Her younger sister had died at the age of 12 while hospitalized for a treatable illness. Sadly, a drunken nurse provided wrong medications to the children's ward, and several children died that day—including her sister. Ukraine does not have malpractice laws to protect the innocent. Natasha's family received nothing but an apology from the hospital. It was clear, from her frequent telephone calls, that she remained close to her mother, Tatiana. We had not known that her mother had moved in with her a short time before, after her parents filed for divorce. She spoke with pride of her mother—with a refined dignity. Tatiana successfully worked as the equivalent of a Mary Kay representative, rising to become one of the top saleswomen within her company, although, her mother could never compete with the life she had been accustomed to, having been married to the chairman of a university. However, living with Natasha made it easier for her mother to accept the fact that her husband was in the arms of a student younger than her daughter.

Natasha blissfully broke the mood, enlightening us concerning her nieces and nephews from her brother's estranged marriage. In his absence, she spent every moment she could with the children. She was hesitant over her feelings of the children's mother, explaining that her sister-in-law was never approved of and was of a different class.

"She has always carried herself dishonorably and parades around with other men." She shrugged disapprovingly.

I was a bit surprised that a class system still existed in Ukraine, although I continued to withhold judgment, especially in someone else's country. She continued endlessly about her love of children, and she spoke of the orphanage for the mentally challenged in Zhytomyr, where she often volunteered. I recognized her as a businesswoman, just as I am, with a heart of gold.

The mood changed in the restaurant, as a group of young men, in celebration, sat at the table beside us. Charles had taken notice early of Natasha's nervousness around men— not himself, but mostly drunken Ukrainians. The night was getting late and the men were staggering drunk, Natasha shrugged in uncomfortable silence.

"I notice you're uncomfortable around the guys," Charles finally said.

"This is not America," she explained. "We are not protected here from abuse or anything, really. If a woman is harassed or attacked, it would be hours for the police to arrive—if the restaurant were to call. That is just how it is here. I have been lucky that people have stood up for me—strangers—but it is not always this way."

I began to really understand. That is a way of life there, or, more so, the acceptance of it. My mind quickly turned to my girls. I felt protective and, more importantly, proud to be able to give them a more secure life. I wondered, though, *is America really so much better? Can you really keep your children safe from everyone and everything?* I had suffered my own sordid pains.

Turning our conversation quickly into another taboo subject of politics, Natasha was profoundly impressed by our sense of honesty about America. We were quick to lay our disagreements with George W. on the table, along with our profound disbelief in the war in Iraq. Natasha was interested, as she had a former adoptive couple of whom the husband was a fighter pilot at a pro-Bush pay grade. Our conclusion was decisive after discovering he was an Air Force fighter pilot of rare credentials and extremely high ranking. She asked many questions. Apparently, most couples don't speak of such matters. I was sincerely honest, although at times I may have appeared arrogant. Charles had served under Bush, Sr., and at least had earned the right to speak about his beliefs of war, Republicans and the entire oil scam.

In all our international travels, it had always been obvious that Americans were less than popular. As our families had served our country, we refused to feel embarrassed. We had proudly voted, and we did not vote for that war, that cause and the president who stood behind it. Nonetheless, in all of our travels assumptions have been made that each and every American believes in whoever is speaking on our behalf. Rarely does anyone recognizes the 49- to

51-percent vote that snaked George W. Bush into office. The other half of us did believe in a better America. I think Natasha was highly enlightened and recognized that the adopted children she was working with might actually be going to a decent place. The intensity of the conversation was broken by the tune of Natasha's little red phone.

She beamed with relief. "Allo?" And she broke into her high-pitched Ukrainian phone voice. "Poka!" The phone clamped closed with her chimed good-bye.

"This was Irena. Her son's wedding was today. She made it just in time from our travels! She says the wedding was beautiful!" Natasha made the announcements with pride.

It was like pouring vodka on an open wound of guilt. We hadn't any idea Irena's only son was getting married on that day! Retrieving a single piece of paper for us, she had almost missed the wedding!

"I am indebted for life!" I said.

Natasha shrugged. "Think nothing of it—this is our job. We are happy to do this for you and the children."

I was stunned, and I wondered why Ukrainians aren't winning Nobel prizes for their grandiose gestures. In viewing the people of Ukraine and their solemn eyes, I realized that when we look deep inside they are truly selfless and giving. While I have seen acts of kindness in America, usually in extreme circumstances such as 9/11, people in Ukraine give everyday, as a way of life. I wondered who accused those people of starting the Cold War. Nothing cold stems from such heartwarming gestures.

As the night came to an end, Natasha insisted on accepting the bill. "It is the Ukrainian way," she said.

I argued profusely with the sobering blonde. "It's your birthday, and we would be honored to treat you. And that is the American way!"

"Well, you are not in America, so when in Rome...." she argued.

She gestured to Aliona for the bill and a corresponding takci call as she excused herself to go to the restroom. When in Rome, I would at least make my mother proud by doing the proper lady-like thing. So, naturally, we stole the bill in her absence and paid it prior to her return. She was less than happy, pleading that she had drunk five glasses of wine—good wine! Charles received his change. We really had not looked at our bill in our hurried frenzy to steal it—until that moment. Our six-hour celebration cost a whopping 225 hryvnas, or $45. I recommended more destination birthday celebrations in Ukraine.

With our priceless Russian documents to deliver on the 10 o'clock nightly train, we bought some time in the city and visited the local Internet café. Our overly zealous friend greeted us in his usual cheerful manner. Beaming from his nearly seven-foot stature, he threw his arms out once again to welcome us. Officially, we were regulars, and it was nice to have a few places with friendly faces to call home while abroad. We wrote home while Natasha printed her Russian-to-Ukrainian translations of the documents she had received in Russia. Vladimir would receive them in Kyiv and, in a chain of events, hand deliver them to the NAC. I sensed a lack of FedEx in that region of the world. With papers in hand, we set out for the central station.

5 March 2006, Welcoming N Back

It is Sunday, and the sun was shining when we visited our girls again today for just an hour or so. N thinks, having missing time with them yesterday, it is good for them to miss us—we surely missed them! N spent the whole hour with us. She was able to learn much about the girls' family history, in a very sensitive way, of course. Anastasia is very much aware of her past and seemed fine in talking about it. Katia knew only a little, and remained her happy self. Both kept their distance from Papa again today. They say they will wait to get to know him a little more. They are terrified by the thought that they might have male teachers at school in America. Anastasia says, "I will not go!" It will take some time, but they gave Charles a quick hug good-bye. For now, they take turns at times and are competitive in obtaining my attention. They are such sweet, well-mannered girls—the result of their strict upbringing. The girls mentioned that today is the day they do most of their chores and iron their uniforms. Even Katia irons her uniform by herself, at eight years of age!

Tomorrow N will go to court and begin talking with the judge about our court date and the possibility of waiving our 10-day wait. Please wish us luck, as we need it at this point. We want to get our girls home as soon as possible. N made it back from Russia safely at 5 a.m. on Saturday after a 21-hour drive in a blizzard. We are so grateful to her and to Irena. Irena barely arrived in time for her only son's wedding at noon on Saturday. N wakened yesterday in a perky mood and was singing. She invited us to dinner. Later, she announced it was her 31st birthday. N refused our generosity to pay for dinner, so we stole the check. She argued angrily that it was too much. I am amazed, considering the fact that she drove across Russia for nearly three days for us. Our vocabulary lacks words to describe N.

Love,

S, C, A & K

The driver waited outside the station for us as we rushed in to meet a train slowing chugging to the platform at Poltava and returning back to Kyiv—twice a day, at 5 o'clock in the morning and 10:00 at night. This is their "FedEx." There is a well-greased system built on bribes for a conductor's word. With no insurance, nor tracking numbers, there is only one's ultimate trust with priceless documents.

The air was crisp and chilly as we walked onto the platform and watched the steel cars roll in. Natasha approached the nearest conductor, offering him the envelope, and returned with the files in hand.

"I do not trust him with the documents!" she exclaimed, and her voice trailed off.

"All aboard! All aboard!"

Natasha's silhouette became faint as she ran to the next car across the black ice. I listened to her six-inch heels crack across the platform of ice, "Click, klack, click, klack." Frost was visible as she breathed, and her fur mishka swayed silently behind her like a ghost in the frozen mist.

"Ezveneetya, pojalzsta!"—Excuse me, please!—she belted out to the next conductor.

Natasha disappeared into the steam, then, moments later, slowly reappeared from cloud bursts. And the train sounded its horns and chugged away from the platform. We stood frozen and were mesmerized by experiencing a black and white film of the '40s.

SPRING **10**

*T*he sun cast morning rays of energy throughout our bedroom, a strikingly unusual weather phenomenon in Ukraine in that time of winter. I took my first breath and smiled peacefully, knowing Natasha was safe and the girls were awaiting our visit on that beautiful Sunday. I certainly wasn't going to let the chill of the Ukrainian morning shower shake the sun from my mind. As we headed to the orphanage that morning, the city somehow seemed new to me in the surreal light. Natasha was delighted by the first glimpse of spring as we left the takci and greeted our Ukrainian angels in the corridor. Anastasia had watched us from her window, perched high above the entrance, and, conveniently, situated at the front of the expansive property grounds. She was warm with her hugs and remained by my side as we walked through the halls, delicately silent on that beautiful Sunday afternoon. We stopped to gaze at spring covering the steel playground, with glimpses of silver gleaming through the snow—calling back to the sun, as if to say, "I am ready."

We had only an hour with the girls that day. I yearned to take them outside, however, it was forbidden on that day of lockdown. We were delighted to hear from Irena that she had arranged an outing for us—the entire day of March 8, International Women's Day. We would indulge the girls in shopping and lunch. My wish on that day was for the sun to shine on us again, and I hoped to then be able to take the girls to a nearby park. Women's Day is an extravagant celebration in Ukraine, similar to our Valentine's Day or Mother's Day. It is to celebrate all women, and only women. On that day, the men are expected to relieve women of all their daily duties and responsibilities, and fulfill them with romance, including flowers and the preparation of a meal—on that one day per year! I was somewhat shocked to find the men of Ukraine still a bit archaic in their ways, with no domestic responsibilities in the everyday household. I remembered, however, to respect the fact that I was in another culture, and I appreciated the differences between us. Nonetheless, I was honored to participate in the holiday during our visit, and I took advantage of each opportunity to experience our new culture.

Natasha spent the entire hour with us that day, a much-needed blessing, considering the communication issues. A great deal of time was focused on Anastasia, being the eldest, and thus considered the guardian of family secrets.

"She is opening up with much progress regarding her past," Natasha said. "I will translate the details to you this afternoon!"

We were grateful for her ability to share her precious past so early on. With so little documented, it could have been years before they would have been able to fully communicate to us in English concerning their emotions. We were happy with Anastasia's progress. As we played and giggled with Katia, she showed little interest in the conversation. Considering her young age, we realized it was best not to force such matters.

We left the school quickly in a takci desperate for a download from Natasha. We stared at Natasha and waited for her to speak and provide us with a presumably earth-shattering glimpse into our daughters' past. She carried herself in her usual Ukrainian debutante manner, and directed the driver to Xytopok. Then our world changed. We discovered more than all the papers could have revealed, but most certainly more than we would have thought could possibly be harbored in Anastasia's short life and enormous heart.

"Anastasia would never live with her mother again; she would rather be at the orphanage," Natasha said. "Most importantly, she knows she has a beautiful family now in America. Anastasia cared for and raised the three younger siblings. This is usual in Ukraine with alcoholic parents." She spoke frankly.

"Anastasia would often go without food—to feed the others."

"She could not even take care of us," Anastasia had confided to Natasha, "and she kept having babies! She was angry as she talked about her two youngest siblings."

I fought to hold back the tears. Anastasia had obviously grown up years before her time. She told Natasha of cooking dinners for everyone, from the age of five—when there was food! Often, she would go out and steal apples from local farms to survive for months at a time. It was obvious that she was very protective of Katia, and Katia seemed to enjoy her sheltered life.

We do know when authorities reported the family for neglect. The home was investigated on December 16, 2003—in the middle of winter. They had no heat and no running water. The house held only one bed, which was broken, and no linens. There was no food in the home and all the children were suffering from starvation. Anastasia, although not thoroughly documented, suffered the worst. She was hospitalized with gastritis for months, when her entire body was affected by appendicitis. She arrived at the orphanage nearly four months after the arrival of her siblings.

Charles and I left for the Internet café, and returned home later that night in a solemn mood. We knew there were many more stories to haunt our daughters throughout the years. Tears rolled across my cheek to my pillow that night.

6 March 2006, Learning and living

N is spending much quality time with Anastasia these days. It is for the best, she says, and it is the only way to unlock the family secrets from the children. N says it is often too late, when children can finally speak in their new language, for them to relate their past experiences and their emotions. Essentially, they will have "moved on." We will have to cope with some very troubling and difficult experiences, but it is selfish to think of our ability to cope, knowing they have survived such grim realities—which I can't bring myself to write of here online. Please know they will have the love and support to heal when they arrive at home.

On a happier note, we were very excited to hear we will spend the March eighth international holiday of Women's Day with the girls. Women's Day is very important here as it is the only day when women are appreciated, when the men have to prepare the meals and clean, or take the women out and buy them chocolate and candy. So, we will have them for the whole day as no one will be working. We hope the weather holds out so that we can get some fresh air at a park. They rarely get outside. Maybe we will go shopping, and we will definitely go out for a nice meal. The girls are excited, too! We were also pleased to learn that the girls will perform in a play, of sorts, on Tuesday, in appreciation of the caregivers and in celebration of the holiday. I am thankful for the video camera we purchased. We will watch Katia read a poem, and Anastasia will do

belly dancing! She is shy about our seeing her perform, but she says
she will just pretend there is no audience. We can't wait!

Love,

S, C, A & K

We were let loose on yet another day of the Ukrainian rollercoaster. The siren that awakened us from our restless night of lingering emotions, was none other than a call from Natasha.

"You must know in confusion, Katia's play will be this morning—in one hour! I have sent Sasha to drive you. He will arrive in 15 minutes, about. He will then return for me at the courthouse. See you there. Poka!"

I had not yet mastered her high English accent and fast paced conversations, intertwined with Ukrainian formalities, however, I did understand play, fifteen minutes and her quick-draw finger on her cell's end button. I knew there was no time for questions.

My newfound maternal instincts carried my listless body out of bed after my sleepless night of analyzing our newfound insight into Anastasia's past. With only 15 minutes, I considered my lack of a shower in—three days, and I knew today would be the fourth. My hair hung from my head as if I had worn a nightcap of vegetable oil, soaking into my thin, stringy blonde hair. First, I dared to overcome my fear of cold showers, which in Ukraine are far worse, and multiplied by infinity. I would simply do as one would do back home in America and quickly, very quickly, I washed my hair in the upstairs bathroom sink. I reached for the handle that turned in only one direction—on. On, because the hot water carried barely enough pressure to run the downstairs shower, much less the upstairs plumbing; therefore, there was no need for hot water gauges. I dunked my head under the stream of water faster than I had done anything in my life, came up with mild brain damage, applied shampoo and went down for more, aka rinse. As the foam ran through my hair and filled the sink, I watched the suds turn to slush, and I continued working the icy slush from my numb skull. My fingers had lost all sensation. Finally, withdrawing my head at the onset of an impending migraine, I negated to apply the conditioner. I was awake, and five minutes remained for a hot blow-dry to defrost the ice cycles from my hair. Literally, I did know that a cold shower has no comparison to the slush just west of Siberia.

After my shock treatment, I felt a little dazed upon arriving at the school. Everyone was in a frenzy, compared to the peaceful Sunday experienced during lockdown. Anastasia greeted us at the door, no doubt having awaited our arrival perched above by her window. In confusion, it was only Katia who would perform that day. Anastasia was pleased to just be in attendance with us. We were soon directed down the hall, up a narrow stairway and into the performing arts room, my favorite room in the school. The entire room was an elaborate mural, from floor to ceiling, with tropical flowers and rainbows pouring colors, and somehow radiating hope into that small corner of the world that is home to hundreds of children the world has somehow forgotten. I looked at the rainbow and wished it could lead them, all somewhere out there, to a home and a family.

The room, within tall, solid-wood double doors, was silent. As they crept open, giggles were heard and faces peered in at the caregivers and at us, their guests, seated along the wall. Within only a few minutes, Katia heard gossip of the Americans inside, and she bolted through the doors like a ray of sunshine. Adorned in a yellow costume and tights, with a yellow-glittered tiara mimicking the Statue of Liberty's headdress, our Katia was the sun. She gave us quick hugs, a hello and swung around like a princess, in a ball gown of felt, Styrofoam and crepe paper in the center of an enchanting room. She was the epitome of pure happiness as she took the floor, all alone. The room was no longer a dream as she performed there for the last time, in front of a family who had come over the rainbow and past many moons to find her.

The dance teacher entered the room and the children ran to their starting positions, only to hear her announcement that the play would be delayed a short time until the arrival of the director. Joyfully, Katia reappeared and scooted herself onto the bench and she snuggled in, on the opposite side of me from Anastasia.

"Hi, Mama!" Unendingly, she gazed at me.

I had become accustomed to the stare from both of my girls, and I realized that I did the same in return. The delay was fortunate, as Natasha arrived a few minutes late and was relieved to have not missed the show. She smiled and complimented Katia on her "harny" costume.

"She is beautiful." I smiled proudly.

"Things are going well with the judge," Natasha said. I will return to the courthouse and continue to gain leverage into getting our 10-day wait waived. We should not get our hopes up. This is nearly impossible, with recent changes in adoption policies. There are still some compromising judges. Well, we'll see." She shrugged in confidence.

The show must go on! After nearly 45 minutes of waiting, Katia was more than eager to perform for us. With vibrant costumes and eclectic music, the play was amazing. The children read poetry and danced elaborately. I had no idea what they were saying, especially Katia, as she read her poem. I was intrigued that three- to nine-year-olds were so keenly able to relay the meaning of their words to us Americans. I found myself very much involved as I began to grasp the meaning of the play. I was profoundly lost in their world as I watched the story of Women's Day revealed through the eyes of children.

The boys sang and serenaded the girls ceremoniously, along with presentations of flowers. They danced in tuxedos and competed to put on aprons, indicating their willingness to help in the kitchen. The beautifully choreographed skits were precious. Katia was confident as she spoke to a young boy during her poem. As we had kept her from most of her classes since our arrival, I am sure she lost some of her lines. Nonetheless, she was not discouraged. After completing her part, she sat beside us again. At the finale, several students from the audience were called to dance. Anastasia was quick to grasp Katia's hand and perform equally well for her parents. They were beautiful together, smiling and laughing! The show was 90 minutes in length and ended with a series of elaborate floral arrangement presentations for, I could only assume, the upper administration and the director, who did proudly make the show—fashionably late.

"Sasha is waiting and I must spend some more time with the judge," Natasha said. "I will call you for supper. Poka!" She rushed from the room, complimenting the girls on her way out.

"Horoshow, ochen horoshow!"—Good, very good!—we exclaimed repeatedly as we met up with the girls in the hall.

They glistened with pride. We were minimal with our vocabulary. However, if I had learned one thing that day, it was that words are not always necessary. They must know that. The words, "Good, very good," with a zillion hugs and kisses upon the tops of their blonde heads from their new family, were worth more than a thousand congratulatory speeches and celebrations. From the sparkles in their eyes, I was certain of that. Nestling their faces into either side of my dark gray wool coat, I watched them hold back tears of happiness.

Again, it was time for good-byes, as we assumed a takci would be our departure ride. I had come to like Sasha as our driver. He was a family friend of Irena and had worked many adoptions, especially when the court processes start and the ladies go from notaries to various courthouses, inspection, birth certificate and passport offices on a daily basis— all day, every day. It is much more affordable and prompt to have a driver waiting. Sasha was young, kind and a very safe driver. Natasha was keen on his brand new Rada, which was unstained by putrid stale cigarette smells, as a result of Sasha's nonsmoking policy in the car; another plus for Natasha.

"Running late, will meet up with you later at Xytopok!" Natasha replied to our text in the takci.

She had forgotten about our safety net Post-its from Russia, as Charles dug into his pocket for Lenina Blvd. I needed communication with the world, I excitedly said to the takci driver, as he looked at the note, accompanied by my cute attempt at Russian.

"Dobry den, computer café, pojalsta!" He nodded, returning the Post-it and looking at me inquisitively in the review mirror.

We arrived at my little corner of Lenina and heaven. Sadly, my heaven consisted of a small two-room semi-basement dwelling, eternally overcrowded with teenage boys playing computer games. However, our young friend in charge was always accommodating. He pulled a chair out from under a boy who was past his hryvnas in game time. Jovially, he motioned with his hand and pushed the seat in for me. Charles, however, was on his own—to stand and look over my shoulder. The computers were outdated, and the room was stank with the smell of a boys' locker room and dirty sneakers. But there, and only there, was my sole connection to reality, to America and home. "Dear Mom," I wrote, holding back the tears of happiness, frustration and sorrow, and I wished she could experience the tribulations of the journey and the joy of meeting her granddaughters. I loved to read my Inbox and soak in the support from my family, friends and clients back home. I quickly uploaded some daily photos, while Charles became agitated. I could type for hours, if Charles would restrain his complaints about holding my "oversized purse". I began typing jokingly about his comments concerning my leather laptop bag.

"It's time to go, Natasha texted. She is on her way to Xotopok." Charles smirked.

6 March 2006, Bringing Sun, Song and Dance to Women

Wow, what an incredible morning! Included was a misunderstanding about Katia's groupa having their play today! We leaped out of bed without a shower, I iced my hair in the upstairs sink and we were off. Like it matters, my five outfits could walk on their own now. N sent the driver, Sasha—who she had hired for the day for her many cross-town errands—for us, and he stopped quickly at the market for chocolate cookies for the little performers, without saying much but the "market" and "N." We made it on time.

The kids were from about age three to nine, so, unfortunately, Anastasia did not perform today. However, they did ask for volunteers to come up and dance. She was so eager to perform for us, she grabbed Katia's hand and danced with her sister. We were so proud of both of them! Katia had a few parts in the performance, reading a poem, as the sun. We do not know what she said, but she was so confident. I think she forgot a few of her lines but, without discouragement, she kept going. She was so bright up there in front of the crowd. I was proud of our normally shy Anastasia, too, for dancing. I did not expect that from her, although we were pleasantly delighted.

I am sure today was the first of many recitals, plays, ballets, and dances, but for some reason I know this is one I will never forget and which will forever remain close to our hearts, as it is a part of their heritage and a celebration for the women of this country. Someday I will have them translate the video for me. I could grasp the concept of love, respect and kindness toward women. There where little boys giving flowers to girls in tradition and in politeness, and competitions to see how fast the boys could put on a skirt and apron over their pants, since the men are to cook for the women on this day only. Everything about it was adorable, silly and cute. I hope to get it e-mailed over to home, but I must find the cable first. Just look for my sunshine when you get the video.

We will let you know more about what the judge says tomorrow, after we have dinner with N tonight following all her legal stuff, but, still no word for now.

Love,

S, C, A & K

The combined news from Vladimir in Kyiv, and the courthouse drowned the mascara off Natasha's rain drenched face like a cesspool of petrol and politics onto her plate, as she toiled with her fork. It was an eternity before she could find the words, in any language, to tell us of the day's numerous setbacks. In contrast to her normally bubbly disposition, bouncing the day's stress off her with the beat of the music. On that day, Natasha could only repeatedly place her hands against her face.

"Wow! Well, it will be okay; everything will be okay." She spoke to us as though only to convince herself.

Charles and I looked at each other, wondering, *what will be okay?*

Looking down at the remnant of her red wine, she carefully explained, "Vladimir has brought news from Kyiv that will cause a slight delay in being appointed a court date. Vladimir has met with officials at the National Adoption Center," she continued to explain. "The NAC director has not been in to review your file. You will not be able to have your court date until later in the week, with the national holiday and the delay in receiving the NAC

131

permissions. Vladimir will spend all days at the NAC office talking with his contacts and, well, we will hope she will conclude this by weeks end."

I knew exactly where she was headed. My heart tore. Closing my eyes, I searched for a breath, which I could not find within me. We had counted the days on napkins so many times over dinner, drawing calendars of possible court dates and worst-case scenarios. The ink had flooded the napkin. There were no more tomorrows.

My soul bore the burden of making a decision to leave Charles and the children behind.

"It will be fine. Well, everything will be okay," Natasha said again. "Your family will be together in America soon and you will forget about all this. Very good news—the Judge indicates he will waive the 10-day waiting period in regards to obtaining legal documents. This will save us a week or two to travel back to Russia in the meantime. And, at 10 days, your adoption will be official by Ukrainian law."

I was happy that we would be united quicker. Nothing changed my fate. As we left Xytopok, my mind was spinning in emotional confusion. Maybe it was selfish, maybe selfless. All I could do was recall the inconvenience of the months leading us to Ukraine for our February appointment date. It had all come rushing forward. Months, days, minutes and moments flashed before us. I could see them reflected in the tears I could no longer hold back. For us, timing was invaluable and, for me, unbeatable. Home was calling, and the plane would have me on it. I would leave for home, alone, without my family.

We knew the schedule and we knew, without compromise, that I would return to the States by the 28th of March to close on the home bought years before in my name, or we would lose everything. This was just the first priority, as my ability to ignore the pressures from Ray, at work, were surmounting. And, if anything, my unsecured leave was not paying the bills, nor would the lost income from a lost job. The sorrow of leaving my children was tearing me in two. However, I knew that if I stayed there might be no home to return to.

Charles and Natasha did their best to ease my burden. "Everything will work out just fine." Their words echoed in my head. I spent the rest of the night trying to breathe and later trying to convince myself that indeed "everything would work out." My girls had bonded to me at that point, with their entire hearts. How would they feel, I wondered when they found their new mother had abandoned them, just as they had entrusted their fragile hearts to me. Could they ever forgive me, or would my motherhood be tarnished in their eyes, as was that of their birthmother? Ironically, for the first time, I knew I was a mother because every part of my broken heart ached for them—not for Charles, and not for me. As I lay in the crook of Charles' arm, I thought, for the first time, of the pain that would be inflicted upon my daughters, and I loathed myself.

"When will we tell them? How will we tell them? What— 'The days just didn't add up right for Mama, so she's abandoning you!'" I cried, as Charles lay speechless, hesitating to calm my irrational banter.

Our mood of dreariness existed in an icy drizzle that was with us from dusk through morning. We first set out for the bank, the first in a long line of errands on the way to the orphanage. The Ukrainian exchange bank erupted in emotional chaos, the banks were a place we had come to know well, and which we had found complex and annoying. Naturally, the morning would prove routine in the denial of our "unacceptable" Ben Franklins. The man behind the counter took several minutes to examine each bill with surgical skill and accuracy; then, with an abrupt nod of his head toward Natasha, followed the inevitable shout, "Nyet!"

I had come to a conclusion as we hurriedly visited every bank in the Phoenix metropolitan area the week before we left. Each teller had the same response, accompanied by laughter. "There are no new $100 bills. The mint does not produce them except in December, based on circulation needs." I spent valuable time sorting through "Call me baby" notes, placing them on the "no" pile, and accepting the usual slightly crisp, highlighter-mark and fold-down-the-middle bills, placing them on the "yes" pile.

After arriving in Ukraine, the nyet-sayer's liked to show me examples of crisp one-hundred American U.S. dollar bills, like I was an idiot. Therefore, I arrived at the conclusion that the Ukrainians and Russians had kept all of them, thousands of them, from the adoptive families traveling through, refusing to circulate them back to us. They habitually held them hostage, just to point them out and say this is what valid currency looks like.

"Well, there are none left in the U.S., until you give them back!" Clearly, I was emotional.

Walking away with our worthless money, mumbling under my breath, we got back into the takci and headed to a bank off Lenina, a Duesche subsidiary owned out of Germany, where Charles and I had experienced better luck. I always liked the Germans! We were much more successful, however, they discounted one of the five bills—one percent for wear. We accepted and went on our way with a fear that we would eventually run out of acceptable bills, having narrowed them down to three categories: good, bad and going back to the U.S. with Mommy.

WOMEN'S DAY **11**

*O*n our final stop after accomplishing a series of tasks for Women's Day, en route to the orphanage. The takci driver silently waited as we made our scheduled stops. Heading for our last stop before the orphanage, the driver frantically threw his arms into the air as we moved around the corner from the flower markets. I deciphered his agitated words as we awaited translation. "The car is no good," Natasha calmly said, "but everything is fine. We are here, and he has called for his friend to take us from here to the school."

Charles paid the distressed driver and left him a tip, as smoke bellowed from the Rada's engine. Sloshing up the sidewalk, we headed to the flower market, which, despite the sleet and petrol, smelled radiant. Though not nearly enough to clear the cloudiness from my mind, the day looked better, surrounded by elaborate bouquets. Charles found the femininity of the place overwhelming, as Natasha prodded him for an opinion. Charles searched for an answer.

After what seemed an eternity of evaluating every bloom for perfection and meaning, I felt confused, having seen very few arrangements and never having preferred them to practical gifts. Also, our cats eat them and toss them about the house, like the aftermath of a tropical storm. We left with four bouquets, one of which I thought would be considered embarrassingly large and gaudy in any country and for any occasion, including as a funeral arrangement.

We headed toward the drivers, as the men hovered, with their heads halfway into the front end of the smoking car. They were quick to receive Natasha's shout, as every man is when the tall, slender blonde catches their attention. They smiled at her as she walked toward the new driver's car, which became adorned with a large ensemble of flowers. Crowded with foliage, we proceeded to see our girls. Natasha disembarked from the car, propping the floral eccentricities in Charles' arms. His facial expression was one of disdain, and I feared he might toss the flowers.

Natasha smirked. "It is only proper for a man to present flowers for Women's Day!" Charles turned beet red in anger; or was it embarrassment?

Strutting toward the door, Natasha was pleased with herself. Although it was only the 7th of March, everyone would be gone the following day for the holiday, hence the early gifts. Upon entering the administration office, Charles was met with a symphony of cooing from the staff of women, "Ahhhh!" followed by what, in Charles' eyes, could only have been seen as Ukrainian profanity—words like lovely and beautiful—as women throughout the corridor fondled the blossoms and smelled them.

"Charles, please present Irena with the yellow arrangement," Natasha said, adding something cordially to Irena in Ukrainian and translating words of thanks, congratulations and wishes for enduring beauty and a healthy, happy life.

Charles looked nauseous but presented a fake smile. I stood back, hoping it would not be followed by vomit. Irena hugged both of us and kissed our cold, pink cheeks. Eagerly, she grasped the key as she eyed the gaudy arrangement the size of a small child, and she knocked on the interior door to the director's office. With a delighted smile, she motioned for us to enter. Charles was silent, as usual, as I searched my mental Russian dictionary.

"Strasveetya, dobry den!"—Hello, good day! I announced our boisterous American presence.

The director was always pleased with my efforts, and she smiled at Charles. How could she not, with such a display? Natasha presented an elaborate speech in Ukrainian, which sounded eloquent. With her high social-class upbringing, it obviously came easily for her. She definitely carried herself like a debutante. For all we knew, she could have been making arrangements for a second wife for him, as the director, with her gold-toothed grin, smiled from ear to ear eyeing Charles and the flowers.

Charles buckled up and readied himself for the big presentation, releasing the glittered tree of flowers into the director's arms. She carried on with the same words of exclamation we had heard in the other room.

"Spaceeba, spaceeba!"—Thank you, thank you! She nodded toward each of us.

"Spaceeba!" I replied.

The ladies quickly turned to the formalities of business. I looked around the elaborate office of wood floors and wood walls and tried to see past the barrage of floral eccentricities, at the importance of this woman. Trophies, certificates and photos by the dozens were displayed, along with important portraits of her shaking hands with the apparent who's-who of Ukraine. A kind woman, I admired her and her success in a country normally suppressive toward, and exploitive of, women.

"Da Sveedanya!"

"Da Sveedanya"—Goodbye, Charles mumbled, mimicking my confident speech, as we were ushered out for their secret conversations.

Natasha relieved Charles of the two remaining floral arrangements as she and Irena set off to the birth-certificate office. "We will present them in your absence, while you care for your girls." Naturally, Anastasia was perched outside the administration office awaiting our release, while Katia, in the aftermath of Irena's call, charged through the corridor. The day had finally found meaning. We had decided not to tell the girls yet that I would be leaving them, and Charles, in Ukraine shortly.

The bitterness of previous days rolled off me as sleet cleared our way for a cold but clear day. The sun's rays pranced through the thick clouds only a few times, as if to remind me of home. I was thinking more and more of home. However, I knew for certain that nothing, including me, would ruin Women's Day and our first all-day outing together with our daughters.

The sight of the city was beautiful as men and women adorned the streets with vivid floral arrangements—some just leaving the market and others wakening to their affectionate display and carrying it with them around town. There was something very moving and uplifting about the city that morning, when the usually gloomy Ukrainian faces were not seen. It seemed more as though we were in Paris, as eyes glistened with happiness—for that one day. Even in my despair, I found the mood contagious.

It was 10 O'clock in the morning when we arrived for the girls. We met Anastasia in the corridor and walked to Katia's wing to release her. The girls had no expectations, having rarely spent a day outside the property, other than their two trips to Italy. They beamed with divine excitement and curiosity. We stood at the door and bundled them up in their usually mismatched coats, scarves, hats and gloves, which were, by most means, communal. Sadly, the children temporarily lay claim to favorites based on a hierarchy of dominance. The tougher the children, the fewer holes in their clothing! Comparably, Anya and Katia looked impeccable.

We were met by a takci for Charles, the girls and me, while Natasha and Irena drove away with Sasha. We headed for the main street first, to take care of the girls' passport photos. Looking at the girls, I felt a burden of sorrow as they removed their caps and I viewed the hair of orphans—knotted, dirt clotted and weaved against their scalps—something I had noticed many times previously. Both girls obviously felt anxious and nervous when they saw the camera. I recognized how embarrassed they were, only they were not longer orphans—they were my daughters!

Quickly, I helped Anastasia shape her thin, greasy locks, which are exactly like mine. The only difference was, I had showered more than once that week, which was their allotment of cleanliness. Although Anastasia appeared brunette, she was pleased. With Katia, it was different. Her hair was coarse, thick and knotted. I retrieved all the clips from Natasha's, Anastasia's and Katia's hair and spit on my hands a dozen times to slick the frayed ends back and make an elegant zig-zag part down her scalp. I pinned and pony-tailed her short bob into tiny knots on the back of her head and left a one-inch line of hair wisping off the curve of her neck. Katia was almost in tears at the sight of her photo on the digital camera. She had not seen a recent photo without her head having been shaved. It was hard to pull her away as the man turned the screen to a black fade.

Returning to the waiting takci outside, Anastasia reacted toward the drive. We were worried about carsickness, only to discover she is profoundly nauseated by the petrol and ashtray odors. Natasha peeked in, and I quickly confirmed to her not to bother. It was by far one of the worst takcis yet. Natasha called for

Charles to pay the man, and his services were quickly dismissed. I felt sad and embarrassed that I could not understand my daughter's distress until translation. With guilt, I told myself that next time I would be more aware of such situations.

"It is important to find a suitable driver for the day," Natasha said with a bit of annoyance, "as you will be with him all day!"

Children must leave the orphanage in nothing but their gifts from God—body, mind and soul. We were more than accommodating. The rest could always be added. Irena, having escorted many adoptive families through Poltava, was cordial and excited to show us to the best and most valuable shopping venues. Shopping in Ukraine cannot be compared to such an excursion in the U.S. There are no malls, strip malls or discount warehouses, only boutiques of mix-and-match Euro-Asian imports.

Due to random importation, shoe sizes do not exist. Shoes are a try-and-buy sizing, with no discount at that. I am accustomed to Wal-Mart and DSW of competitive America. Our first stop secured a pair of shoes for Anastasia and, consequently, the first sibling rivalry of our new family. After visiting four boutiques, Katia had found nothing in her size. After giving up for the day and heading to the equivalent of an overpriced small galleria, we visited the local children's store for coats, gloves and undershirts. We found hair clips, too.

Shopping was a new and tiring experience for the girls. Nothing had ever been purchased just for them before. They were filled with mixed reactions, however, mostly confused. Anastasia could not decide on shoes and had no concept of being asked her opinion of which pair she liked best—was one color better than the other? The girls warmed up to expressing themselves more as the day wore on. We knew, however, that the shopping could not possibly be completed in one day.

We retired from shopping and headed for Xytopok, hurriedly and slightly late for our dinner reservations, which were required for the holiday. Our new friends at the restaurant were accommodating. Irena and Natasha toasted one another and me with glasses of red wine, an unrefuseable custom. However, I promised Natasha a rain check for later in the evening, not wanting to burden the children's eyes with the sight of alcohol—especially concerning Anastasia's animosity toward drinking, a result of experiences with her birthmother. The girls ended dinner stuffed, and, as usual, Katia refused to leave a morsel, including ice cream topped with bananas, kiwi and oranges—strangely, a more common custom than drinking. No chocolate? Irena and Natasha were out of sorts in their appreciative acceptance of our offer to pay the tab for Women's Day. We were surprised and delighted, as we had no other means to show our appreciation. We did not have an escape route or translated Post-it to a flower market.

We made a quick stop at our apartment for Natasha to retrieve some papers for Irena and, at the girl's request, to see where we lived. Amusingly, they had not quite grasped the reality that it was not our real home. They did not fully understand that our home was thousands of miles away, in America, although we had shown them on a map many times. For now, that was home. They rummaged through our things and smelled Mama's perfume bottles as though they were works of priceless art. We showed them some of the clothes we had brought from home for them. They fell in love with their jeans, which were crisp and new, with sparkles. They lay them on the carpet and brushed them up and down, as though they were the finest cashmere sweaters from Bloomingdale's. They felt like princesses, which, in our eyes, they most certainly are.

As the takci pulled away, the girls had left all their bags in the living room and had changed back into their worn and tattered clothing. They would see their clothes again when we picked them up for forever. Then they would walk away feeling like royalty, in their own clothes and with their own family. They waved and held their hands pressed to the frosted takci window, waiting for that day.

8 March 2006, Heavy Heart on Women's Day

Happy International Woman's Day. Today is a very special holiday in Ukraine, more special even than I had imagined. Much of the city was closed today, but we did not mind as we spent the day with the girls—the whole day! This was a first for our family, and very exciting. We had a wonderful lunch and treated N and the orphanage lawyer for Women's Day. N and I were welcomed at home with flowers from our housemaids. It was a lovely gesture.

We were able to have the girls' Ukrainian passport photos taken, which they will need to exit the country and maintain their citizenship here. I fear Katia is weary of me after her first public grooming ritual with spit and polish. Fortunately, we retreated to do some shopping. Finding open stores was a challenge, but we managed to find some garments and shoes for both girls.

I left yesterday on a sad note as we have discovered that the worst-case scenario with Russia is now the most likely situation. I am forced to leave my girls and Charles here and head for home on the 28th of March. I will wait for their arrival in the U.S. about ten days later in April. This decision has not come lightly, and I feel I am forced to abandon my children at a time when they need me the most. However, it is necessary for me to return home, sell our home and get our finances and income back in order, since we did not expect to be gone nearly this long. I am sad, and we have not yet told the girls. The girls have bonded with me so much and are still very shy around their father. I know we will all survive this and that we will reunite happily, and stronger than ever, in our beautiful new home in America!

Thank you for your kind wishes through all of this!

Love,

S, C, A & K

SOOT! 12

*M*y final days were spent biding our time waiting for answers and waiting for the political forces surrounding a court date. However, a signature, along with acknowledgment that there is a family waiting, is the furthest concern in the hierarchy of this system. We have continued to not question and to live out our days appreciating our girls in the moments with which we have been blessed, and looking forward to the lifetime we will share. Every day we waited, I began to absorb more of the Ukrainian culture, it became attached as another part of me. I had not yet used my camera to capture the landscape. The stark reality had become too depressing to view through the lens. I collected receipts, subway tickets, labels from the grocery and anything, really, to remember we were there. I felt that one day I would be able to paint a mural from memories of the wonders I had seen.

Our former Russian professor, who always struck me as odd, was beginning to make sense. He had spent much of his life on that side of the world. He once advised us to never use the sidewalks, for fear of falling vodka bottles. I was never struck, but I saw the evidence of truth painted on the sidewalks, along with glass slivers in my shoes at day's end. I watched mothers nestle open vodka bottles in the corners of their baby strollers for a warm bite from the cold during an evening stroll. Groups of people gathered below our apartment drinking all but the last drop in the bottle and igniting the shattered remains into trash bins. They stood around the blaze until all hours.

I had learned one sound piece of advice, that it is best not to waken the sleeping drivers as they are usually "sleeping it off." The ones parked on the sidewalk are sobering up and are there because they always drive on the sidewalks. In general, we found all the drivers were crazy, driving on ice as though it were a sport, sidewalks or no sidewalks—whatever! And seatbelts—well, those are, of course, needed for wiring harnesses for their stereo systems and takci meters. Seatbelts are ridiculous and unseen—as they are certainly useless for much else.

We were thankful for the days in which we were blessed with our hired driver, Sasha. Sasha was a safe driver, had seatbelts and even stopped for pedestrians! Unfortunately, we did not see Sasha everyday. On our usual evening trip to the market, we had our takci driver wait while we picked up a few things. Upon our return, his friend hopped in to share a drink. Natasha and I glared at one another. Annoyed, she shook her head as we entered the car, and his friend exited.

"Is it a good thing that our driver is drinking?" I asked.

"Voy Piyani?"—Are you drunk?—she shouted in his ear.

"Nyet, Ya Horoshow."—No, I am good—he mumbled in embarrassment.

"It will be Okay." Natasha said, comforting us, with disdain in her voice.

I remained nervous, as I was still recovering from my automobile accident back home. Natasha shook it off as we drove toward the house, trying to find humor in a bad situation. I recalled a story of another adoptive family Natasha had facilitated—a priest. She had told us of how the priest would, at random, refuse drivers for "having a bad soul."

"We should get another driver," I whispered to Natasha. "I think he has a bad soul!"

Laughter echoed from the back seat during our bumpy ride home. In the front seat, Charles held on for dear life, wondering what was so funny. Unfortunately, that is all too common in Ukraine, and there was little choice but to go along for the ride. Thankfully, the girls were not with us on those evenings.

We awoke grateful for having survived the previous evening, but were soon disappointed by a call from Natasha as a messenger in a long line of power in canceling our court date. We stood dressed in our one clean, pressed set of court clothing, all dressed up with no place to go. Carefully, we removed our slacks, stepped into our walking clothes—which could have walked on their own—and headed out for a visit with the girls. We were grieved as we told them it was not their day; we would not be able to take them home on that day and celebrate being a family. *If we continued to bring our love and broken bureaucratic promises, would they feel they were still orphans?*

It was most unusual, upon arrival at the orphanage, to discover that the girls were nowhere to be found. Anastasia had not watched from the window, nor had she run to greet us in the corridor. The day, however, was not like most days. Natasha had explained to them that it would be a special day. We were scheduled to make our visit late, after court, and as their parents. The change in our timing essentially changed our entire routine and left us to fend for ourselves. Our pathetic Russian language presented a problem. Unfortunately, our favorite secretary, Natasha, was not on duty that day. We became a challenge for the entire administration staff to translate. Eventually, the director came out to see what the fuss was about. Naturally, she found it was the Americans!

Immediately, and with surprising confidence, she began a conversation in Ukrainian, as though we knew exactly what she was saying. We had no understanding of her words. She knew, we were Americans. Maybe she had become overly confident of my understanding of the language as a result of my frequent Ukrainian formalities.

"Soot, soot, soot?" She repeatedly said, in increasingly louder volume and with apparent frustration.

Not wanting to disappoint her, I smiled politely and replied. "Da, da!" Da sounded so much nicer than "nyet," and I certainly did not want to disappoint her with the word "no!"

With a smile, I kept nodding, and I elbowed Charles in the ribs. "Call Natasha!"

Charles quickly handed the phone to the director. She talked for a moment and, smirking, sent someone off to get the girls.

Everything seemed so complicated that day. I missed the secretary and her very limited English, but it was English, nonetheless. How I appreciated her at that moment! I was certain I had lost some points with the director. I was profoundly disappointed, as I had worked so hard on my Uk-Russian formalities. Until then, I had been so polite. I recognized that her position was extremely prestigious. Few people speak to her, except to offer greetings or bow their heads in passing. I had done beautifully with my nods and strasveetya, dobry den, spaceeba and da sveedanya. Charles had even presented her with that horrid flower arrangement on Women's Day—she had become so impressed. As I sat in the musee, I quickly pulled out my

Russian/English dictionary, eager to know what she had asked me. "Soot" means court, and I had said "Da," meaning, "Yes, court went well." Translation: "Da, we are absolute American idiots!" Hopefully, our gift of the human-size, glittering flowers that graced her office would offset the whole "soot" thing.

Eager to see us, the girls ran in, and I wondered, Have they been told our court date of that day was canceled? *Did they call out 'Mama' and 'Papa,' thinking it was official?* I mustered the courage, in the hope that they were just happy to see us, knelt down and grasped Katia and Anastasia's little hands.

I found the words: "Nyet soot gorodnya"—No court today. My voice shook.

I felt the words hurt me more than they hurt the girls. Their faces remained unchanged—their smiles remained painted like perfect little matrushkas. Confident that I would always be their mama, they leaned in and hugged me. It seemed apparent to me that a lifetime of waiting had left them with a disregard for tangible things like documents. Anastasia and Katia felt loved and knew their family was in the room with them. Again, two young girls had opened my eyes to reality and had somehow shed light on what seemed a most disappointing day.

10 March 2006, Another Day, Another Delay.

Today we awoke in anticipation of our official court date, however, despite N's exhausted attempts while spending the morning at the courthouse, news from V in Kyiv was disappointing. The NAC director is in and has been in all week, but has yet to sign our permission for court. We are becoming exhausted as we try to determine exactly what the NAC director does all day, when she does show for work, of course. We are trying our best not to judge. And, of course, we will follow the golden rule—Don't ask why. With that said, our court date is now rescheduled for Monday at 3 p.m., assuming the papers are signed. Keep in mind, poor V is spending his entire days sitting in his car outside the NAC waiting for a signature on a piece paper—for days now. Then there are the two civilians (jury, so to speak), the judge, the orphanage lawyer, the state inspector and the prosecutor (who challenges our abilities as caretakers, financially and morally), all of whom are rescheduled.

So, with disappointment, began another groundhog day in which we got to see the girls, but not without challenges. N stayed at court, still trying to get a hold of the Russian Parliament and the birth certificate office, to see if they will accept our decree. We arrived at the orphanage on our own, and the girls were nowhere to be found. N had informed them we would not make a visit, or would be late, due to court. So we stumbled through our pathetic Russian, in the office, causing a huge fuss and ultimately embarrassing ourselves.

The girls are interested in going home as much as we are. Increasingly, the girls are being made fun of and taunted by the other children. I find myself being both protective and angry. I think I am still between worlds. My mentality is: "I will not let that boy talk to my little girl like that. I'll go give him a shove." However, as a mother, I know I must choose much more socially accepted paths. I will find my way, but I have such a hard time watching them struggle. I also struggle with things they have accepted as normal living conditions. It is hard to know they sleep in this cold place that smells and that they have not bathed, nor do they know when they will. And I can do nothing to correct such matters. For now, we are all in limbo. We are only able to give our love. They ask us to come live with them at the orphanage, and I cannot explain why we sleep at night in a nicer place and eat in a nice restaurant. I do not like this middle ground in which I have no peace and no control.

Love,

S, C, A & K

QUARANTINE **13**

*C*louds shifting and turning across the world every day, in Ukraine I observed dark clouds that hovered and lingered. I began to wonder why there was never a break in the monotony and the unchained series of obstacles. Our usual arrival at the orphanage was met without concern, as we caught Irena in the corridor, with its weekend stillness. Irena seemed in pleasant spirits and made no mention of the rude awaking that lay ahead. She sent us up to find Anastasia, which was certainly not unusual for a weekend. With Anastasia at our side, we made our trek to the other wing of the orphanage for our little Katia.

Katia's caregiver, a tall, large woman with ash hair, was normally kind and attentive. On that day, she abruptly scolded us. We were quickly led from the room as she shouted at Natasha in a fast Ukrainian tongue. Clearly, it was unpleasant, and I recognized that dreaded word again and my skin began to crawl: "Nyet, nyet, nyet! She hurdled, waving her arms about. The woman ushered us farther away, into a room down the stairwell. And Natasha continued to banter with her.

"Katia's groupa had been quarantined with measles, and it was believed Anastasia may be a host," Natasha informed us in a chilly voice.

"There is also concern for you; you could get sick or … possibly carry it on your clothes." She hesitated.

"Now what; what can we do?" I asked, as we were hurriedly ushered farther downstairs to speak to the supervisor of Katia's wing.

"There are nine children hospitalized from Anastasia's wing, although not from her groupa. They are all older children!" Natasha did her best to calm us while she translated the supervisor's concerns.

"Anastasia, included with the older children, were given immunizations last week, however, the incubation period will still be a week from now, with the outbreak."

"Why are we just now being told?" I asked. "We sat and watched Anastasia line up bravely for the immunization, and nobody said anything; not even what is was for. Why now? And what about Katia? She was not in that line." I demanded an answer.

The supervisor and Natasha spoke. "They can't afford immunizations for this wing, and there have been no outbreaks."

"Natasha, measles is an airborne virus. The older kids are still in the halls cleaning, and Anastasia was allowed out? What can we do? That just isn't good enough. We need to get Katia inoculated."

The supervisor phoned the orphanage physician.

"She cannot just treat Katia and not the other children," Natasha translated, as the physician headed down to meet us.

"What will it take to inoculate all the kids in this wing?

"The physician estimates, nearly two thousand hryvnas," Natasha said, as the physician nodded.

"That is only $400 to protect these kids, all of them." I was shocked.

Charles and I nodded and asked Natasha for the required prescription.

We sat in the supervisor's office for most of the day, while Natasha tried to make sense of the alarming situation. We had no idea what that would mean to our family as we waited for Natasha to provide us with the details later, over dinner. The supervisor remained cordial and eventually changed course, as Natasha had managed to find information about Maryana, their younger sister.

Despite everything, our afternoon ended interestingly, sifting through photos of children who had passed under her wings. In fondness, she remembered Maryana and seemed saddened at the separation of their family. With emotion, Anastasia and Katia pointed out their sister among the small faces in the photo album, and they asked if they would ever see Maryana again? We kissed Katia good-bye and left her to be escorted and held under lock and key. We walked Anastasia through the halls, hoping to find her well the following day, as she braved the infested dorm.

We left the orphanage and immediately hailed a takci for the nearest pharmacy. After visiting at least 10 pharmacies, we returned with measles inoculations for Katia's wing and for all the remaining children who had not been inoculated. And we had vitamins A and C to boost the children's immunity. The cost was a little more than $400. Natasha ran the supplies up to the physician so that she could begin treatment immediately that evening.

We pined away concerning the trillion-piece adoption jigsaw puzzle that had just shattered. Wasting no time, we went straight to the question and answer portion of dinner.

"What does this mean for our family, and what are our next steps?" we asked Natasha.

"You may visit the girls for 15 minutes each, outdoors and separate of each other by the director's request," she answered solemnly.

"That's it?" I asked, searching in a pit of emptiness for the strength to persevere.

"We will hope for court Monday. The director is favorable of an immediate execution to allow you to take custody of the children after court, just so as you remain in Poltava for the 10-day wait." In a businesslike approach, she continued, as Charles and I grasped for hope.

"The permissions have not even been signed at the NAC back in Kyiv." I pointed out the obvious, as I felt the devil's advocate in me show its snarling teeth.

"Then what?"

"The director is concerned, if the outbreak should worsen, the city would be notified and officially quarantine the orphanage in its entirety for approximately 21 days, or however long they determine necessary." Natasha's voice was shallow as I pried for the possibility of a further delay in court.

"What if court is delayed again? I don't want to hear, everything will be fine." I repeated myself in an attempt to corner Natasha harshly with my words, sensing her resistance to tell us the whole truth, behind the political bureaucracy of international adoption.

"No child will be allowed to leave for any reason, including adoption. This is the law." She was terrified as the words left her mouth.

"Your laws aren't the only ones we have to contend with. The burden of fear is with our own country! Anastasia and Katia will be denied entry into the U.S. for what could be months. And what if, if...."

I could not force the words to escape my mouth. Measles was a serious risk to their lives. I would not say it, I would not enable that possibility.

We left Xytopok with few words. The quiet was eerie. As we drove through the streets, I ached for home. I found myself at the Internet café looking for a piece of family, love and advice. The keys gave me strength and familiar guidance.

11 March 2006, Quarantime

Some days here are better than others, however, today, I think, has brought me to the next level of—what! After another shouting match of "nyets," We discovered Katia's groupa had been quarantined for measles and that our Anastasia could be a host. A supervisor finally revealed that nine older children were hospitalized from Anastasia's wing. Although immunizations were given a week ago, a seven-day incubation period remains. I can't believe we have heard nothing of this until now.

So what does this mean to our family and the adoption, you ask? Today we do not know, of course! The best-case scenario is we are able to go to court with our signed NAC papers on Monday, which the director, has yet to sign. We would be granted immediate custody given the new circumstances concerning their health; however, it is not "official law" until after the 10-day wait. We believe the director had hoped for our Friday court date to go through, knowing full welt there was to be a quarantine in their midst, and now it will be harder for us to remove them— especially if court is delayed further.

Bad scenario is we wait the seven-day incubation period and we are allowed only 15 minutes a day with each of the girls, separately and outdoors only. We will not be allowed in the

153

building, and, to top it off, I will leave two days later, having little to no bonding time with my girls from this time on.

Getting worse scenario, the outbreak gets worse and the city officially quarantines the orphanage as a whole for approximately 21 days, or however long is randomly determined necessary, and no child will be allowed to leave for any reason, including that of adoption.

Worst-case scenario is one or both of the girls contract measles and are hospitalized or worse. The U.S. Embassy will then refuse them entry into the U.S. until further notice.

I am supposed to be their mother, I do not believe they should be made to sit in this place where the disease is spreading rapidly, when they have a home to go to, both here and in America. Katia has not even been immunized due to lack of funding. They say things like, "Since it has not even spread to this side of the orphanage." "'This side?' It is airborne, people!" For now, we have purchased a supply of immunizations and a suppressive antibiotic, along with much-needed vitamins suggested for Katia's wing— totaling four hundred U.S. dollars! For now, despite everything, we just hope to keep her groupa and the younger wing well while they are confined, and hope that we can take them with us on Monday.

Obviously, all of this is an open wound and with each situation thus far, we have absolutely no control. For now, I am left broken-hearted for my children. For those who are following along, please prey for our daughters' health. For now, I shall remember a biblical verse for these trying times.

Love,

S, C, A & K

God grant me the serenity to accept the things I cannot change,
Courage to change the things I can,
And wisdom to know the difference.

There is something draining about spending a month visiting a foreign orphanage. The poverty and the faces of despair and loneliness redefine each day and burden the soul with a new reality. Having been redefined, and having accepted my surroundings, I yearned to continue the fight I had started, forever ago.

We arrived at the orphanage drive, when Sasha was halted behind an entourage of ambulances. We were bound to the car by quarantine and watched with a newfound level of horror. Familiar faces of children were carried from the building in droves by men in surgical masks. The children were pale, sullen and scared. My eyes welled up, and tears drizzled down my cheeks. I was unsure how much one's heart could bear. I watched each face closely and prayed not to look into the deep blue eyes of my sweet Anastasia. Charles was silent as he clutched my hand. I knew he was searching for the same face, the same eyes and the same smile. As ambulances drove away, the two that remained awaited stretchers. Frail blue limbs protruded from cloth draped over their faces. We waited and wondered, *did she survive another night as we lay comfortably in our beds?*

The doors closed and the last of the ambulances pulled away—no sirens, no fuss— crossing into the fog of the icy city. I did not see her face, but I continued to observe each child in the paramedics' arms, and the bodies of those who did not survive. I was numb as Irena emerged from behind the large wooden doors holding Katia's hand.

"We need to see Anastasia," I cried loudly to Irena. "Is she is okay?"

"Yes, Anastasia is good. You no see her today." Irena gestured toward her window high above the orphanage doors. The shape behind the frosted window was indefinable, but I knew the swirled hearts on the frosted pane were from my Anastasia. I pressed my hand to the car window and shed one last tear. Sasha pulled away

155

from the drive and into the city. I gathered myself and found strength as Katia curled up beside me. I was grateful for my stolen moments with Katia and I felt a tremendous need to remain strong for her.

Poltava bustled with weekend shoppers, and Katia was caught up in an excitement she had never known. She was still shy about making decisions and was, at that time, completely void of the "shopping gene." We were able to find shoes for her, and nightgowns and undergarments for both girls—the remaining items we needed. We had lunch at a delicious bakery with confectionary artistry unlike anything Katia had ever seen. She was confused as to whether to eat her cake or simply look at the pink iced sculpture. She was pleased when we convinced her it was okay. But she ate only a small amount, having no tolerance for an overindulgence of sugar.

The mall beckoned, and Natasha was able to find a new pair of boots to replace the beautiful brown suede boots that were destroyed when she pushed the Rada through the snow banks in Russia. Although she refused to let us pay for them, we were happy to lend money to her for the purchase. We invited Sasha in for dinner, I had always felt awkward on the nights he waited outside, at his insistence. Natasha reassured us that it was proper for a driver. On that day, he accepted our invitation and enjoyed a lovely steak. Despite our dinner guest and attempts to lighten the darkness of the day, dinnertime was filled with silence. Having one of our first family dinners without our entire family was mournful. All of us felt Anastasia's absence. I sensed that Katia felt it as much as we, if not more.

Before our return to the orphanage, we made one last stop to pick up the girls' passport photos, taken on our last outing together. It was uplifting to admire Anastasia's smiling face, if only in a photo. Irena collected photos from her son's wedding, too. It was a beautiful wedding, and all of us remarked on the fact, remembering she had almost missed it on her delayed return from Russia. Nonetheless, she had fond memories of the day, and we passed the photos around in the car on our drive back. Before any of us realized what had happened, we sat in the silence that comes after the shattering sound of mangled steel—a sound all too familiar to me.

I reached for Katia who was sitting, unbelted, on Charles' lap in the back. She was scared, but okay. Fortunately, we found that everyone was all right.

Sasha, in an attempt to swerve around a pothole larger than a car, caught the tail end of a man speeding from his driveway. Sasha was quick to assess the damage to his three-week-old car and to talk with the driver.

"He is obviously drunk, but it will be a matter for the police," Natasha said as the man and woman, slurred their words and stumbled about behind her.

"Sasha will stay for the police," Natasha said sternly, "but it is best if we pay him for the day and go before they arrive, or we will all be questioned."

We understood her meaning in a country unfavorable to U.S. passport holders. We retrieved our stash of shopping bags, enough for a diva's spending spree on Rodeo Drive! Peering up at the icy incline that awaited, Charles placed Katia on his shoulders for the long haul. Each of us took a load of bags and forged up the hill nearly a half-mile to the next major road, for a takci. Slipping and sliding, I caught Natasha falling downhill toward me. It was a close call, but I kept my balance and avoided taking down Charles and Katia, who were behind me. Finally, we succeeded in reaching the road. In the takci, I inquired about Sasha and wondered if they had insurance there. Natasha explained that they do, however, very few people can afford it. Irena said she would check in on him and let us know if everything was okay.

As I sat down to the keyboard, for the first time, I found myself grimacing at the irony of the day's events. It seemed absurd, as I wrote about the emotional tribulations of the morning, and topping off the afternoon by becoming involved in a car accident. I was beyond expectations, and resigned all sense of control. I would sacrifice every last breath for the safety of my children and the ability for us to escape that place.

> *12 March 2006, Riding the Gauntlet*
>
> *Today, we consider ourselves lucky for the stolen moments we were able to negotiate with Katia. Since her quarantine is more lenient, Irena managed to have her released from the orphanage for the day and into our care. So, we were able to continue shopping for the girls. Anastasia was not far from our thoughts all day. We came to grips with the seriousness of this disease and the risk to Anastasia as we waited for Katia outside this morning, watching ambulances take many children to the hospital. Sadly, some of the children did not survive. I cannot think about that, and am only happy to know our Anastasia is still well. I am heartbroken by the knowledge that Anastasia is trapped there. I wish for her strength and health and to be able to take her away from all of this.*
>
> *Later, we were involved in a car accident not far from the orphanage on our way to return Katia. Everyone is okay, with the exception of Sasha's new Rada, which is only a few weeks old. The other driver was drunk—welcome to Ukraine! We slid around on the ice and caught one another on our hike to find another takci.*
>
> *For now, we must keep our spirits focused ahead, and hope for court tomorrow. If the NAC will sign our papers before 3 o'clock, we can request permission for immediate custody of the girls from quarantine.*
>
> *Love,*
>
> *S, C, A & K*

I tried to remain peaceful and worldly in my outlook while residing in Ukraine. I had not yet made public judgment, however, today I found it impossible to resist the slinging of political sludge from across the dinner table. Bad news rolls downhill through translation, straight from Vlad at the NAC, where he spent another day waiting. I felt anger, as the news was filtered through the polite social etiquette of Natasha's high English tongue. Alarmingly, the NAC director did review our request for permission, although she found herself abruptly concerned with the separation of the girls' younger siblings in November. First of all, I was delighted the woman showed up for work and, then, that she actually did something while in her political position. She has been nationally chastised in that regard in the past! But why research a dead case? She could not undo that which had already been done. I was on fire concerning the woman, and I directed my question at the only person who might have answers:

"Does she plan to visit Israel and unadopt Maryana and Mikola?" I asked. "Here's an idea. Why not just consider the eldest children fortunate in having a family now?" My words spewed forth.

"She is most certainly looking for someone to blame for the illegal separation within her office," Natasha said, "when it was most likely herself taking a bribe." Natasha tried to explain Ukrainian politics.

It was obvious to all of us that she assumed no one would ever come for the "older children" and that she could get away with it. We had created a political paper trail, among many black marks on her scandalous, highly publicized record. At the time, she already faced forced resignation effective May 1, under the new ministry. Why should our children suffer for her tarnished record?"

159

With many theories in the local adoption circles, as well as the international adoption communities, one thing was most certainly unanimous in regard to the corruption overflowing the deep pockets of that for-profit child retailer, otherwise known as the National Adoption Center director. I had read numerous stories of the woman having chastised innocent couples, crippling their adoption dreams and sending them home empty handed. Up to that point, however, we had steered clear of her, as she had spent most of our time in Ukraine on one of her notorious vacations. It is not until someone directly affects one's family that one feels free to pick up a sign and become a part of political reform—even in a foreign country—in my children's country!

Natasha was hesitant to open up, but she shared similar stories of meetings she had endured with the woman. Clearly living six feet above her human rights status. Natasha had been in such meetings, where families were sent home because they already had biological children; or because of not accepting severe physically or mentally delayed children who had been referred to them. The families were sworn at and condemned for being Americans seeking only cherub perfection, and were hastily dismissed from her presence and sent home thousands of miles. I began to accept the truth, and I felt both hatred and sorrow for a woman who had sold out her country, the children and herself. But for the time, having vented my demons, I stewed for the remainder of the night as she held the future of my children in her calculating hands, covering her own erring ways.

13 March 2006, Political Sludge

Another day has passed, and the news is less than desirable. For court today, the NAC director has reviewed our papers, however, she was somehow suddenly troubled when she realized the split from the girls' siblings in November. Since a law was passed in May of 2004 banning the separation of siblings in adoption, she is appalled that this was allowed in her absence. So, today she is reviewing the siblings' adoption paperwork to find out why, and, more importantly, to her, who allowed this? Then she can—what— verbally punish them? What is done is done, and the important thing is that we are here now to provide a loving family for the older of the children, which is next to impossible odds in the adoption world— less than 2 percent. We are here just waiting for her signature! We are saddened that they were separated, but they cannot be unseparated; so it is important that we move on, especially given the current health risks to our daughters. Does this woman understand nothing? So again, we will remain with hope.

Love,

S, C, A & K

We yearned for some kind of rationalization in our second home. We continued to be unsettled by the lack of effort to grant our family a final commitment. We strived to endure each day, weathering the challenges and thankful for the moments we were given, under strict supervision. As promised, we were finally able to visit with Anastasia in the front foyer for a mere 15 minutes. Surprisingly, we were allowed, and invited, through the towering doors of infestation. Anastasia was brought to tears at the sight of us, surely in fear. With an unrelenting grip, she held her arms around me during the entire visit. Nuzzled against my wool, double-breasted coat, I wished I could take her away from all that. But the ever-watching eyes of broad-built babushkas of boorish Russian decendents deterred such action. Our tears could have flooded rivers as my daughter was torn from my arms and escorted to the depths of what had become the infirmary wing.

Natasha was directed to escort Charles and I to the back entrance of the expansive campus where the younger groupas were housed. The walk was long and the weather severe as we make the trek through knee-deep snow, thankful for a few wide pathways in between. In the 10 below temperature, we caught only glimpses of the sun, shadowed by the massive buildings. Our breath froze on impact with the early morning air as we searched, through watering eyes, for the door to our daughter. Natasha tried several large steel doors, all of which were locked. We began to recognize parts of the children's wing through the frosted windows and stained glass.

A young woman appeared thorough the glass pane of a steel door. Natasha knocked for her attention, and she said she would find Katia's caregiver, as she directed us to another door within sight. Under cover, we hovered against icy wind and waited for our dear Katia. Then she leaped from the doorway with childlike enthusiasm. The caregiver pointed to her watch and gave a foreign command to Natasha. Charles braved a playful snow fight with Katia as I began to nurse the onset of a migraine, the result of intense cold and snow blindness. In less than ten minutes, we sent Katia back to her room. The harshness of the weather was too much for a child so young. She kissed both of us good-bye and smiled as the door closed and latched behind her.

The walk back seemed even longer, with no reward at the end of the path—no Katia waiting there for us! The snow was crisp under our feet and the wind echoed in my ears as the fast- paced crunching sound resounded. We turned, with arms locked, to become stable from the wind, and found ourselves staring into the eyes of an angry, hungry pack of dogs. Four of them eyed us with scrawny legs, matted fur and teeth of wolves.

"Stay very still and do not look into their eyes," Natasha said. We stood immobile and silent until the beasts moved toward a capsized trash can and released us from their stare.

"Remain fearless and just keep walking," Natasha said, adding, "walk slowly, just walk slowly." We did as told, moving increasingly farther from the pack.

"They were frothing and probably rabid," Natasha said after we had moved to the opposite side of the building. "Most strays are rabid in Ukraine."

We continued to walk slowly, with all the adrenaline necessary to reach the front drive. Sasha met us at the bottom, near the back gate, the Rada was nearly stuck in the icy snow. Ukraine constantly reminded us of little things for which to be grateful.

JUDGEMENT 14

As our wait continued, I feared we might have tried the judge's patience. That morning, he sternly advised Natasha that he would no longer appoint a court time for us until she had the document in her hands. We were sympathetic toward all the parties who had arrived for court those many days, and had taken time from work to do so, for yet another no-show. It was not favorable in our case, either, as the witnesses were tiring of our semantics. One of the ladies was insulted at the offer from Natasha to cover lost wages and takci fare home. She considered her court appointment as a witness part of her moral duty and was quick to point out the fact that few citizens qualify. With the theft and alcoholism statistics, I was not surprised. On the other hand, the second witness asked Natasha to escort her back to her office and speak to her employer, verifying she had been at court and providing a service, the woman was terrified of losing her job.

Having Natasha make such a request was almost the equivalent of a bathroom pass in elementary school!

There we were, in a society with no protection for jurors, and we thought of our rights and the fact that we complain about jury duty, and take advantage of our privileges at home. There was still no word from Vlad at his new office, in his car in the parking lot at the NAC. As the day closed and night arrived, we wondered if there would be any justice for our daughters.

Finally, over dinner, came the jingle and chime of Natasha's cell phone, and Vladimir delivered news of the receipt of the document upon the close of day. He promised to notarize our permission and have it on the 5 a.m. train to Poltava. We remained in a strict "believe-it-when-we-see-it mode." We had discovered that was the Ukrainian way. The judge was pleased with the news, however, he agreed with our sentiments, telling Natasha to telephone him only in the morning when the papers were in her hands. We were pleased with the good news that the judge might fit us onto the docket the following day.

As we stepped along the icy walk outside xytopok, Charles gestured over the snow bank for a takci home. Natasha and I got in the back, and I listened to her usual pitch of directions guiding us home. I asked Natasha more about the court preparations, when bam, out of nowhere, someone else chimed into our conversation—in English. The speaker was our weathered, snow-haired takci driver, and I understood.

"You from Australia?" he asked with interest.

"No, we are American."

"Ahhh, yes, yes, America," he replied.

I smiled. "Where did you learn to speak English so well?"

The driver smirked, as he elbowed Charles in the arm. "Australia!"

"Ahhh, you speak very well. It's nice to hear English again. It's been awhile!"

Our jovial takci driver was as excited to speak English as we were to hear it. As we drove the icy roads and potholes in the dark of night, we enjoyed small talk with the driver. Suddenly the brakes slammed and the car jerked and slid over the thin black ice from snow bank to snow bank. We peered around and, in shock, saw another scraggly, thin legged mutt running circles around our takci.

"This dog is mad. Someday, I tell you, I just run him over." With a squinted eye, he stabbed his finger at the window.

"Oh? He just looks cold and hungry," I said, pleading for the pups safety.

"Yes ma'am, that dog hungry all right. He eat you if he get the chance. You see, he got the foam. He try to eat the bloody machina if he could. I know of this dog. He chase the machina always, but he no catch me! Look, he chew on the bloody bumper while I drive. Crazy beast!"

"He's rabid too?" I inquired of Natasha after our second run-in with dogs today.

"Yes, I suppose," she responded.

"Rabid? Yes, yes, that's it. That dog, he got the foam and he mad, he mad as a hat.

The driver spared the dog and, swerving around him, cursed. It was a short jaunt from that point to the large iron gates of the house, and the dog chased the machina much of the way. We were all certain we had lost him as we stepped into the snow banks and ran for the safety of the gate.

"You lock that there gate. That dog come get you!" The takci driver roared with laughter.

There are firsts for everything, and there were many firsts that day. I had never seen a rabid dog, and now I have seen five of them. I had never had a rabid try to eat my car. Nor had I met a sober Ukrainian takci driver who spoke English, much less English with an Australian accent. It was a colorful night!

The ring of the telephone did not awaken us that morning, as we had succumbed to the worries of parenthood, which had kept us up at night. It was without taking a breath that we answered Natasha's call, hoping for something to relieve us of the anxiety we felt.

Natasha was brief but exuberant in telling us she had met the train that morning and had delivered the permission to the judge. We would need to be prepared for court at 3 o'clock. It was early when we lay our one court ensemble on the radiator, to air the hint of mildew and remove creases from the moist Ukrainian elements. Until that day, we had dressed and undressed in our court attire five or six times, only to be a "no show." After cold showers, we spent the day staring at the radiator, awaiting arrival of the moment. We had practiced our lines and our answers for the judge and prosecutor, which were always the same. Natasha, having spent so much time with the judge, had coached us concerning his expectations. I was sure we would mess up and stumble, as imperfection is human nature. I would speak on our behalf. I was not worried. As a business woman, I speak to clients regularly. Charles, on the other hand, is much better with inanimate objects. It was evident that he was nervous.

Sasha arrived sharply at 2 o'clock to pick us up. We went to the office of the notary for the zillionth time that month to fetch Natasha, and made a quick stop for flowers and chocolates before arriving at the court. Although with many court dates in the past, that was the first time we had been in the presence of the court. The building, not different from any other in Poltava, was very much in a state of disrepair. We waited patiently in the car while Natasha presented chocolates to two middle-aged women nearby. I noticed Charles' sweaty palm as we stared at the pale green concrete-block building. Natasha opened the door and reached for my hand. We walked toward the building, and observed the many cracks beneath the peeling paint, dating from soviet times. Judging all its flaws, and the fact that it was not a white marble courthouse like one we might find in the States, we wondered how Ukrainians might judge us.

We had waited for that day for what seemed a lifetime, and were finally able to present our illegible blue passport to the court guard. Natasha translated our purpose and, in Russian Cyrillic, signed us in and signaled for our signatures. Climbing the stairwell of unfinished concrete block, with a stench similar to that in our apartment, we were seated on a row of wooden benches across from courtrooms. Natasha pulled at her mouth repeatedly, gesturing for us to smile. Charles appeared silly to me, as the expression was contrary to his usual demeanor. He had taken his natural stance, a military pose—reflective of his earlier days as an MP. I nudged him at least a dozen times, flashing my pearly whites, but tried not to speak due to the attention drawn by my native tongue. We had wanted to be in and out expediently to retrieve our daughters from quarantine. Natasha and Irena worked the corridor of women, all of whom I presumed were appointees to our hearing.

Natasha ushered us to our seats on a wooden bench at the back of the room, seating herself directly behind us. The courtroom was long and narrow, with desks aligned against a wall of windows. Irena sat among four women poised over microphones. She was there as a representative of the orphanage and the girls. Next to her was the city inspector, whom I had met only once. Unfondly, I recalled her cursing and her waving of Anastasia's Russian birth certificate about in a barrage of "nyets!" Irena seemed friendly with her, so I was hopeful they had made peace. It was after all, at the inspectors request that Irena and Natasha made the grueling 40-

hour trek across Russia, for a single piece of paper. At the next table was a woman I had not seen before. Tossing folders and handfuls of papers about the platform where she sat alone, she was an older woman who glanced crossly at us. She, we found, was the prosecutor, whose duty was to prove us unfit parents.

"Don't worry," Natasha said, "this is normal."

Normal? I wondered. We had traveled half way across the world and had fought for our children. At that point, nothing we had experienced had been normal. I stood tall. *She is welcome to challenge us*, I thought.

At the next table were the two middle-age women who Natasha had introduced to us as our witnesses. Throughout all of our "no-shows" and the risking of their jobs, they had tried to remain impartial. Both seemed pleased with my coy attempt at greeting upon our arrival, "Srasveetya, dobry den." I had tried to dissolve the reputation that accompanied my U.S. passport—the reputation of being arrogant and barbaric. At times, it had worked, with a reciprocative smile, but it almost always worked when we tried to speak to others in their native language.

The folders shuffled and the women acted busily interested in their piles of paperwork, however, for the most part, all eyes were fixed on us as we waited for the judge. Strangely, we were first greeted by another guest of honor. I waited for carnival music to begin through the ancient microphones, as police officers brought a prisoner into the courtroom in iron shackles. His wrists and ankles were bound by black dangling chains. He was attired in a worn, faded, gray and white horizontally striped jumpsuit. Still, no carnival music! He was seated in a locked cell, a cloth was placed over his mouth, and an officer stood guard. I wondered, as the bars slammed shut, if there was an apple behind there? Was he a juror? I turned to look at Natasha, and her expression mirrored mine at the shock of such an unusual event.

"I have never!" she whispered beneath her breath, in her elite voice.

The judge, a short, portly, balding older man, entered the courtroom. He was not at all the man we had pictured while teasing Natasha many evenings before. In politeness, Charles and I stood, which confused everyone!

"Sit down!" Natasha whispered sternly.

The judge and Natasha talked through the introductory portion of the proceeding, and all attendees were accounted for with a quick response of, "Da."

"Okay, you may stand." Natasha instructed, and she began her translation.

"Please state your full names for the court."

We have this one in the bag, I thought.

"Please state your place of birth."

"Phoenix, Arizona, United States." I said.

Uhh, Phoenix, Arizona, Sir." Charles said.

"Phoenix?" Natasha nudged his shoulder and the judge repeated the question to Natasha.

"Where were you born?" She whispered, as the judge asked if the paperwork were incorrect.

Oh, La Porte, Indiana." Charles said, quickly correcting himself.

To err is human nature, but…. I checked my sense of humor and held my husband's hand, with an adoring smile.

The judge asked that we read our request, which we had written with Natasha's help and had unitedly decided I would read, considering my lack of fear of public speaking, even though it involved a group of Ukrainians and a shackled criminal. As yet, there was no carnival music! The Ukrainian echo of Natashas voice covered my words from over my shoulder. The echo was unnatural as I read our two-page formal adoption request,

171

breaking after every two sentences for translation. We were halfway through when the echo became all too familiar. Natasha's words mimicked mine in English. Perplexed, I noticed a stare from everyone in the courtroom, including our guest prisoner who seemed enthralled by our theatrical-like adoption performance. I turned to Natasha and smiled. The judge let out a roar of laughter, whereupon, Natasha smiled in return and apologized profusely in the right language. We were thankful for the commradery she had established with the judge, most likely over the glass of brandy she could not rudely refuse on Women's Day.

Irena and the city inspector provided favorable determinations concerning the fact that all the documents were in order, the rights of the girls' mother had been terminated, the fact of her subsequent death and the unknown status of the fathers of both children. The witnesses continued to nod, and the prosecutor took her turn at the microphone, preparing herself for the inquisition by arranging her array of folders and clearing her throat.

"This question is for the mother. How do you intend to educate and care for your children and family when you have a career that provides the majority of your finances?" She hurled the words at me.

I smiled at the woman and responded, "I am fortunate to be blessed with a wonderful career that allows me to work from my home computer. I work in a field in which I have college degrees allowing me to thrive professionally and be at home to teach my children as they advance into higher education. In addition, we are blessed to be surrounded by family, all within five minutes of our home. My mother is retired and eagerly awaiting her first grandchildren, to love and spend time with."

Apparently she had no more questions, as she collected her piles of folders and made a statement to the judge.

With a sigh of relief, the judge dropped his gavel. We were greeted by everyone with congratulations, the first having been from Natasha. I felt that even the prisoner was happy. We met the judge in his chambers and, with Natasha and the notary present, we signed our official adoption decree. The judge quickly pulled us aside to hand us a small manilla paper with an address that read Sderot, Israel. The transaction was made covertly as Natasha whispered his intent to provide us with the siblings information. The judge said, "for girls," smiled and ushered us out from his chambers.

We then joined Irena in the corridor for another hug. Sasha waited outside in our chariot to drive us to our daughters—yes our daughters!

We arrived at the orphanage at nearly 5 o'clock, frantic to catch the director before she retired for the day. Irena assured us she would be waiting, knowing that we certainly would have had court that afternoon. I was eager to make up for my earlier blunder and tell her that court was very good—"soot ochen horoshow!" More than that, I was eager to retrieve my daughters in good health from the orphanage-turned-infirmary. We unloaded the car, with a large shopping bag for both girls, including one full ensemble of clothing, from head to toe—with butterfly hair clips, and purple hair bands to top them off.

Natasha and Charles went in search of Anastasia, while Irena escorted me to Katia's room. The kids were playing outside as we looked for them. The caregiver called the class in so that Katia could say her good-byes. The children stood and watched Katia change into her new clothes, then suddenly, like a wake of vultures, they frantically dove, to collect discarded shoes, pants, shirts, underwear—everything! It was a sobering sight—and nothing like the farewell I had imagined. Most of the girls' friends had all but alienated them upon our arrival, however, I had still expected some hugs, tears and good-byes from the only world Katia had known. But there was nothing, as the children scampered away with everything that had formerly belonged to her, after having huddled and fought over each item.

Anastasia came to Katia's room within a few minutes. The behavior of Anastasia's "friends" had been even worse, though I could only imagine a less friendly farewell. So, it was with the same possessions with which they had entered the world, in their pale skin, blonde hair and optimistic blue eyes, that they would leave Poltava's Regional Boarding School for Orphans and begin their journey to a new world, a new language, a new home and new parents. I admired their courage in previous days and that which they displayed as they faced the future. Neither girl shed a tear. As we stepped onto the front stoop in the dimness of evening, Natasha took a quick photo of our family together, at last, forever!

Dinner was a celebration, for the first time in weeks. While we ate and laughed, we explained to the girls that they would not return to the orphanage. From the expressions in their eyes, it was obvious they did not grasp the idea of "nyet internat," nor did they see beyond the following day. There had been many steps in the adoption process, most of which challenged the spirit, however, that night was our triumph after having surmounted those challenges together as a team. That night was filled with unforgettable moments.

It was late when we arrived at the market. The girls would surely be up well past their usual bedtime, however, we had a family to feed, and they ate three hot meals along with two snacks. Natasha helped choose most of the food selections, and we knew our children were not like any we had known—they had no concept of choice. Anastasia and Katia's faces were in sync and the eyes of both opened widely each time they were asked, "What would you like for dinners?" We tried less broad options, like, "Do you like chicken or pork?" Their heads continued to tilt in confusion, as if we were crazy. I remembered the same expressions from our shopping trip in the mall while choosing their clothes, but I had learned that Katia liked anything pink and Anastasia liked anything blue and green. Food was another matter. Apparently the luxury of choice was beyond their comprehension. Until then, most of their food had been pureed due to dental needs. I had assumed they did not know the difference. Collectively, we decided to carry on with meat, lunchmeat, bread, eggs, soup—lots of soup—and plenty of fresh fruit, and head home for the night.

The girls met Luda, who graciously provided a tour of the apartment. Before long, they began running around like children with no past, only a blissful future. Suddenly, frivolity was cut short with the foreign discipline of brushing one's teeth—a new routine and definitely unfavorable, despite the Barbie® Princess berry-flavored toothpaste we had brought from home. Natasha had an interesting night of translations as the girls giggled their way to sleep on a sofa bed down the hall. With a sunny dawn, it was not long before the giggles began, and tiny fingers tickled our feet at 6 o'clock in the morning. It was official—we were parents! After a month of restful mornings, it became obvious that the vacation was over. Those little angels of ours, we discovered, are morning people.

Convinced we were prepared to dine on a breakfast of what I considered to be ham with scrambled eggs, a la avian bird flu. Instead I chose packaged croissants with and extra helping of preservatives—just to be on the safe side. Afterwards, we went into town for more notaries and birth certificate papers. Most of the morning was spent waiting in the back the takci, following behind Sasha and the ladies. Natasha and Charles obtained Katia's birth certificate later that afternoon, about an hour away in the town of Mashivka, where the girls lived last. I was happy the birth certificate office only needed the signatures of one of us, and that I was allowed that precious time with my daughters. I was scheduled to leave for America three days without my family.

16 March 2006, Announcing—

We are proud to announce our new daughters, Anya Anastasia Schadowsky and Katia Katerina Schadowsky after our court decree was issued yesterday, March 15th of 2006. We are especially happy to have had the immediate custody of the girls granted to us in lieu of recent health concerns with the quarantine.

Last night was our first night together. It was wonderful. We celebrated with a nice dinner and then we took the girls grocery shopping for their three meals a day! We put them to bed a little late and discovered this morning that they are morning people! They woke up around 6 a.m. and wanted to be entertained. The joys of motherhood have begun!

We are now beginning our paper trail of birth certificates and passports and N will set out for Russia on Monday to complete the process for Anastasia and hopes to return by Wednesday. On Monday, I will head to Kyiv and on to America. Charles will have his hands full for a couple of days alone!

The girls are happy but nervous about all the new changes in their lives. This is a new beginning for them. They had to leave the orphanage last night with no clothing or belongings unless they had been personally gifted, such as photos and earrings that were given to them in Italy. All the shopping we did was to prepare for this, from underwear to socks, shoes, hats and gloves—the works!

We are all doing well and will be busy until my departure. I am excited to see my family back home, but I am torn and am terribly sad to leave my family here. There are no words for the enormous thank-you owed to Mom, Dad, Greg, Becky and Grandma for everything they have done at home! As some of you may know, despite being half way across the world in Ukraine, Charles and I managed to move homes yesterday as well as adopt our two children—all in one day! So thank you, thank you, thank you, all! I can't wait to come back to our new home and get everything in its place for our new daughters.

All our love,

The Schadowskys

The afternoon went by quickly with the girls as we watched music videos and danced about the house. The girls had a dress show with the handful of clothing we had brought for them from the U.S. Most of the clothes were too loose on Katia, but she paid no mind. Natasha and Charles had returned with belated news of success from Mashivka and a laminated passport reading Katia Katerina Schadowsky, in its Cyrillic form, and listing us as her parents. It was momentous. We were quick to assure Anastasia that we would be just as proud upon returning with her passport.

The hourglass was daunting, hanging over my last few days with the girls. I stretched each moment, hoping for an eternity, but the nights fell upon us and I felt distanced by language. Katia's cold had finally caught up with me and my pathetic excuse for an immune system. I could not complain as I watched her wipe her nose on her sleeve and bounce back to her activities. I spent a full day in bed, despite my best attempts not to do so. I knew I would not make the long journey home without rest.

With every obstacle in our communication, Anastasia became quickly withdrawn and shut down since learning of my departure. Everything with Anastasia swirls into a thunderstorm of emotion. With a love of dancing, she was most happy when watching music videos on television. Apparently, it made her feel carefree, so for the time, I let her have that, knowing that soon the voices on the screen would be foreign and confusing—something I have been all too familiar with.

Katia shed a few tears during overwhelming moments, but mostly she hugged us and attempted to learn everything she could. She enjoyed watching DVDs in English and reading English/Russian picture books, taking breaks to play "Go Fish" and "Solitaire" with anyone who was willing. Bursting with energy, she watched TV only briefly at Anastasia's side. She only wanted good old-fashioned love and attention, and we were happy to give it.

As the hour grew close, I withdrew in guilt and sat in our room sorting our shared luggage into mine and theirs. I felt selfish and alone in leaving my family behind. *How can a boss, a job and money drive one to such regret? Would I ever forgive myself?* The tears began to fall on my silver suitcase as I tried to justify my actions. *Was America really a better place—with more opportunity—if one has to sell one's soul for the roof over one's head?* My path had been paved, and there was no turning back. I held my head high for our silent last meal together.

DEPARTURE 15

*V*ladimir, who had arrived that evening for the night, prepared to leave at 4 o'clock in the morning to take Natasha and me into Kyiv. With the knowledge of his intention, the girls were unwelcoming, but did their best to mind their manners. Everything boiled down to tying up loose finances with Vlad. There is something very primary about the exchange of money in Ukraine. There are no emotions when it comes to tens of thousands in crisp one-hundred-dollar bills. Perhaps it falls from trees in America, although I don't have such trees. I was left with a total of $57 to fly halfway across the world and not a credit or debit card to speak of. I felt naked and terrified. I was to wire another $4,700 back to Vladimir upon my arrival at home.

The girls had asked me to waken them, and, despite my own selfish sorrows, I kept my word. Katia cried at the last sight of me and sweet Anastasia refused to turn over, covering her head with the covers. I could not blame her. My tears fell on her blonde hair as I whispered to them in a raspy voice, "I love you. I'm sorry!"

In darkness and in pain, we drove away from the house. I could see nothing through the ice on the windows, and I rested my head against my wool coat until daybreak. The three-hour drive was a silent one, with the exception of my coughing. As we pulled into Kyiv, the city bustled with rush-hour commuters. We arrived early at the Russian Embassy so that Natasha and Vlad could make process inquiries prior to Natasha's trip to Russia again for Anastasia's birth certificate. I spent nearly two hours watching the people, young and old, pass by bundled in fur coats and rabbit-spelt hats. The vast sea of unanimated faces was not as unfamiliar as before. Mostly, I sat, wishing I were back in Poltava with my family.

Natasha and Vlad returned to the car, engrossed in conversation. They continued to talk anxiously while, as usual, I was left to my own imagination as to the goings on in the Russian Embassy. Next, we arrived at the U.S. Consulate office so that I might notarize my portion of the documents in front of embassy officials, and Charles could later return without me. The consulate office was hidden in a maze of city streets and was unrecognizable as an official building that represented a little patch of America. I watched a crowd of people huddled near the entrance. Natasha said they would not accompany me as it was my embassy's consular office, and it would be somewhat of a hassle for them. I glanced over the frenzied crowd and searched for the energy and willpower to forge ahead. Natasha walked there with me, as I made every attempt to find a structured formation of a line, something everyone learns in kindergarten where I am from.

"You do not wait in line; you're a U.S. citizen!" Natasha said with a cackle in her voice as she grabbed my arm and attempted to push through the crowd.

"I guess I forgot already. It's all right, I can take it from here." I pulled out my blue passport and smiled at her.

Until then, my passport had proved useless in Ukraine. Suddenly, it had turned into a glorified VIP pass. I left Natasha and Vlad behind and mustered up my street smarts, politely shouting excuse me, "eezvenetya!" Shoving men, women and babushka's alike, finally, by force, I approached a massive steel door and pulled it open, which took almost every ounce of my strength. I was quickly halted before waving my little blue U.S. VIP pass. I was greeted with smiles, and the Ukrainian voices politely turned into English—American English. I was asked to place my bag on an X-ray machine and walk through a security detector. The voices, though loud, were familiar and pleasant.

"Have a nice day." I was motioned toward a security booth in a tiny patch of America.

Natasha and Vlad waved from outside the massive barbed-wire walls. I was alone as I watched hundreds of Ukrainians in a maze of lines. Each was hoping for a golden ticket, an immigrant visa, into the United States of America. Since Bush W. had taken office, I knew the tickets were more elusive than ever and many of these people were standing in line for another broken dream.

I entered the U.S. Consulate and proceeded through several more security counters, bulletproof windows and steel-bolted doors and, with each, a friendly nod following the simple wave of my blue VIP pass. Inside the room, I encountered a soldier in a familiar uniform that was similar to those worn by my grandfather, brother and my husband years before. He smiled and asked me where I needed to go, pointing down the hall, around the corner, to the end.

I felt comforted in a home away from home as I took a seat across from three women. They whispered among themselves in

Ukrainian for several minutes, then noticed me with my blue passport.

"Are you American?" one of the ladies cordially asked.

I smiled. "Yes."

"You don't have to wait here. You just need to ring the bell." She pointed toward a small silver bell, much like those found in desolate diners in places like Kansas.

"Thank you." I rang the bell and was quickly greeted by a young woman.

"Allo?"

"I am here to see Olga," I announced, as instructed.

"I am Olga, yes?"

"I am Shelley Schadovsky—Schadowsky."

"Yes, I told you are coming," she said in a pleasant manner.

Olga was friendly as she asked to review my U.S. Embassy paperwork. She retrieved only a couple of the documents and placed the remainder in a folder prelabeled with our name. Inside the folder was our 171-H sent there many months before—a paper I had submitted, notarized and apostilled long before I knew who Anastasia and Katia were. It all seemed surreal.

She smiled. "Have seat and someone call you in moment for notary." With those words, she closed the window.

Within minutes, my name, my real name, was called from around the corner. I peered for the male voice and kept walking, looking past each partition, until I arrived at the last window. I was greeted by a scrawny, red-haired man who was quick with his unpleasant candor. He shrugged and asked why I was leaving without my family. I wondered why it mattered to him, and I wondered how I might justify my action to him, when, in my own conscience, I was unable to justify it.

"I must return for work and reasons of finances." I said.

"Hmm." He nodded, not looking at our papers.

"I also have to close on the sale of our house." I felt a need to add something more.

It sounded logical, I suppose, although my mother had the power of attorney to do that for me in that the house was in my name alone. While reviewing the two forms, he appeared satisfied, and he notarized the first one without question. With a grunt, the wicked man reviewed the medical acknowledgment form.

"You state here your children have no medical conditions?" He inquired suspiciously.

In confidence, I replied, "Yes!"

"Well, certainly you know that is extremely unlikely in Ukraine?" He forced the issue.

"I am aware of the common Ukrainian medical conditions," I said, "However, if you take notice of their ages, we are adopting much older children who have sought medical attention and evaluation over the years, and any obvious abnormalities would be on record by now." With irritation, I added, "So, we are quite confident concerning their records,"

With a snide grunt and sniff from the irrational man, he spoke. "Well, I must advise you take a form with you so you are able to fill out the medical conditions found by the embassy doctor. You will need to notarize a revised acknowledgment and mail it back to us before the visa can be issued." He thought nothing of it other than formality.

"May I please have two forms, for both of my medically challenged children?" With a sarcastic smile directed at my red-headed nemesis, I took the forms, which he pleasantly handed to me without hesitation, obviously ignorant of my sarcasm.

Upon reaching the other side of the fence, I provided Natasha and Vlad with a recap of the encounter.

Kyiv paraded before us in a melancholy manner during the last steps of my journey there. I prepared, over a silent lunch, to part with Natasha and then made a final trip to the market for bottled water, cough drops and necessities for the night. Vladimir, in his kind and gentlemanly way, found an apartment for me in his complex, where he kept watch over me, while I was on my own. I was no more nervous than when I arrived initially, but I was grateful for his thoughtfulness as I observed the same lock-and-key mimes remembered from one month ago. Natasha was cautious with her emotions as she shed a casual and semisweet good-bye. She packed a file folder with the final remains of our adoption papers, and she returned to Poltava by train to care for my family. I was envious of her at that moment.

In loneliness, I paced my apartment, searching for a peace not offered in that place. I changed into my sweats and turned on BBC-Europe for the first English television I had heard since leaving home. I walked out to the balcony and watched Ukrainians arriving home from work. With my last Slavutich beer from the market, I curled up in a chair on the balcony and watched the night fall over people huddled around their fires, with the ever-present bottles of vodka. Following a call from Charles and the girls I cried myself to sleep as I prepared for a sobering trip home.

Vladimir arrived promptly in the morning, and we set out for the Kyiv Borispol airport. We found the airport crowded by day as we made our way to the passenger gate. Vlad, grasped my arm for a forlorn shake in attempt to say good-bye, and I reached out to hug him in thanks, a genuine gesture before a long journey. Apparently, hugging, like smiling, is socially unacceptable in Ukraine. Vlad looked terrified, so I stepped back and smiled, and with that I walked through the gate into a crowd, not looking back, and forged my way toward home.

"Da sveedanya, spaceeba!"

"Da sveedanya!"

The flight to Frankfurt seemed short. My cold medicine had kept me quite loopy throughout my journey. I was accompanied by a kind woman on her way home to the Midwest. Her family still lived in Latvia, since her immigration as a child. She was my mother's age and offered me her shoulder to sleep, although I nestled against the window instead.

Frankfurt was a marathon of security checks, and I made my connecting flight with sheer luck. I was completely backward in time when I reached Detroit, where I spent most of my layover trying to change a $50 bill in the middle of the night, to make a call home to Mom. I managed to get a few words in and "I love you" before heading to Denver for four hours of sleep in a hotel. I arrived in Phoenix the following morning.

I pulled myself through the orange-carpeted airport and felt the warmth of the Phoenix sun through the corridors. It seemed unreal to be there, to be walking without my children's hands cupped in mine. I was not the same person who had walked through there so many weeks before. I could feel them—the children—missing.

My mother stood at the security gate, as though she had never left. The sight of her brought a flood of tears from everything that was left of me. I pulled from her strength as I walked the distance between us. After retrieving my luggage, we headed for the new home I had never known—wherever and whatever that might mean. First, we stopped at Mom's house to retrieve the animals. How I had missed Sierra and Bella, our beagles, and our two cats, Phoenix and Ansel. I waited for my mother to bring clean clothes and shoes for me, and I tossed my boots and gloves into the trash. I remembered the rabid dogs, urine-soaked stairwells and syringe-strewn sidewalks. I stood in my underwear in the garage.

From within the house, the beagles wimpered uncontrollably at the scent of me—bringing tears to my eyes. They wandered

185

back and forth to the door, looking for Papa. For the first time, he was not behind me. He was not coming home—not yet. It was never spoken, but somehow we all knew it didn't seem right, but we managed to just love each other through it all.

We got into the car and headed for our new home, I was terrified at the thought of how it would feel. Charles and I had talked our last night in Ukraine about the strangeness of spending my first nights in our new house without him and of the fact that it seemed unnatural. We had never spent a night apart in nearly seven years and had vowed to spend all our nights together.

As the door opened, the dogs ran into our new home as though out of habit. Mom reached to show me the way, as I lingered on the porch, avoiding the threshold. With persistence, I joined them at the unwelcome sight of layers of boxes and piles of tools, scattered furniture and a futon in my kitchen. My mother sat upon it and pointed out the tile in the kitchen and the remodeled entertainment center. I was afraid to see the master bath, knowing of its chaotic mess my mom had endured in its unfinished state. I glazed over and sat beside her in tears. I had wanted to come home to a nest for my children, but the place where I found myself was not home—just our things in transition. I was overwhelmed. Mom kissed me and recognized that I needed to be alone. I crawled into my half-assembled bed with its scattered linens and cried myself to sleep. It was nearly midnight when the shrill sound of my cell phone wakened me. I was lucid, but alive at the sound of the girls' and Charles' voices, for the first time in nearly two and a half days of traveling.

"Hello Mama," The girls said, giggling. Being at a loss for words in English, they returned the phone to Charles.

His voice sounded distant, and then I realized he was carefully breaking bad news from Russia. "The birth certificate office is refusing to give us Anastasia's birth certificate. Nothing is certain yet. Natasha can't travel until she finds a solution. She and Vladimir are contacting everyone they know to find out what to do in this situation." Charles felt as battered as I did. I could hear his voice crack.

"But how? They said everything was fine when I got on the plane—that you would all be here in 10 days. How is this happening? How can they do this? The girls are Americans now. They cannot keep her there!" I could not believe what I heard. I had left just a few time zones before and had entered hell.

"I need for you to go to the U.S. Embassy in Kyiv, and tell them what Russia is doing," I said. "This is a Ukrainian adoption, and they cannot hold our child hostage over a document—she is an American!" He agreed, but we both knew Charles was not the type to start a confrontation.

We changed the subject after agreeing to work together on both sides of the world to make things right. He had been packing the girls' suitcase for the train to Kyiv. They would stay at a large apartment Natasha had arranged for through a missionary organization that rents to adoptees. We were told it was comfortable, I assumed it was more comfortable than the chaos at home without them. Concerning his curiosity about the workmanship and the state of things at home, I avoided his questions and simply cried, assuring him that Sierra and Bella were well, and sleeping on his side of the bed next to me and that the cats were wandering around curiously. I held onto our respective "I love you," and cried myself back to sleep.

Mom arrived bright and early to begin putting the broken pieces back together. I am not sure if that meant me, the house or both, but she didn't leave my side for the duration. I was grateful, as I dragged myself, in all my resentment to my computer, which was not working. My father and my brother had worked hard to put my home office together so that it would be ready for my return, however, upon several re-evaluations of all connections there was no power to the computer. We took the computer in for a rush repair, and found the problem was a dead battery. Apparently, if a computer is unused for a period of time it will die. Clearly, a month was an extremely unusual period of time for my workaholic 80-hour work weeks. Nonetheless, I was relieved to find an easy fix and no data loss. And I was delighted to delay starting back to work until the following day. Mom and I chose paint to replace the greenish gray prison walls throughout the house, which clashed with the warm beige carpeting.

1 April 2006

Dear Shell,

How are you? We are finally in Kyiv and have an Internet connection. Did you get the pictures I sent? I tried to send as many as I could. If you want more, let me know. Today, we went for a walk around the neighborhood. It was not very pretty. The snow has melted, but the grass is still dormant. The playgrounds are either sandy litter boxes or mud.

Yesterday, we went to the movies and we did a lot of walking. Natasha pointed out all of her favorite buildings in Kyiv. She had a safe agenda and managed to keep everyone entertained. Natasha went back to Zhytomyr today. She has an appointment with a tax inspector on Monday, which she can't miss. We met her mother the first night in Kyiv. She stayed the night with us.

The girls are doing well and we miss you!

Love,

Your husband and daughters

The days continued in monotony, as bitterness grew with the insincerity of work and the expectation of overexertion. The bad news the telephone brought each night incurred political efforts by day and homemaking by evening. Mom continued to work tirelessly, while I worked from my office. I had already made enemies with our new neighbor over my unbearable barking dogs. Like a shrew, I said he could go to hell, as he was the least of my worries. "The friendly neighbor," as he had introduced himself, continued to harass me, including in his calls to my new homeowners association and the police; however, he never showed his face again. Again, he is the least of my worries. I have taken to daily writing and calling our local senators, the secretary of state and various parties in the state department, along with George W. himself. "We'll look into this further," was a common response. My phone was not ringing off the hook—it was not ringing at all with concerned politicians.

Time was closing in concerning the travel date for Charles and the girls, with no resolve. Our only hope was to appeal to the U.S. Embassy to grant Anastasia a nonimmigrant visa to travel for visitation until we could return and finalize the process, which Russia had negated from a two to three year Russian adoption and declared a two-month wait. We stood stern and felt secure enough in our government philosophy of leaving no man behind, a philosophy my family and my husband had practiced for generations for our country. It seemed simple at the time—they had to allow Anastasia into the country. Our legally adopted daughter, they could not separate her from us. We were her parents! Confident in America, we delayed their travel date pending their scheduled appointment with the U.S. Consular. The delay cost us several thousand dollars and put all our hopes on the line.

It was then I received word from Ana Armendarez, a kind woman employed by Arizona Senator John McCain. I knew it took miracles to get someone to listen, and I was grateful for their help. Ana worked with me in preparing our plea to the U.S. Consular in Kyiv, attempting to have all paperwork on our behalf waiting for Charles and Anastasia's arrival, even copying Vladimir by fax. The preparation across time zones and the struggle to contact political parties became exhausting. Frustration grew as documents did not arrive, faxes were not received and telephones were constantly busy.

Charles and I began to fight endlessly. I knew we were living and fighting from two different worlds. I had not forgotten what it was like to be in Ukraine, in quicksand, with no power or control. But I would never surrender! It was somehow easier in the United States to take on the fight in my familiar concrete jungle, playing with the big kids, fighting for control, maybe redemption. But I was fighting harder than I had ever fought for anything.

It was 3 a.m. when I heard from Charles.

"Well?" I asked anxiously.

"No go."

"What do you mean, "No go? This can't happen," I shouted.

"They didn't receive any paperwork," he said, "and even if they did, the man made himself clear—no senator is going to push his hand. He was an asshole!"

"They did receive the papers? We have confirmation receipts! How could he just lie?"

"He said I could appeal to the consular general herself next week. We should have time for our travel. You will need to have the senator's office resend everything."

"Are you kidding me! Do you know what it took to get this done?" I was shattered, yet determined to start over.

> *3 April 2006*
> *Dear Charles,*
> *I am doing okay and getting by, but working so hard. I am very tired. Most days, I am lost and depressed without you and the girls. But you know me, I just want my husband back and I want to*

hear my children's laughter again. I feel like I am still traveling when I have to carry all my things into the other bathroom. It's not worth it most days. Mom made me shower this morning. Mom and dad called an intervention last night and made me leave the house and go to dinner and a movie. I guess I figure if my family is in such a lonely place, I should be too. I refuse to do anything enjoyable without you and the girls. I have not even turned on the TV or done anything routine—it just hurts too much. Please come home soon. We don't belong apart.

Love,

Your lost wife

Ana, at Sen. McCain's office, wasn't surprised at the consular's response, concluding that it was normal behavior. She agreed to resend everything and keep trying. The next appointment ended with a call to Ana from the consular general—one that would condemn the fate of our family for the unforeseen future. Charles and I were without words as he read the paperwork explaining that my daughter would be separated from yet another sister and her parents because her Ukrainian passport still bore her former Ukrainian name, as opposed to that of her name on our adoption decree. The only way for the passport to be changed lay in the issuing of an adoptive birth certificate in our names by the issuing birth certificate office in Russia.

I fought with myself, and I fought with Charles. If only I hadn't left, if only he had tried harder. I condemned Russia and I lashed out at Ukraine. I had lost all sense of pride in America. Charles and Katia were to leave in two days. It had been nearly a month since my return home. Our agents and lawyers in the United States and Ukraine hurled advice on exactly the best way to abandon our daughter for two months. Anastasia was no longer an orphan and could not return to the orphanage, nor did we want her to. Nannies came back with expenses ranging from two to four thousand dollars per month, although it was Natasha who pleaded to take Anastasia home to Zhytomyr with her and her mother. Vladimir and his cousin and boss, Dimitri, disagreed. I spoke with Dimitri and his wife Galina.

"Everything will be okay. Two to four months is very short, and Anastasia will be home before you know it. You will all be a family and forget about all of this." They tried, calmly, to rationalize.

"How would you feel if I took your son away for a couple of months?" I shouted in anger. "You would be back together soon enough! Could you forget about your child being torn from your family?"

"Natasha is unfit to care for Anastasia," he said. "She is a young, career woman. What if she has another adoption couple arrive?"

I reminded him "Natasha is my age, and I am a career woman, does that make me unfit? And if I might remind you, Ukraine is currently closed—a moratorium on adoptions until May! Natasha knows Anastasia, and Anastasia is happy with her. It is our choice."

Our family was being torn apart during the final days before Anastasia's moratorium in Ukraine. I wept for the loss of my 11-year-old daughter as I prepared for the homecoming of my husband and my dear Katia. I felt an infinite amount of love for my husband, and respect for my husband, for his strength and courage to carry on for the sake of the girls.

Natasha calculated a modest monthly fee of $750, in United States dollars, for expenses and full time care, although our agency in the United States was hesitant about the fee, as foster families receive less than $500. It dawned on me that I was calculating and negotiating the hostage of my eldest daughter. I broke down in tears and told Charles he was there in that world with Anastasia, it was their decision.

"Anastasia will stay with Natasha!" Charles said. He and Anastasia had made the decision jointly.

> *9 April 2006.*
>
> *Dear Shell,*
>
> *This is the zoo. Yesterday, we started the day wanting to go to the zoo, but the weather was a lot chillier than we expected. So, we went to the souvenir row instead and got Katia a traditional doll to remember Ukraine. Today, we were going to go to the zoo again, however, Anastasia decided she did not have to wear her coat or listen to me. Katia followed Anastasia's bad example, so I sent them to their bedroom. Unfortunately, I phrased it wrong, and they put on their pajamas and went to bed. Later, when Natasha returned, she went in to see them and Anastasia said some hurtful things to her and had to be reprimanded again, by Natasha. Later, Katia tried to apologize for Anastasia. Then, about an hour or two later, Anastasia offered her own apologies. She needs to respect Natasha because she will be living with her for a while. Anastasia argued, "I will go back to the orphanage, rather than go with you."*
>
> *Later, I tried talking to them, Anastasia tried to say I was not her real father. I reassured her, "You're my daughter and I am your father now."*
>
> *All our love, I will be seeing you soon!*
>
> *Charles, Anastasia and Katia*

> *10 April 2006*
>
> *Dear Charles,*
>
> *Please have Natasha translate:*

My dearest Anastasia,

Please know that everyday we are apart my love for you still grows with each day that passes. Please never forget that we are a family, no matter how far apart we are, distance cannot separate us. Just look up when you miss us and always remember—we, too, are underneath the same big sky.

I miss you and I love you!

Mommy

My little Katia,

We are very anxious to see you here in America. We wish you very safe travels with daddy. He will take care of you. Just hold his hand and never let go during your journey, and you will be in my arms before you know it! Give your sister lots of love and be brave for her, too. I promise she will be here soon with all of us shortly.

I miss you and love you!

Mommy

10 April 2006

Shelley,

The girls were really touched by your words! They loved hearing from you! I am translating the girls' words to you:

"I miss Mommy very much and hope to be home sometime soon." - Anastasia

"I love her very, very much and miss terribly." – Katia

Charles and Katia have left us and entered customs. Your husband and youngest daughter are on their way home to you. If you have any questions, I'll be glad to answer them.

God bless!

Natasha

I felt fortunate to not bear witness to the event. I prayed bitterly that higher powers correct those who had done this to our family. In the morning, Charles and Katia said good-bye to Anastasia as Charles and Natasha fought to tear our two daughters from a hug that, obvious to God and every soul bearing man, is a bond that can never be broken.

Before they turned the corner to the ticketing counter, Charles found Katia was denied entrance onto the flight because their itinerary had two European layovers. It was not until the moment of check-in that we were notified her U.S. visa would allow only one layover before landing on U.S. soil and being sworn in as an American citizen through immigrations. I was unsure how I missed the frantic midnight call from Charles, however, he was able to get through to my mother. Mom was able to purchase tickets on her Visa Card for both of them directly through Frankfurt for several thousand dollars more, and they were able to keep the remainder of their connecting flights. Charles was out of money. I spoke briefly with him, to say one last farewell before their long journey home.

10 April 2006

Dear Natasha,

First, let me thank you for all you have done for our family. And thank you in advance for all you will do for our sweet Anastasia. I am pleased to know that you fought to take Anastasia into your home and to include her in your family. You are truly an amazing woman! Charles and I have all the confidence in the world that Anastasia will be happy and well cared for under you. It is most important to me that, as I cannot care for my daughter during this time, someone most like me shares that responsibility. I am honored that she will have someone to look up to who is educated, successful and takes great pride in everything she does. I will always encourage

*my daughters to be inspired by you and the wonderful things you do
for your country and the children of Ukraine.*

*Please give my Anastasia love, protect her and let her know that
we think of her each moment. Tell her to enjoy her time in Ukraine
and cherish every memory that you are able to give her during this
time. Please inspire her to believe in the adventure she is embarking
on and not wish for that which cannot be for these months. I could
not live with the burden of her sadness.*

Sincerely,
Shelley

10 April 2006
Hello Shelley,

*The pleasure is mine! You are a very beautiful, friendly family
and will be very soon together!*

*Anastasia misses you and sends her love. I do think your
daughter will do okay and this waiting period will just fasten her
willingness to be your daughter for the rest of her life! I will update
you on everything.*

God bless!
Natasha

MORATORIUM: SEPERATION 16

$\mathcal{T}$ he few weeks following my return home had flown by in a flurry of preoccupation with the fate of Anastasia and new house, which was then on a timeline for completion. It had come a long way, with Mom painting the walls and everyone working at assembling furniture and hanging curtains and photos. We worked hard, mostly mom, while I worked endlessly at my job, which I had grown to loathe, as a result of their lack of concern for my family and Anastasia.

With every detail carefully in place, stuffed bears and tigers on the bed, along with ornate drapery to complete the girls' rooms, with a touch of luxury, modestly priced from IKEA. The hammers were neatly tucked back into the garage. The beds were made and pillows were fluffed. I was satisfied in my relentless path to nest.

It was nearing noon and time to head to the airport, when we received a call from Charles. Their last flight had been canceled, which would delay our reunion another three hours. I already had a flurry of butterflies in my stomach, much like the day I met each of my darling girls. It felt like another lifetime to hold my little Katia again. I had grown weary of waiting.

To offset our delay, Mom and I stopped for lunch, washed the car and found some welcome home gifts for Katia. I did not want a big welcome, with everyone at the airport with signs and giant balloons. We bought a small foil butterfly balloon and a little pink tiara. I thought Katia might be fearful of the eccentricity of America, but mostly, a fanfare didn't seem right without Anastasia. So, mom and I would go alone to meet her first grandchild, and for me to reunite with one part of me that I had lost.

The airport bustled with children, and the faces moved past me in slow motion. I wondered if I would recognize my own daughter; would she recognize me? It had been only a month since we parted in the bitter dusk of Poltava, but we had only shared a month of our acquaintance. I sweated my fears into the palm of Mom's hand as we waved our small butterfly balloon. I held my head in my hands and choked back tears at the thought of their appearance on the security ramp. *What would I say?*

In a glimmer of light, the six-foot stature of Charles appeared through the corridor. I followed the wavering sight of him through the crowd, as I searched for a glimpse of our little angel. As the crowd broke a few feet away, her hand in his, I saw my little Katia. She had come home!

"Mama, Mama!" Katia shouted, throwing her arms around me.

I had lost all my breath, and I showered her with tears. No feeling can be compared to that of being reunited with one's child.

Standing beside me, Mom wept, begging for a sight of her smothered granddaughter. I can never imagine meeting your grandchildren through photos. My mother swept Katia into her arms with her whole heart, loving her beyond borders and languages. She had been terrified of what to say to her.

"I am Grandma! I love you!"

"Katia, eta Babushka." In a flood of tears, I introduced Mom to her first grandchild.

I had explained to Mom that the girls were quick to understand the language of love. As my mother and Katia became acquainted, Charles threw his arms around me. I could not stop the of tears as I grasped him.

"I am not whole without you," I said. "You are my strength. I love you so much!"

We were a family again! Charles directed us to baggage. As we walked, I was very much aware that one of my hands swung empty at my side, and I mourned the absence of Anastasia. I vowed, though, to be grateful for the moments I had. Looking down at Katia's smiling face, I remembered the days and hardships in Ukraine when I was able to draw strength from my girls through their courage. There, before the spinning baggage carousel, once again I found hope in Katia's big eyes.

We gathered our things and stepped onto the platform of our new life in America. Katia felt the heat of the Arizona sun in springtime caress her pale white face and soak into her winter wardrobe of oversized jeans, a pink sweatshirt and denim jacket— the clothes I had purchased in Phoenix so many months before, without a face or name to go with them. Katia eagerly nodded at Papa as she pried off her jacket. Without words to tell us, we knew she was hot, and tired too, by her unusually calm demeanor.

Everything was new to her, having known a world surrounded by walls and gates with only frosted windows to the outside, teasing with an imagination of fresh air and a breeze. Katia stared admiringly at the glittered women and flashy cars moving beneath the rows of palm trees, beside bougainvilleas of brilliant pink. She clutched my hand and pointed with a smile as we drove past inviting playgrounds. They were, in fact, golf courses, but they were big and beautiful to Katia. To her, everything was miraculous, although her arrival was the true miracle. We drove into our cul-de-sac and Katia recognized our home from the pictures we had shown her many times.

"Papa's machina!"—Papa's car—she shouted, recognizing it from photos.

"Eta doma?"—This is home?—She asked with her little head cocked slightly off center.

"Da, eta doma!"—Yes, this is home!—I smiled.

The house silently awaited us, and we nudged Katia to enter. As she wandered through the house, she noticed the large silver "K" and "A" emblems mounted on two doors, and smiled. She did not walk to the "K" door, but stopped short and placed her hand on the large silver "A."

"Anastasia?" She asked in sadness.

Katia held her hand on the "A" for a moment but did not enter. Curiously, she walked to the "K" door and opened the lever. She was taken aback by the sheer draperies surrounding her iridescent bedding and modest cotton-covered toy chest. In addition, was her craft table with an iMac for both the girls and rolls of butcher paper to color on. The plush animals seemed to call to her as she leaped upon the bed and began petting them, a grin spread across her face.

Grandma kissed her good-bye, for only a few hours, promising to return for a special dinner. The remainder of the afternoon was devoted to exploration. The silver "A" did not detour Katia for long. I feel she found reassurance in her sister's room. Knowing there was a room for Anastasia meant she would be coming, too—someday. A flurry of questions flowed from Katia.

"Shto, shto, shto?"—What, what, what?—She asked pointing at objects throughout the house.

Although we did not have the exact words to respond, using English was naturally our first step. Katia would politely nod and adjust by mimicking. By dinnertime, I am quite sure she had tried each piece of her clothing for her debut. She remained curious and appeared to question whether the clothing was to be returned. Obviously, the concept of ownership was just one of many obstacles that would have to be overcome.

We made our way down the road to the Red Robin. Introductions were exhausting for such a young girl. As in every situation since our first encounter, she was hesitant toward men, except Papa. Grandpa and Uncle Greg had anticipated her rejection and, like the men they are, took it well. Greg ignored her shyness and showered her with love, laughter and childlike enthusiasm. Dinner was nice and Grandma had already made a new best friend, particularly when it came to protecting her from the hooligan, aka Uncle Greg. As I watched her interact and warm up to the rest of the family, I felt sure she would learn to get along well in her new country.

14 April 2006

Dear Anastasia and Natasha,

I hope these words find you well! Papa and Katia have made it to America safely and Katia is doing fine. She is very curious and keeps rather quiet. She is quite taken with the family and is bonding with everyone very quickly.

I can't wait for Anastasia to join us, although it will be much hotter here in July! I hope you will enjoy the attached photos. We look forward to hearing from you both!

We miss you terribly, and love you very much!

Mama

Natasha and I began writing almost daily. I waited for the e-mails and hoped for a translated word, a photograph or a scanned picture. The little words that formed short sentences and small paragraphs were the only connection we had to our Anastasia. Natasha continued in her attempt to teach Anastasia English. And, as she was no longer in school, her Ukrainian studies continued. Natasha's dog, Macho, was hesitant to accept Anastasia in the house, and he growled fiercely in his Chihuahua voice. I read of their daily walks to the market, the meals they cooked each night—duck and lamb!—the strawberries that were in season and the recently discovered cavity in Anastasia's new, sweet tooth.

Letters from Charles, Katia and I were short and filled with photos of Katia and the family. I refused to let anyone take a photo of only the three of us. To me, it would have seemed an acceptance of Anastasia's absence, flaunting "us" in her face, as though we had moved on and away from her. I wanted her to know how welcoming America would be toward her. Our letters spoke of encouragement, and we always tried to reassure Anastasia that we loved and missed her, and we would return for her soon. I wrote each word with a tear and hit the send button on the cold keyboard. Those were the only words we had, with the exception of our weekly phone calls on Sundays. Katia and Anastasia spent at least an hour talking each week. Katia always carried the phone to her room, to talk in private. We didn't understand anything she said to her sister anyway, as she spoke Ukrainian in a rapid, high-pitched voice. Charles and I could not yet speak to Anastasia in a mutual language. We were only able to repeat, "I love you."

After two weeks in America, Katia had a distinct routine, spending her days watching Spanish soap operas, insisting they were speaking Italian. She understood some Spanish words, but we were still communicating on the same level, "da," "nyet" and "toilet." It was time to start school. I knew I would have only a short time in life before choices and opinions would rule the girls' lives, and that was something I would encourage, but, for the time, I would be strong. After all, the support groups had taught me forever ago that sudden immersion was best.

Together, we decided to immerse Katia in public school with ESL (English as a Second Language) courses for the last five weeks of the school year. Many decisions had to be made. So that she could benefit from phonics and learn English quickly in those last five weeks, we chose to place her in first grade, although she had been in second.

It broke my heart to drop Katia off at school the first days. The teachers encouraged us to remain at the school and comfort her, but remembering Natasha's Ukrainian advice, I stood my ground. Her advice certainly made it easier to walk out of the classroom stern and assertive rather than in tears.

"Ukrainian children expected to be told what to do," Natasha had said. They do not question authority or talk back to adults."

Katia jumped right in and never looked back. When I dropped her off again on the second day of school, all the girls ran to surround us.

"Excuse me, why doesn't she talk to anyone?"

"Katia is from Ukraine and she only speaks Russian. She'll learn English quickly. You'll see!" I replied.

"How do you say, hi to her?"

"'Pre-ve-yet!' That is how you say hi in Russian."

"How do you say, bye?"

"'Poke-ah!' That is goodbye."

"Wha' about 'thank you?'"

"'Spa-see-bah.' That means, 'thank you!'"

"I know how to talk Spanish, like, 'gracias.'"

"Wow, that is great, but Katia doesn't speak any Spanish."

"That's okay. Anyway, Katia is so cool. She beat up all the boys yesterday."

"Excuse me?"

"Yup, all of those jerks! They were making fun-o-her and pushing her around and—POW!" The large girl struck her fists.

"Pow? Katia, did you hit somebody?" I tried to ask, smacking my fists together.

Katia looked up at me with a smile and continued to hold my hand like mommy's little girl. I mimed, and I tried English, Russian and Italian, to explain that fighting is not good—nyet horoshow! Then I walked off with a gleam in my eye, thinking, you go, girl! Needless to say, Katia didn't have a problem making friends, and those boys never bothered her again.

Life, as they say, moves on, and I continued drowning myself in work on school days. I found school a relief from motherhood and my ability to mother only one of my children. Meanwhile, I leaped at every chime of my e-mail, eager for word from Natasha and Anastasia. The routine was staggering and painful at first. I continued to write the department of state and the president, George W. Naturally, he held up to all his expectations with no action. Relentlessly, I continued in my desperation for Anastasia's homecoming.

Most days, work was hardly a vessel of solitude to drown in which to drown although I sought the support of my clients, sincerely remained at my side. The fight to justify my roles as a mother and a political victim became as staggering as the effort of fighting the government. I could no more prove my worth than save my daughter, and not for a lack of effort.

Ray, coy in his false intensions grew to loathe my priorities and increasingly became my nemesis. The pressures of more hours, more face time, more meetings and returning to the office full time were only some of the serrated edges on his increasingly sharpened blade. With dignity, and driven by my work ethic, I remained steadfast and dedicated. Although, I remained dedicated to my client, who provided me with sufficient self-worth to continue through the difficult days.

My affairs swirled endlessly into chaos. I recollected days when I had felt a certain level of power—that I could control important matters in my life. I had always managed to get things done. I was fixated on the helplessness concerning the political tyranny over Anastasia. The moment I stepped off the plane into Ukraine, I had lost all control, and that had accompanied me on my return home.

As I lived and breathed for my children, I was becoming more and more in need of an oxygen tank and, some days, most certainly resuscitation! Anastasia had kept us at a distance, hesitant in her in-between world, questioning our return, and rightfully so. She had begun asserting her opinions, with arms crossed and lips sealed. Natasha had her hands full and was up to her neck in pre-teen "nyets!" Natasha's kind-hearted and unequipped approach to discipline was unexpected and left us all overwhelmed.

Anastasia said "nyet" to English lessons, healthy food selections, clothing choices and well … anything she felt like. Natasha pleaded in her letters for some sort of guidance. I had little to offer, with things—errr—moving so smoothly at home!

Discipline was ruling our home! Katia had become less impressed with America when it didn't bow to her every whim. I suffered the burden of her pain. If only she had known that each moment she sat in a corner for refusing to do her homework or clean her room or eat her vegetables, I, too, was trapped in that corner. As moments became weeks, the girls challenged us harder, pushing their boundaries to see if we would run, send them back and ultimately still love them. Katia had a whole slew of new phrases for me:

"I hate you!"

"I want to live with Grandma."

And my favorite:

"I want to go back to Ukraine!" when she really wants to tear me down.

"Katia, I love you and you will live here forever! Now go to your room and think about respect," I calmly and repeatedly replied.

I cried myself to sleep each night, for Katia, for Anastasia, for myself. I felt I was experiencing a sort of hell I had never known, and which I hoped would pass. The mornings brought new days and a calm solitude that allowed me to resurrect myself and push forward. On the outside, I appeared to everyone to be strong. On the inside, I was losing it, especially when it came to questions about our Anastasia.

I had developed a standard reply, with a standard phony, grin, "It shouldn't be long now. Charles is expecting to return with his itinerary on June 29."

The words sounded less convincing each time they passed my lips. Natasha was strictly hesitant to make any promises, as was everyone in our legal camp. There was little action or response from Russia. I continued to ask, nay plead, in our scattered e-mails and scheduled Sunday morning telephone calls, although answers proved to be nothing but elusive.

30 April 2006

Shelley,

We are really busy these days. Everyday, we make outings to the country or local parks. Anastasia loves swings! Today, we stayed outdoors for almost the whole day! She looks refreshed and "blossoming" now. The weather is getting so nice!

Shelley, I contacted the Ukrainian Ministry, and they said they mailed the proper documents to Russia already. They told me to inquire about our case only in the middle of May. Then they will tell us whether the documents are being processed and when we can expect them to be approved by the Russian Federation. So, in mid May we'll have more information thereabout.

God bless,

Natasha

Anastasia is forever "doing well" by Natasha's report, in her reassuring but melancholy words. Anastasia has still learned little-to-no English since we last held each other. Our phone conversations had become frustrating for all of us and painfully short. I constantly reassured her by repeating such phrases as "I love you" and "I miss you!" I was certain she understood, from our days together in Poltava. Katia was beginning to struggle with speaking three languages and had started fighting with Anastasia on the telephone over constant linguistic misunderstandings. Although, Katia was now able to translate for us a bit, it just wasn't supposed to be that way.

"How is Anastasia?"

"Anastasia is good."

"Is she happy?" I asked.

"Yes!"

"Is she excited to come to America with you?"

"Yes, I miss her!"

By May, Anastasia had essentially become accustomed to Natasha's lifestyle in Ukraine, and had gained seven pounds. At the age of 11, she had started a diet. She visited the first space museum of the former Soviet Union and volunteered at the Zhytomyr orphanage for cerebral palsy. She had learned to cook, dance and mimic the social etiquettes of the upper eschelon in

Natasha's society. I felt I had lost my innocent little girl. Really, I was just jealous, and so was Katia—who only leaves home for school and does nothing at home except homework.

> *13 May 2006*
>
> *Hello, Shelley,*
>
> *Per our telephone call, I am as much curious as you are to hear more details about Anastasia's paperwork. Yes, the Department of Justice I talked to is the Ukrainian entity. I contacted them since they were the last institution in Ukraine to approve the court decree and mail it to Russia. We were told two to three months, in the best scenario. Could be longer if it takes Russia longer to examine the case. We are tracking the paperwork. We know all the documents were approved by Ukrainian laws in three institutions. They are in Russia (at the Federal District Department of Justice) at the moment. Afterward, they will be sent to the regional court for processing and allowing its execution on the Russian territory. And it is totally up to the Russian party how and when to process and approve the paperwork.*
>
> *I know it is emotionally stressful for the family to be separated, however, we have no influence upon the Russian Federation and their policies to expedite anything there. We can only ask. I am calling the regional court, which will be listening to the case, but they will have our documents only approved in a month. When they get those, I will call them to ask to listen to our case as soon as possible. Though it will depend on how many other cases they will have hear before us. Then, after they listen to it and approve it, all the documents will be mailed back through all the same entities (regional court, Federal District Department of Justice, Ministry of Justice in Russia, then Department of Justice in Kyiv, Department of Justice in Poltava, Poltava court) to get international validity.*
>
> *Shelley, it is your right to involve your government if you think it will help, however, we have never been officially promised any*

dates. All we were given— just approximate expected dates of two to three years to procure a full Russian adoption. However, in the best scenario, they are working to make an exception in our case for two to three months. Besides, half of the current month has been off because of the national holidays in both of the countries—Ukraine and Russia. So, they most probably were not complying with the case because of the days off.

Again, Shelley, sorry, but it is not our competence to "push" the Russian entities in any way. We will call the regional court in Russia when the documents get there and bring up our special case so that they could expedite things to listen to it and mail it back. But the final decision will be up to them. In other words, after half a month break for the national holidays, it will be really good if we wait only for two more months. I agree, it is wrong for everyone involved, but we cannot force them to help, because it is a different country with its own laws and policies.

Sincerely,

Natasha

For each brick wall I have faced in my journey I suppose I have become a stronger voice for my family and justifiably less susceptible to corruption and greed. As all things must come to an end, I have reached that inevitable standstill of human truth with Ray and work. In late May, I faced daily threats and false accusations. In all truth I had tired of vague promises and mismatched assortments of kiss-ass and lies about my adoption. Ray ultimately blamed his decision to let me go on the request of my client. I did not feel justified in insulting them with his lies; I had spent the previous four years covering up his shady business practices, financial kickbacks, printing scandals, false promises and unreasonable deadlines. As I sat across the conference table from my former "friend" and his pit-bull, Elaine, I had yearned for longer than I could recall to stand-up to the downfall of a once respectable company. I was forced to call his bluff and surrender to myself and my family. I felt relieved in my decline of his proposal.

"I don't see a solution for us to continue our working relationship." I stated, as their faces turned pale, obviously not anticipating my response.

"You have a family to consider now, and we both know you are the bread-winner! Please reconsider what you are saying," Ray pleaded. "I will give you some time to think this over so you don't make any rash decisions."

I made myself clear. "I am thinking of my family and have always done so! I don't see any way that this will work."

He pursued his plea and smugly placed his arm around my shoulder "Take a week."

I glared at him.

"No matter what, we will always be friends!" he said as he smiled confidently.

Walking away, I wiped the dry salty tears from my face and gazed into the sun, optimistic about my future for the first in a long time. Having faced my fears and finding courage in two little girls from across the world, I had learned to commit, sacrifice, give whole-heartedly and, more importantly, to live. All that remained were a few loose ends to sever the past four years. Unfortunately, it ended in lies, legal papers and separation agreements to hide the truth of my termination for having become a mother. Everything was well hidden, neat and tidy like the remnants of a good divorce, bought off and paid for.

When all was said and done, I was then an unemployed mother of two beautiful children, one of whom was being held hostage in another country, and I could no longer afford her ransom.

MORATORIUM: PARENTHOOD 17

*A*djusting to my new responsibilities, which came in time for summer release from school, and Katia's exceeding demand for care, I had come to terms with my decision and found honor in my choice, however, I wondered if I could ever forgive those who condemned my family. The attack felt calculated and the knife wound was difficult to heal. I felt the forces of greed that walk the ranks of the corporate world, as I began on my own as a freelance marketing and design consultant. I nudged the doors, making my way in beside my former comrades, although banned from my natural role beside my clients. In the end, I had stood them up on my last day, the day of my adoption shower. I was forbidden to contact them, to say I could not attend, to tell them I was sorry and I would miss them.

14 May 2006
Dear Shelley,

Happy Mother's Day! Our best wishes to you on this wonderful day when we honor and thank our mothers for their kindness, consideration and unconditional love!

I know you are a great mom and will be always loved and highly respected by your daughters!

Sincerely,

Anastasia and Natasha

Summer had arrived and June welcomed our extended family from everywhere. Becky and Greg were expecting their first baby at any time, and my parents would become grandparents a second time. I kept adding it up and could not make sense of the idea that Anastasia would be their third grandchild. That someone else would be born into our lives, before her arrival.

We had a big dinner for Grandpa's 60th birthday, while everyone was in town. Katia had asked Grandpa for his birthday wish that night.

"Mmmmmmm, okay!" She hummed loudly.

"Whooooooooosh." With our help, she blew out sixty candles.

"That's it. What did you wish for?" I asked.

"Mama, I wish Anastasia home for me birthday," she said quietly, and lowered her head into her arms.

"Rrrrring, Rrrrring, Rrrrring." All I could think was that it was morning in Ukraine as the phone blared at 4:30 a.m.

"Hellooooo?

"Shell? It's Mom. The baby's coming! Becky just checked into the hospital. Dad and I will head over there in an hour or so."

"Wonderful! When should I come?"

"It will be awhile, I'll call when I get there. Go back to sleep for now, Auntie Shelley."

I lay in bed with anticipation. Motherhood was something Becky and I had found together that summer. We had spent weeks in the heat talking about how much our lives had already changed and how much they would continue to change as we waded around the deep blue pool. It was no real discovery that we realized bringing a child into this world, naturally or by adoption, is nothing short of extraordinary. Becky was finally getting her baby, and I lay awake thinking of Anastasia. I had no conception, no trimesters and, ultimately, no due date for her arrival.

I had slept little, and I was filled with anticipation at the thought of meeting Julia Grace. As morning shone through the windows, I felt happiness for Becky and for Greg. I waited eagerly for Katia to rise from her sleep. I wanted to share the beautiful news and take her to meet her first cousin. Katia finally stumbled into the kitchen at about 9 o'clock, groggy and with the appearance that an entire flock of birds had nested atop her head.

"Katusha, It's a magical day today! Guess who we're going to go meet?"

"Is Anastasia coming home today?"

"No, Anastasia won't be home today, but we are going to meet your baby cousin."

She seemed confused. "Who is my baby cousina?"

"We talked about your new cousina, Julia Grace. You remember, you talked to her and sang to her in Aunt Becky's belly. Today is her birthday and now you can meet her."

"Ooooh, what is she like?"

"We'll have to see, now hurry up and get dressed so we can go meet Grammy at the hospital!"

"Whyyyyyyyy is Grammy there?" Katia demanded.

"Grammy will be Julia's grammy too, and Grammy wants to meet Julia Grace, just as you and I do!"

"NOOOOOOOOO!" Katia screamed, throwing herself on the kitchen bench, arms and legs latched.

"Katia, what is the matter with you? We've talked about this, and you were excited for Julia's birthday?"

"NOOOOOOOOOO, I won't go!" she shouted, as tears streamed down her face, soaking into the scratchy cotton bench.

"Katia, we have to be there for Becky, Greg, Grammy, Grandpa and Julia Grace. We are going!"

"Mama, I won't go, I won't share Grammy with that stupid baby!"

"Katia, Grammy has more than enough love to go around. She will love you and Julia and Anastasia—all of you just the same!"

"No-hooo-hooo, I won't share her, and Anastasia can stay in Ukraine, too. Grammy is my grammy."

At a complete loss for words, I waited for the tears and slobber to subside. I picked Katia up from the bench in the fetal position she had rolled into and carried her to her room. We managed, with great difficulty, to dress her and get ourselves into the car and on the road to the hospital. I decided that only Grammy could solve the problem.

We arrived at the hospital in plenty of time for Julia's grand entrance. Everyone was seated patiently in the waiting area. Becky's mom, Grandpa, Uncle Greg was in the room with Becky, and there—how dare she—sat Grammy. Katia crossed the room and sulked into a chair with her back to everyone—arms crossed, lips perched. I sat next to Mom and explained the earlier tantrum. Mom, with her usual glow, smiled, walked over to Katia and asked her to go for a walk. I don't know what she said, but they returned hand in hand, and Katia had a music box, an ice-cream cone and a smile. Nestled in Grammy's lap, she waited with the rest of us throughout the day, as we all took turns visiting Becky.

Moments of silence hovered above the room as a sliver of sun drew through the curtain from across the way. I sat beside Becky. Between gasps of agony, she clenched my hand, which pulsated from her grip. Our eyes were fixed on one another as I watched the pain well in her eyes during each contraction. Very little was said while both of us gained a profound empathy for the other's journeys en transit to motherhood.

My sister-in-law, in all her dignity and strength, struggled to bring my niece into the world the natural way. However, like most things we venture to control, after 23 hours of labor, tempered by fevers, vomiting and other unimaginary pains, Julia Grace arrived in the most sterile of surroundings via caesarian section, without her mother's clear consciousness. Like Anastasia, Julia Grace can always say she made a miraculous entrance into our lives.

Julia Grace drew her first breath, clenched her tiny fingers for the first time and held her head up straight. Meanwhile, I was still somewhere between home and Ukraine. I was already a mother to one and lost to my own demons in a struggle to reunite with the daughter I had abandoned.

As summer moved forward, Anastasia was still held hostage between the tyranny of three governments, awaiting her own miracle. Julia Grace was here and healthy, and Becky and I both knew there was no medical intervention that could deliver Anastasia to me.

11 June 2006
Hello Shelley,
Congratulations!
We love the pictures, Julia is an adorable baby!
We are back from Crimea. We just made home! Anastasia is doing good and misses you very much! We had a wonderful trip, with lots of sightseeing and good rest. We stayed at my friends' and Anastasia made friends with their son, Sasha. Every day, Anastasia is opening up more and more, I would even say she has absolutely no

communication problems and gets well along with other kids, and also adults. I hope you will enjoy the pictures!

Yesterday I talked to the Russian court. They said the documents arrived and they are processing them at the moment. They also said they're making an official inquiry (as they need an additional confirmation) about Anastasia's citizenship and are waiting for the Ukrainian judge to confirm it. This is a usual procedure to double-check, nothing special. I also contacted our judge to make sure he's responding immediately after he gets the inquiry. Our judge has not received it yet, but assured he will provide the necessary information right away.

In terms of a time frame, the current situation means we still need to wait another month, at least. Nothing changed. I just wanted to update you on where we are in the process. Papers are in Russia (in the final institution before approval) being processed.

First, they will approve your adoption on the territory of the Russian Federation and mail their approval back through the same Departments of Justice (five institutions). After that, I will travel to Russia to get Anastasia's post-adoption birth certificate. Then I will go to Poltava to get her passport issued on her Schadowsky surname.

Only when a birth certificate and a passport are on my hands, Charles will return to Ukraine to pick up Anastasia. Then we will do the physicals at the American Medical Center and get a visa at the Embassy.

I still hope to be done with your process by late July.
Sincerely,
Natasha

P.S. Anya has prepared some special pictures for her daddy in celebration of Father's Day and his birthday. I will e-mail them shortly.

The temperatures had soared into the hundreds, while the heat kept rising with flaring emotions throughout the house and across the ocean. Katia continued to grow a love/hate relationship with family life and discipline over the summer. She began to loathe Charles and me for everything we did not offer. Anastasia became loathed for everything she was enjoying without her. Katia built fury as she read our daily letters from Anya about camps, parks, markets and a vacation to the Crimea; and, more importantly, about Anya's new best friend, Masha. Masha was the 10-year-old niece of Natasha who came from St. Petersburg to spend the summer with them. As Katia viewed Anastasia's photos of fun and friendship, she was filled with envy.

Natasha explained to me that Anastasia was equally jealous of Katia for being American without her. She was angry about Katia's days spent at Grandma's house swimming and making crafts. The truth was, Mom was my only buffer to sanity with Katia. I had denied her so much. I wouldn't take her to Disneyland, to amusement parks or to sporting events. I simply could not bear the pain of doing anything special until our family was reunited. I could not, however, deny Katia time with Grammy, which was the only thing that kept her happy.

Mom's pool became Katia's sanctuary—for swimming, snorkeling and even scuba diving with Uncle Greg. Katia was fearless and wanted to try everything. It was Saturday, as we ladies sat, bouncing Julia Grace on our knees. Intermittently, we watched Papa and Greg toss Katia from one side of the pool to the other.

"Katia! Are you okay?" Papa screamed.

"What happened?" Terrified, we all stood.

"Toot's okay!" Katia giggled as she swam to the edge of the pool toward us.

Upon careful evaluation after pulling Katia from the pool, Mom, Becky and I concluded she would live. Katia was bleeding from her lip and had cracked a baby tooth.

I broke my daughter. What kind of mother would let this happen! I wallowed in shame.

Charles and Greg pleaded their innocence, and Katia begged to go back for more. Doctor Becky certified that Katia's health was sufficient and that she could continue swimming, and back she went, shouting to reassure us each time she flew across the pool.

"Toot's okay!"

I never did find a translation for "toot," but I think "Evel Knievel" was simply trying to say, "That's okay."

Anya had left for camp with Natasha, where they volunteered with disabled orphans from the local orphanage in Zhytomyr. Anya was there for several weeks in the lush, cool forests of Ukraine. For Katia, it was another hit to her pride. However, for us, it was a long, dreaded void with no e-mails or phone calls from Anya.

Family remained ever curious of the "other one," dare we speak her name. For the time, it was too emotional, with her living in Ukraine, and then with no contact. Eventually, we all began overstepping our boundaries in our ever-opinioned family. When the letters from Anya stopped, my dedication and diligence concerning her quickly came back into question despite, painstaking efforts. I was constantly challenged to try more departments, never accept no for an answer, go to the top. I certainly did not need anyone to remind me of my priorities or of my daughter.

"When you encounter yourselves in a triage of post soviet and U.S. immigration political mutiny, you are welcome to share your opinions!" I screamed at everyone who suggested that I could possibly do more.

The seniors in the family became more impatient about news of Anastasia's arrival. I was faced with another confrontation, of proving my effortless struggle. I appeased my brother's wishes to call a former contact from the military, a high-ranking official in the state department. I was again politely detoured with the usual response, generating false hope.

"We'll look into this further and follow up with you," he assured me.

'We'll?' Who exactly was 'we' when the government was talking down to us? I wondered.

I bit my tongue and quickly asked, "Would you actually like to take down my phone number to follow up with me?"

"Yes, certainly," he replied in his rush to hang up.

Much like the others, I was certain I would never hear from the likes of him again.

To add insult to injury I made a last-ditch attempt to satisfy my mother as well and convince her of her country's worthlessness. In a sorrowful effort, we dragged three generations of women, Mom, Katia and me, to Sen. McCain's Phoenix office and requested to speak with Ana Armendarez. Ana had been most helpful in previous months with the Ukrainian and Russian ministries. I was pleased to hear she had agreed to see us unannounced.

Ana was lovely in a blue pressed suit, her dark brown hair falling over her shoulders. She leaned down to Katia and introduced herself, indicating she had recognized me on announcement of my name. She shook our hands and asked how we were doing. I responded in a weathered voice, not one of optimism and expectation that she would have recognized from the previous April. She was disappointed and clearly held a soft spot for our unresolved situation with Anastasia. Ana asked how she could be of help and promised her continued efforts in Moscow and Kyiv.

As we prepared to leave, I reached for my things and Mom lashed out for an answer. "Is this all you can do? I don't understand. Anastasia is an American! Our government must do something—now!" I shall always recall the desperate echo of words in my mothers voice—words I had cried so many times!

"I am deeply sorry for your granddaughter, however, under new Immigration and Homeland Security laws, there is nothing that can be done. I cannot make someone break the law. I understand your pain, and please know that I work with families everyday who have family members who are living in refugee camps, for over five years now, and we continue to fight for their freedom into this country."

My mother shed a tear of defeat. I was relieved that someone other than Charles, Natasha and I finally "got it." I held Katia's hand tightly as we waited for the bulletproof door to unlatch and release us. Mom understood the pain I had to put all of us through to help her finally understand. The day was hard on all of us.

It was the first time Katia had seen me cry since our reunion. I was not sure she understood why, until she spoke.

"Mama, are you sad for Anastasia?"

"Yes honey, we are fighting to bring Anastasia home."

"Good, I miss her." She cried and gave me a hug.

Breakthroughs are few and far between with attachment and adoption, however, after we arrived home, Katia broke her silence for the first time in an emotional outpour. "Mama, I don't really want to go back to Ukraine, I want to be an American. Mama, I just don't want to be an American without Anastasia!"

I reassured her. "You and Anastasia are already Americans, nothing can change that!"

"Why do I have a Ukrainian passport, if I am not going back? Why not a blue passport, like you, Mama?" She wiped her tears on her little pink tank top.

"You will always be an American and a Ukrainian, but you must promise to keep your Ukrainian passport until you're 18." Clearly, it was a bit much for her to comprehend.

I smiled at her. "Mama does not want to get you a blue passport until Anastasia is here, so we can celebrate together!"

"Mama, what will happen to Maryana and Mikola? Will they come to America too?"

"No, dear. They have their own family in Israel now."

"I dream of Anastasia and them every night. Will I ever see them again?"

"I hope, someday."

I returned to my office and again wrote Condoleeza Rice and George W., along with state department appointees. I could not shake the realization that Katia felt she had lost three siblings, and not just Anya.

I dug through our adoption folder and removed a small piece of paper the judge had torn from a manila envelope after court. He had pulled us aside and had Natasha explain that it was not right what the NAC had done when they separated our children, and he handed the note to me. We all recognized the fact that his gesture must be kept between us. The information was a breach of confidentiality and therefore could be construed as illegal.

"It rightfully belongs to your daughters." Natasha translated.

The note included a family name and address in Sderot, Israel.

I decided to do some research on the Internet. I found Sderot situated on the northern edge of the Gaza Strip, and I began wading through countless news stories of bombings in Sderot and death tolls. One article, dated the previous week, told of an elementary school bombing. Not only was I interested in the possibility of Anya and Katia reuniting with their sister and brother one day, but I wrestled with the thought that they may no longer be alive. In my research, I found the link to a Jewish nonprofit organization, helping to locate displaced family members in and around the Gaza Strip, including Sderot. I placed a call to the phone number listed on the page in the hope of learning something about Maryana and Mikola.

"Allo?"

"Yes, hello. Do you speak English?"

"Yes, how be of help?"

"I am hoping you can help me find a family. I am interested in their safety."

"Are you family." She asked.

"Well, yes. I have two daughters adopted from Ukraine, and they have a sister and brother who were adopted to Sderot, Israel, in November, 2005. I want to inquire about their safety."

"Do you know their names or any information? Without that, I cannot be of assistance."

"Yes, I have their family surname and address. I don't have any phone number."

Politely, I gave the information to the woman, and she asked me to wait a moment as she placed me on hold. It is awhile before she returned to the phone.

"Allo?"

"Yes, hello! I am still here."

"Yes, I have wonderful news for you, I was able to find the family in our phone database. I just rang the mother and have her on the line for you."

"She is on the phone, now?"

"Yes, please hold while I connect her in."

"Hello?"

"Hello, you don't know me. But please hear me out. We adopted our daughters Anastasia and Katerina Yurchenko from Ukraine in March. I believe they are the biological sisters to your adopted son and daughter, Mikola and Maryana?"

"Yes, I know of them. What do you want?"

"My daughters talk of Mikola and Maryana all the time. We really just want to know if they are okay, and maybe just have a chance to know them. May we write? I could send pictures."

"No, please leave us alone."

"Please, just listen. My daughters raised those children. They love them!"

"Just leave us alone. My children are Israeli. They know nothing of Ukraine, and they never will. You will leave us alone. We don't never want to hear from you or your daughters again."

"I am sorry, I can't do that. I won't make that promise. They are blood, and you cannot break that bond."

She hung up somewhere in the middle of my plea.

The kind lady who had found her consoled me, but she refused to provide me with their telephone number, as she had been a party to our three-way call—a call that ended abruptly in an attempt to forever sever my daughters' relationship with their own flesh and blood. I did not know when I might find the heart to tell Katia, but I was certain it would not be until after Anastasia's arrival. I walked away from my computer screen of war photos consoled knowing Mikola and Maryana were alive and well—for the time being.

Just days after we celebrated the Fourth of July at Tempe Town Lake, on the cool grass below a colorful extravaganza of fireworks, Anya finally returned from camp. I felt relieved and close to her as I viewed the dozens of photos she and Natasha had e-mailed. It was obvious they had a wonderful time. The photos showed T-shirt designs, potato-sack races, swimming and even a crazy hair day. Anya glowed across my screen in bliss and laughter. The American flag caught my eye as Natasha had an American flag and a Ukrainian flag painted upon each of Anya's cheeks in celebration of our Independence Day with dusk and fireworks in the background. That photo with the flag made the whole sky seem smaller, and our sweet Anastasia felt closer, just knowing we were all looking up on that night.

> *7 July 2006*
>
> *Natasha,*
>
> *Upon your return, please update Charles and me on Anastasia's paperwork. Dimitri and Galina have not returned our calls or calls to our agency in nearly a month! We were assured we would be given their full attention until Anastasia was reunited with us in America! We are running short on money, with me out of work, and have become desperate to get our daughter home. Can you please update us on your current information, as last we spoke you had hoped for a late July completion? In the meantime, I am still working with senators and the department of state to put pressure on the embassy in Moscow, however they have not yet given us any official response.*
>
> *Charles and I have become skeptical about his July 29 return since we have heard no word from all parties. Should his travel plans be canceled, I will personally return for Anastasia myself. Please advise on a timeline and, if I will be traveling, any additional paperwork I will require in Charles' absence.*
>
> *Sincerest thanks,*
>
> *Shelley*

7 July 2006

Shelley,

Today I contacted the Secretary of the Rustov region court today. She said they have not received the letter yet. I contacted the Ukrainian judge, who said it must arrive at the end of this week for sure, because he mailed it longer than two weeks ago.

The Rustov secretary said that the assigned judge (her surname is Kornilova T.G.) to hear the case, is on summer vacation. However, taking into consideration the importance of our case, another judge will be assigned immediately after they get the reply, and this substitute judge will hear the case. Then they will issue their permission to get Anastasia's post-adoption birth certificate.

Shelley, this is so much tough time for your family, and I wish your reunion happen as soon as possible. Unfortunately, Russia is a different country and we must abide by their laws. If you can pull the strings with the help of the senators or your embassy, it would be good! Though the Russian court secretary told me they will work on your case right away. Again I think the aid or additional explanations from your Embassy will be really helpful!

To specify on the dates we need to wait for the Russian court to approve it. Let me first talk to them after they get the reply from the Ukrainian judge next week. I do estimate at least one additional month.

Anastasia will feel more comfortable to travel with you overseas! She sounded glad about the news! She is still shy and timid when men are around her or just talk to her and its been awhile since she's seen her Papa.

Sincerely,

Natasha

The summer became long while days, nights, seasons, births and birthdays have passed without our sweet Anastasia. What was apparent was eventually confirmed; Charles' July 29 return for Anastasia would not happen, as we canceled more costly flight plans. We had determined, with my new career status, or lack thereof, that I would return to Ukraine to reunite with Anastasia—someday. Knowing I would return, granted me a minute piece of redemption toward the guilt I had leveled on myself for abandoning Anya. I had lost a precious and valuable month with my daughters the previous April for regret of a wasted job, not knowing of the moratorium that would separate us.

I continue to fight to gain control of my daughter a thousand miles away. Our phone conversations had dwindled to nothing, and Katia had refused to speak any Ukrainian due to embarrassment and a complete loss for words. After several sibling outbreaks over the telephone, Natasha and I discovered Anastasia making fun of Katia's mispronunciation of Ukrainian and her inability to understand her conversationally. Natasha and I counseled the girls separately and regrouped online from across the world to negotiate the parenting and reconciliation of my children. It occurred to me that I had become more defensive of her "parenting" role and it was not long before jealousy would prompt me to wrongfully question her place.

12 July 2006

Natasha,

Thank you again for sending pictures! I am so anxious to see my daughter again. I hope she is as excited to come home. I am concerned after her last conversation with Katia, Anya has expressed how happy she is there with you. We all realized this would happen and we would need to deal with attachment issues, however she has made Katia very upset and crying again. I am not sure what to make of the situation as Katia expressed to me that she wants to go live with Anastasia and you because I don't make her happy and take her fun places like Anastasia and you are able to go. She too has now expressed feeling upset with Anastasia's photos of camp and vacations in her barrage of emotions to me yesterday.

I am not sure the girls realize the financial situation in that I must send much of our money to Anastasia for her to have fun and that you are able to spend your days with her because of this arrangement. Katia only sees that I have to work and does not realize that we cannot afford to do fun things back home. I know there is little to be done now except to help Anastasia understand the situation and expenses we have provided for her and to remind her how sensitive her sister is when speaking to her.

In the meantime, to prepare Anastasia for coming home in the next month and all the changes she will face, I would really appreciate focusing much of her time on learning English instead of playing. I had hoped to hear a more substantial change in her conversations by now, but sadly, I am still unable to speak with my daughter on the phone. I am only able to communicate hello and that I miss and love her. Despite her resistance to want to learn, at this time it is absolutely necessary to make her sit down for several hours a day and learn instead of watching television. This is what we have had to do with Katia, and the same will be done with Anastasia when she gets home. If she refuses, please take her television privileges away from her for the following 24 hours. I know this will hurt her for now but I need her to feel proud of her accomplishments when she is able to speak to Katia and her Mama and Papa, rather than discouraged on her arrival home.

Please let me know when you talk to the Russian birth certificate office this week, as discussed travel dates will be hard to come by during August.

Thank you for your assistance and kindness,
Shelley

13 July 2006

Shelley,

I am always glad to send the pictures of your daughter. She is a beautiful, kind girl. Yes, she is absolutely excited to travel home with you! She never expressed any doubt or fear! Even her zero-English knowledge doesn't scare her off the trip to America. She is very optimistic about picking it up.

I was very surprised to read the letter about the girls' last conversation on the phone. Anastasia said that Katia is doing great with Mommy and Daddy. I was more concerned about my being over-strict with her here in Ukraine. Thanks for thinking she is happy with me, but trust my word, I am strict with her and these words were a big surprise to me.

There might be a kind of attachment issues, just because we have been staying for a long while together, but I am not her Mommy who she is so proud of and she has known from the first day she is going home to America! This is her dream and biggest wish! We agreed on keeping in touch per e-mails and I explain to her how blessed she is to have you, and she is emotionally prepared to travel to the US. She was even several times patriotically offensive; she joked (sometimes in a bad way—which I disliked) about other nations. She is sure America's the best country in the world, and she tells everyone she is neither Russian, nor Ukrainian, she is American!

Anastasia understands the financial situation you are in and that you work hard to provide her stay and fun in Ukraine. She is happy as much as an orphaned child can be. I just taught her to appreciate everything she has now in comparison with her previous life. She has loving parents and family. Children forget all the bad they used to have when they get all the best (love, care, material things, etc.) in abundance. By the way, Katia said you buy her whatever she asks you about and Anastasia was jealous and said she wished she had been there.

Shelley, correct me if I am wrong. I got an impression that you think I benefit from this situation when she's with me. It is not true. First of all, I have not expected to stay for that long with Anastasia in Zhytomyr. Most of my friends are in Kyiv, and my boyfriend has not seen me for ages. Besides, usually I earn at least $1500 monthly! Shelley, despite all my liking and getting along well with Anastasia, I am the person number one who is incredibly interested in her going home as soon as possible, because it is a waste of time and money for me. Sorry if I sound too straightforward. Every medal has its reverse. From your point of view, you pay lots of money, but from my point of view, I am financially negative. All the money's spent on her, not on my sitting with her. I hoped I would be able to perform some written translations while at home, but this turned out to be very hard. I have very slow productivity with a child beside me. I have savings and monthly incomes from investments, which I am spending now. And thanks to those, I survive. So, I am very interested in your family reunion.

I quite agree with you about Anastasia's learning English. Sorry to upset you again, but it has never been a mandatory requirement, yes, it was preferable and desirable, but I didn't think I had enough power to force her into doing it. I made numerous attempts to teach her. My mom even volunteered to be a co-student, but it didn't work out either. After getting your letter today, we seriously talked and Anastasia said she will do her best in learning it. Hopefully, there'll be a change soon.

As for Katia, I don't think she meant it. Her mood swing was down, next time, it'll be up. Anastasia has the same attitudes sometimes, especially when she sees Katia happy, swimming in the pool, for example. We don't need to take it personally. It is not us doing something wrong. The girls are experiencing and are doing different things, so they wish they were in the same place together. They need each other.

229

Shelley, I did contact the Russian court today. The secretary said they have not received the reply yet, unfortunately. So we are still waiting for the special delivery mail to get to Rustov court. Please don't make any flight arrangements before we have definite news from Russia. I hope you will come to pick up your daughter soon, but I cannot encourage you to purchase tickets before we know anything definite from Russia. What if they decide to check on something else? Hopefully, we'll be down in the nearest weeks, but just in case.

Shelley, Please let me know, when exactly did you wire the money? My bank officer couldn't track it in the system. Please, verify.

Sincerely,

Natasha

14 July 2006

Dear Natasha,

I am very surprised at how you have read into my letter and simple requests. However, I feel your need to be so straightforward obviously shows a need to release your feelings with the situation. I am most concerned and disheartened that you feel our daughter is a burden financially and socially. This, however, was a concern of mine in the beginning. Although I was not present in Kyiv in the final days, all parties agree that you were insistent on wanting the responsibility of Anastasia and even offended at the idea that we were looking into other nannies. Despite what has been said, I do not doubt your care and feelings for her at any time. However, I must ask, why you agreed on providing care for our daughter for this fee if it was a waste of your time and money? I am hurt and confused.

At the same time, all parties agreed that your ability to teach Anastasia English was a particularly important part of your service, and Charles did give you the authority to appropriately discipline her in her education and respectful behaviors. I do accept some *responsibility for not addressing these language delays earlier and for letting her English lessons stray for this long, as our guilt for leaving her behind has allowed us to let her do anything to keep her happy. Nonetheless, the English was part of our arranged fees and agreement. Although you say she is optimistic about picking up the language, in our conversations on the phone and e-mail you have expressed that she has no interest or that she would simply like to wake up one day and know how to speak English, but never has any mention been made of our daughter showing an interest in learning the language. In any circumstance, at this time my request is that she learn the language. She speaks to Katia of how she watches television as much as she likes and has a TV in her room. This I do not care for and would like the behaviors modified and replaced with more learning in preparation for her coming home. Two to three hours of TV a day are acceptable.*

I apologize if you misunderstood my e-mail to imply that you are taking advantage of this situation for financial gain. This was not my intention. I was simply asking you to make it clear to Anastasia that her current lifestyle and having you available to her to go to the park is made possible by our arrangement; otherwise, you would be a working career woman. This is not how Katia is understanding Anastasia's words. She believes that you are taking her on these wonderful vacation adventures and providing this wonderful life for Anastasia right now. Believe me, I understand Katia's emotions are fluctuating. From one moment, she loves us and could not be happier. If we discipline her for something, she tells us she hates us and wants to live with my mother, or she says she wants to go back to Ukraine. Now she says she wants to live with you because I don't take her on vacations to the sea and to summer camp. Yesterday she loved me again. I know what they are both dealing with and neither of the girls really grasp what a true family is as they try to find their place here. It is hard and confusing every moment for them, especially Anastasia

231

since she knows you and your family, better than ours. There will be a transition of attachment for her, and overall I just need everyone to be sensitive of each other's feelings.

Anastasia talks so much of her wonderful vacations this summer and Katia is disappointed she has had no such adventures. Anastasia makes fun of Katia for being in soccer practice and says she needs to tell me that this does not make her happy, that she wants to dance. Katia tells me she loves soccer, but she would like to dance too. She only thinks soccer is bad because Anastasia makes fun of it. The truth is, I could not afford both activities for the summer, and Katia chose soccer over dance. These are the financial sensitivities I was discussing, as I am certain Anastasia will be disappointed with her working mother and small dinners out of a bag instead of roasted duck and fresh fruit and vegetables from the market each day.

Now, after reading the defensiveness of your letter regarding the financial issues, I am confused about your financial analysis regarding the care of my daughter. It is understood that part of this monthly sum is a fee for your services and we do not expect every cent to be spent on Anastasia. You are doing a job and a service for her care, so I would never accuse you of taking advantage of us. Therefore, some of the fees should be yours, and that is a small financial gain to you. Where I am left confused is how you spend the full amount on her, as we don't even spend that much, nor do we have that much to spend solely on Katia. It does not cost nearly that much to raise a child in the U.S., I believe the American foster system pays less than $450 per child. In addition, I have sent all the clothes to Anastasia and extra fees for dental and phone expenses. Is my daughter requiring extra expenses I should know about that are unrelated to your vacation to the Crimea and the recent camp you were hired to attend as a translator? Please let me know if this is the case.

I empathize and feel for your loss of other financial opportunities, however, I don't' understand how Anastasia is such a *threat to your translation services, as she speaks of how much time she spends in your mothers care and watching television. I am managing to care for Katia over the summer and start my own business, I know of the distractions, yet I am able to work a solid six to eight hours a day while starting my business. I have never expected you to be at Anastasia's side for every moment. It is good for her to read, color and entertain herself at times too.*

In regard to the wire, it has not been sent yet as all parties involved (us, our agency and Dimitri) were anticipating to travel in less than a month's time. There was a need to calculate this month's payment. However, the travel information that was to be provided this week was not. We received Charles' paycheck deposit today and can only now afford to make payment. However, I expect to travel before the 11th of next month and I need as much money as possible to afford travel. So, I am working on a budget and would prefer not to overpay and reimburse on my arrival. We lost several thousands of dollars, (again!) on June 29th when Charles was made to cancel his nonrefundable tickets that we were told would be more than enough time for the paperwork to have been ready by both yourself and Vladimir back in April. I realize this situation is no one's fault, however, we are in dire circumstances, as we have used all our savings, bonds and mortgage to complete this adoption, which has now become almost triple the expected cost. We are terrified that we won't have enough to even fly our daughter home when the certificate does come through. With that said please help me to evaluate a travel date and calculate payment for your services this month.

I am not sure what we need to do to correct this situation and get our daughter home. I am sad to discover that you harbor such negative feelings. I feel we do need to work on a resolution, as we are still in this situation together. I continue to respect you and appreciate your honesty, and I am sincerely and continually grateful for your ongoing loving care for Anastasia. I hope we can work together for a resolution to the recent tension between us.

Sincerely,

Shelley

14 July 2006

Dear Shelley,

First of all, I don't think we have any recent tension. This is life, and such things happen. I got an impression you think I take advantage of your money, and decided to ask directly whether you really think so. I am glad you didn't mean it. I don't harbor any negative feelings. Your maternal instinct makes everyone admire and respect you a lot!

Your daughter is not a burden, financially or socially, because I feel a wee bit responsible for the situation in which, as you mentioned, there's nobody's fault. We cannot blame Anastasia, you or me for your daughter's being born in a different country and a different country having its own legislation. So I feel it more like my moral obligation to keep her in my home. I just felt right for Anastasia to stay with me and not to just any nanny. No matter how good she could be, she would be a total stranger to your daughter. And yes, I thought, and still think, it's the best for her! We love her and she really opened up and became a self-confident young lady despite this difficult phase in her life when she is already yours and not yet with you!

The sum was given just approximate. And I still regard it covers Anastasia's stay and fun. I cannot explain why it is more expensive for me to support a child in Ukraine than a child for you in the U.S. I try not to limit her in her requests to buy this or that, if can, but I don't spoil her. Everyday I go to the market to buy fresh fruit, vegetables and meat, because I cook every meal from fresh products, no fast food or preservatives, using purified water. I cook at least three times a day. Sometimes Anastasia helps me with making salads and she is very inventive. She loves making fruit salad, which is her favorite now.

The reason I wrote you about my financial situation was not to complain or swindle more money from you; my intention was to explain to you that I am in the same boat with you. We are dealing with the same adoption which is not over yet, not only for you, but for me as well; I also (like you) didn't expect it to take that long as I had different plans for this time. I, too, feel as much deluded, confused and shocked at the time frame.

Learning English is very important. I am sorry, but I only remember my saying I would eagerly do it to help her. But I didn't say it is a part of the payment. But, please, I don't want to discuss it anymore. I just say, it is important and she is compelled to learn it now, no excuse.

As for watching TV as much as she wants, Shelley, I am very surprised to hear it. This is a big piece of news to me! I don't want to know whether Katia misunderstood Anastasia or Anastasia just wanted to say something to tease Katia. It doesn't even matter. I just want you to know, I don't encourage anyone in my home to watch much TV. This is a rule for everyone, your daughter included. She usually watches TV for two to three hours a day when I make meals, do the dishes, clean or iron. Usually our choice is good quality cartoons, children's movies, intellectual shows or documentary programs. But maybe, in comparison with the orphanage regime, two to three hours of TV a day can qualify as "as much as she likes" in her understanding, however she doesn't even have that much time for watching TV. We walk in the park, visit my relatives, my friends, she draws, paints, colors, she makes clothes for the doll you mailed, she plays a lot with my cousin's daughter, we go to the river beach, I make her read. She just doesn't have time for watching TV for that long.

As for a TV set in her room, Shelley, from the very beginning she was given a choice of which room to sleep in. Though we have two bedrooms, she chose a living room, which has a TV set. But her choice was caused not by an easy access of TV, but by her fear to sleep alone in a separate (as she said "secluded") room. Two weeks ago she changed her mind and she is in a secluded room now.

Shelley, I really don't have any spare time, time for work or for myself. Maybe because I don't have a dishwasher and a food processor, I do everything with my hands. It does take long to make fresh food, do the dishes, clean. Then we go somewhere, and so goes my day. By the way, when we went to the camp, I was not hired; every year I volunteer this job to help handicapped kids.

Dear Shelley, I am terribly sorry for your family in this predicament, for all the expenditures tripled now and for all the frustration you are experiencing! This is an unbelievable, horrible and cruel situation. I do everything possible to smooth things in Anastasia's eyes. But what else can I do? We were not told four months, but we are almost there. And we cannot change anything. It will take as long as it will.

The worst thing is I cannot predict any travel dates yet. It drives me crazy and I do feel deceived, as they still need time for issuing a resolution and mailing it back to the Ukrainian court. I did negotiate with them, but they refer to an international legislation and much stricter rules for foreigners. And I cannot encourage you to purchase airline tickets before they finally say, "We are mailing it," so that we could calculate the exact date. Hopefully, the next week will give us more understanding of the current Russian situation.

Anastasia will call you tomorrow at 8 p.m. Ukrainian time.

Sincerely,

Natasha

19 July 2006

Hi, Shelley and Dimitri,

Tomorrow I start getting medical treatment. Tomorrow my physician will say whether I am going to stay at the hospital for a week or I can be an outpatient and spend nights at home. Anastasia will stay with my aunt and my cousin's ten-year-old daughter during the day. They will be going to the beach, to my granny's summerhouse, the Museum of Nature, and she will be with my mom at night in my home.

Natasha

Natasha's letter had caused serious concern at home. Its brief and vague nature had left us no real understanding of her sudden leave of absence and no real connection to Anastasia. I called Scott immediately and pleaded with him to pry Dimitri for more answers. I heard the following day from Galina, Dimitri's wife with some alarming news about our caregiver.

"Allo, Shelley?"

"Yes, this is Shelley."

"Shelley, this is Galina calling. I need to speak to you of Natasha's circumstance."

"Circumstance?" I asked.

"Well, Natasha is not well now. She urgently admitted herself in sanitorium of recenct days. She is not well, I said. She tells Dimitri she is to be treated for nervousness and stress of environment. But please, Shelley, you need not worry. Vladimir is certain Anastasia will be good with Natasha's mother. Vladimir does visit regularly and comes to know her family kindly."

"Galina, I really had no idea this had all become to much for her. Why did nobody contact me?"

"Shelley, everybody worries for Anya. We can't worry your family any further."

"Will Natasha be okay? I am not worried about Anya with Natasha's family. Anya loves her mother, her aunt and Masha. I know, and I can see the happiness in her pictures. I know she will be well cared for. I just wish I had known how hard this had become for Natasha. I feel I am partly to blame. We have had some recent tensions, and I wrongfully took my feelings out on Natasha. She is not to blame for Anya's circumstance, for Russia, Ukraine or America. I was just desperate to have my daughter home, and we were all jealous of their time together. Please tell Natasha I am sorry. We love her and are very concerned for her recovery. Please, Galina, tell her!"

"Shelley, yes I do tell her your kindness. This sanitorium just temporary, and she be home very soon. And you tell her yourself, okay?"

"Yes, Galina. Thank you for calling and letting me know."

"Okay, well, good-bye."

"Good-bye."

I set the phone down and sank deeply into my chair remembering all the scornful words I had darted at Natasha from my keyboard. I had literally drove the only person who was trying to help us and save Anya—insane! Natasha is a good person and I had no idea how long it would be before we would know anything about her recovery. Fortunately, it was not long before we heard from Anastasia. Our first conversation did not go well since Natasha was the only person in her family who knew English.

"Allo?"

"Hello, this is Shelley."

"Da, eta Tatiana e Anya. Strasveetya!"—Yes, this is Tatiana and Anya, hello!—Natasha's mother called out.

"Ya govoru Anya, spaceeba?"—I speak Anya, please?—I asked.

"Da, Anya ochen horoshee!"—Yes, Anya is very good.

238

"Ya govoru Anya?"—I speak Anya?—I pleaded again.

"Da, da! Da sveedanya!"—Yes, yes! Goodbye!—And with a click she hung up.

My Russian was rusty, I knew some of the words, but it was not enough to get my baby on the phone. Luckily Vladimir called later that morning.

"Allo, Shelley?"

"Vladimir?"

"Da. Yes, Vladimir. You speak Anya now."

"Preveyet, Mama!"—Hi, Mama!

"Vas horoshow? You okay, tvoya okay?"—Are you good? You okay, are you good?—I held out for something to know she was well.

"Da, Mama, Ya okay!"—Yes mama, I'm okay!—She replied. At least "okay" was one of the few words she remembered from our time together.

"Horoshow, Mama loves you!"—Good, Mama loves you!—I assured her.

"I looova yo, Mama. Poka!"—I love you, Mama, bye!—She said all she could, but it was enough to keep me going.

"Poka, Anastacia, I love you!"—Bye Anastasia, I love you!

27 July 2006, Worried about you?

Natasha,

Galina tells us you are home now. We are so worried about you. I am so sorry for everything I said. I know that Anya's circumstances are nobody's fault, I am sorry I blamed you. Please know how much I appreciate everything you have done and continue to do for our daughter. I know you are a special person with amazing things to offer Anya. Please send a note that you are recovering well!

All our love,

Shelley

27 July 2006

Hi, Shelley,

Thank you for the kind words. I am relatively fine now, I am recovering from nervous exhaustion. At the moment, I am still suffering from giddiness and skin rash from medication to help it.

I returned home today. Anastasia is doing really well. She's enjoying the company of Masha. I am sure you know, they are close friends now. Anastasia will feel less entertained, when Masha leaves for Saint-Petersburg tomorrow. Her visit is over.

Thank you again for your concerns about my health. We will call you shortly.

Natasha

Katia was delighted to hear Anya's voice again and was beaming with excitement to tell her big sister news of her first boyfriend. Tyler played on Katia's soccer team during the summer, although Charles and I noticed that Tyler did not so much play soccer as stare at Katia while the goals went flying past him. His parents, sitting next to us, had also noticed and were arguing to pull the lazy boy out of soccer. We said nothing, but they were obviously paying more attention to his lack of defense than his tactile offensive strategy as, stammering, he coyly asked Katia to be his girlfriend. It was all so adorable and innocent. Tyler had always been kind to Katia since the season started. He would point her in the right direction when she spoke little English and was plowing down her own teammates toward the wrong goal. Again, Katia was fearless and Tyler seemed to like that about her. Nonetheless, she said yes to being his girlfriend and, although they never spoke again, the only important thing was sharing the news with Anya.

28 July 2006

Hello, Shelley,

The news for today is that I contacted the Russian court and they said they have not received the reply. I contacted the Ukrainian judge, who is on summer vacation and is out of the city, and he agreed to return to the city for a day and sent the additional package today. The documents had to be re-translated into Russian and certified by a Russian translator, however this was arranged and everything was mailed. I asked him to use express mail, to be delivered in earliest terms. He will come especially for our case. The secretary in Rustov said they will listen to our case as soon as they get it.

This is taking really long, and they assure they have not received it yet. They might put blame upon bad mail or anything, though the lady I am talking to on the phone sounds very trustworthy and nice. I explained our case to her, and she said she is paying special attention to Ukrainian-Russian correspondence (and remembers your name, Schadowsky, by heart) and will process it as soon as they get it.

I do hope you will take your daughter home very soon! She misses you very much!

Sincerely,

Natasha.

I spoke with Natasha that weekend over the phone to get a better understanding of how things would transpire when the judge in Rustov does receive the letter. The conversation left me more concerned. Apparently, the judge would rule on our case and either issue an immediate decree for the issuance of the birth certificate or submit her ruling back through the regional and ministry courts of both countries, which could take an additional two to three months. It was of the utmost importance for all us to convince the judge to issue the birth certificate immediately. The judge who is hearing our case would be a substitute since our assigned judge was on summer vacation. We were all concerned by the possibility a sit-in judge might hesitate to make such a drastic decision. I knew I could not bear an additional two to three months!

MORATORIUM: RESOLUTION 18

6 August 2006

Shelley,

Happy Birthday! Many wonderful blessings to you! It is a most wonderful day with best news from Russia!

I just called the Russian court. The secretary said the original letter (dated last June) from the Ukrainian judge arrived there early this morning. It took it almost a month and a half to get delivered! The secretary who informed me about the judge's appointing the court session for August 25, 2006.

The judge is going to be the original one. Her name is Kornilova Tatyana Germanovna. The rest of the information I got from her. She sounded very understanding and compassionate.

I asked her whether we could request to appoint the session date earlier. Her reply was negative, and she explained it by the fact that within these two weeks they must inform the Krasnozorinsky village administration of Bokovsky district of Rostov region (the place of the

243

state registration of Anastasia's birth, which is a local birth certificate office) and invite/oblige their representative to appear at the court on the exact date. They are informing the birth certificate office by mail. They also need to get their confirmation, which will be mailed back. This is a procedure by their law.

After approving it, according to the Russian legislation, it'll get a legal validity only 10 days later, which will be September 5 or 6.

I asked the judge about the procedure afterwards. She said 10 days after the court decree annunciation I can pick the birth certificate up and go to the local birth certificate office to get the post-adoption birth certificate. And, Shelley, when we get a birth certificate, I need another day, too, for getting Anastasia's passport in Poltava. The judge's direct contact information is attached, in case you would like to get more information to contact them.

Natasha

P.S. Please see attached birthday picture from Anastasia for your pleasure!

7 August 2006
Natasha,
Attached is my letter for the judge on behalf of Anastasia for translation. Please let me know if something should be added. Thank you!

Dear Kornilova Tatyana Germanovna,
I am writing you on behalf of my daughter, Anya. My husband and I finalized our adoption in Poltava, Ukraine, on March 15, 2006, of both Anastasia and Katerina. We have spent these last months raising Katia in our home in America, separated from our beloved Anya and watched our Katia suffer great hardship without her sister. These months apart have been emotionally trying on both

our daughters as they struggle to find their place as Americans and their new culture and language without each other. Anastasia has made us proud with her unending strength throughout the struggles she has endured during her short life.

Today, I plead of you for our family to favorably unite us by court decree, and request issuance of her birth certificate to read her adoptive surname. We plead for an expedient resolution to this matter on behalf of our daughter Anastasia so that she may finally reunite with her sister and her new mother and father here in America. She has proven herself courageous during these last five months as she has blossomed into an impressive young lady. Additionally, I plead of you now as a mother to expedite her return so that she may have a small but most valuable amount of time to finally learn how to be a child without sacrifice and without burden, and experience the carefree childhood she has yet to know.

With sincerest gratitude and respect,
Shelley and Charles Schadowsky

I had received the best birthday wish of all—a date! The court date would allow us a time frame, a light at the end of Anya's moratorium. With that little piece of information, we began our travel plans in preparation for bringing Anya home. Anya would have her day in the Russian courts on August 25, after the additional 10-day wait and two days for Natasha and Vladimir to travel back to Russia to retrieve the birth certificate. That put my arrival around September 8. All flights had been sold out to Ukraine through September, so I had Scott arrange travel plans through the agency for adoption and special needs. Of course, it would be costly but we were ready to spend every last penny we had to bring Anya home. Scott was able to come through for me and secure flights leaving on September 9, and arriving in Kyiv on the tenth. Anya and I would finally return home, leaving Kyiv on the fourteenth and arriving on Katia's ninth birthday, September 15.

> *11 August 2006*
> *Hello, Natasha,*
>
> *I have just placed a hold on my airline tickets. I will arrive on Sunday, the 10th of September and we will leave on Thursday, the 14th. I have allowed enough time for any delays and I will have four business days in Kyiv. I am hoping Eastern Europe is not on holiday that week—from my research I cannot find cause for holiday! Please make arrangements for our stay in Kyiv. I look forward to seeing you again, and my heart aches to reunite with my baby.*
>
> *I am happy to hear your friend wants to help tutor Anastasia. It will be interesting enrolling her in school. I thought much about it as we attended the open house last night to meet Katia's new teacher! School starts on Monday and Katia is nervous all over again. But she is quick to make friends, and her English is amazing. She has read two "Harry Potter" books. She loves to read. I know she can't comprehend the entire vocabulary, but she puts the paragraphs together and understands the story. It is amazing how determined she is to be American. Katia wants no mention of her being Ukrainian anymore. She is embarrassed. I tell her she should be proud to be Ukrainian and embrace her heritage. I think, in some respects, the time Anastasia has spent with you, will give her that pride in her culture! I can't wait to see how the girls interact with each other. They have both changed so much, apart. I will feel blissful to be a family again and together.*
>
> *I can't wait to see you both when I arrive in Kyiv!*
> *Sincerely,*
> *Shelley*

I was brought to tears at the thought of reuniting our daughters on Katia's birthday. Charles had arranged to take the following week off from work, and we would excuse Katia from school so that we would be able to spend Anastasia's first week at home, together as a family. It appeared that all our birthday wishes were finally coming true. I was filled with elation as I began to prepare for my trip back to Ukraine, back to Anya.

America was finally becoming real for Anya. She continually asked for more photos of us, Katia, home and Arizona. She wanted to see every detail so that she could be prepared for fitting in as an American. Ironically, since we received our court date, Anya suddenly took an interest in learning English. Although, after all her blow-outs with Natasha, Natasha had found a friend to tutor Anya, with her fiery temper. We were hopeful that would keep all concerned parties out of the sanatorium.

13 August 2006
Shelley,

Anastasia had her first lesson with the tutor today. First, she really did try and even seemed to enjoy it! Then, shortly, she became moody and wouldn't talk. I had to push some buttons and to explain to her the longer she keeps silence and plays truant, the less she'll learn. She wants to make you proud, so she then obeyed.

Anastasia is so excited to see you soon and go to America. She loves repeating the same words in English, "I am going home!" She is talking about her family all the time and loves you very much!

Shelley, It could prove beneficial for you to write a letter of encouragement for her. She is eager to make you proud, and maybe such words from you would help her through her moodiness?
Natasha

13 August 2006
Hello, Natasha,
Please translate the attached letter for Anastasia, as requested.

Anastasia,

I am so happy to speak to you each Sunday, and I am proud to hear how well your English is coming along! It is music to our ears when Papa and I are able to hear you speak new words in our, and, more importantly, your, new English language. I realize that learning is a very difficult process, one that Papa and I can relate to since we spent a year in school to try to learn what little Russian we could before going to meet you. I remember struggling with headaches and confusion with your language. However, I wanted so much to understand you, if only a little bit. It is important to see the rewards past the hardship, and you, my sweet Anastasia, are truly an amazing and intelligent girl, and I know that learning English will be a beautiful triumph once you find the confidence. It is very important that you respect everyone who is making great efforts to teach you English. This is a gift they are giving you, not a punishment. Please honor them by accepting their gift and embracing the knowledge they are able to share with you, and recognize that you are among women who Mama resects for both their dignity and intelligence. Natasha is someone whom I hope you to admire and aspire to be like someday. For each day you share with her, learn everything you can. You will miss her later.

Anastasia, it is also most important that you know that Papa and I have requested that Natasha teach you the language during your stay with her, and we support Natasha in any disciplinary actions she deems necessary to help you learn. I know that you hear Katia speak English now in these short months, however, she did not learn without struggle or discipline. Katia has not learned English, simply just from living here. Katia has been in school and does two hours of homework each day in addition to reading from her book each night. She has done this without any Ukrainian translation. I need you to understand her time here has not been easy. Imagine how frightened she must have been to go to doctors and dentists and not be able to have anything explained to her, and to walk into school after one week in America only able to speak the words, "hello", "good-bye" and "okay" in a classroom of 30 children. Katia was very scared, and she became fiercely determined to learn the language for herself. She cried everyday and fought with the words and the letters and wouldn't talk to other kids until she had the courage. I am sure you also are aware that Katia has lost her ability to speak Ukrainian. She is unable to remember simple phrases. It will be emotionally trying for both of you to communicate at first. I tell you this so that you will respect your sister's great efforts and so that you will understand that just living in America will not give you the ability to speak English. You will have to work for it, just like you do now, only you will do it on your own without a translator. I hope that telling you of Katia's struggles will open your eyes to the blessing Natasha and your tutor are bestowing upon you. You have the opportunity to come here with much more confidence and knowledge.

I love you, my dearest Anastasia, and I request that you accept your gifts in life. They are often few and far between. I request, as your mother, that you are guided by the one and only rule we have in this family, and that is "respect." I hope that word will guide you in all your life's endeavors. We cannot ask of others what we are not willing to give. With that said, please go forward in your lessons. Respect yourself by accepting these gifts of knowledge. Respect others by participating in their efforts with appreciation. You cannot ask them to respect you if you are not willing to reciprocate.

Anastasia, please know I love you and I am proud of you everyday during these trying times and always know that all your efforts will be rewarded. You will see when we are reunited in America!

All my love,

Mama

August 25 was a scorching day. Katia was back in school and I was left alone, waiting for news from Ukraine. I had pleaded with Natasha to call, write or text when the news arrived concerning the resolution of Anya's court decree. Like most experiences throughout the process, my nerves over-wrought as I watched the clock and seconds turned to hours; then the inevitable—ding.

25 August 2006
Shelley,
Congratulations! The judge confirmed her issuing a positive resolution regarding Anastasia's case.
In 10 days, it gets legal validity and a new post-adoption birth certificate can be issued.
Sincerely,
Natasha

It had been nearly six months of paperwork, fees, and bribes between Russia and our agencies. There were many possible outcomes concerning the court case, and, with only a few words, I finally believed the judge in Russia read my letter and heard my plea with all its love and sincerity. Someone had finally answered our prayers and granted Anastasia her family. After celebrating over dinner with Charles and Katia, I took a moment to e-mail everyone we loved and whom had supported us through everything. It would be only a matter of days until I could hold our sweet Anastasia again. I began researching travel plans, flight restrictions and temperatures, and I started to pack for Kyiv the following morning.

28 August 2006
Hi, Shelley,

Sorry it took us a while to specify on the costs. Unfortunately, many changes in our plans have occurred since we last discussed with you in Poltava. Vladimir has helped me to compare all the information and possible itineraries for our trip back to Russia for the birth certificate.

We have talked to several airline and taxi companies to compare prices and find the most reasonable solution is for us to drive.

First of all, because Rustov is geographically situated on the way to the Southern resorts of Russia, it is next to impossible to purchase any train tickets this time of the year. They were blocked out months ago. Secondly, there are no longer international flights from Kyiv to Rustov. The only route by plane is first through Moscow and on to Rustov. Tickets are available at a maximal price of $1,040 each way. I would also need to hire a taxi to Bokovsky district, which is 300 km away. In addition, this would require stay for three nights, as I will need at least two working days in Rustov region.

Thus, we came to the conclusion the best way is to go there with Vladimir by car so we can be more flexible in our travels. We will travel Kyiv to Rustov, from Rustov to Bokosky Birth Certificate Office, from Bokovsky back to Rustov to get an apostille stamp on the original of the new birth certificate, from Rustov to Poltava, where I'll need two days to get the passport and finally back to Kyiv.

So, below are the costs for the trip to Russia. They were changed because of the price increase for petrol and the calculations are for two now with Vladimir's attendance.

Transportation: 2800 km x 0.3 = $840
Customs on border: $60
Rustov Accomodation: 2 nights (2 rooms) x $90 = $180
Food: 3 days x $40 = $120
Gifts and official fees: $100
Poltava Accommodation: 2 nights (2 rooms) x $90 = $180

Phone conversations: $55
TOTAL: $1,535

The sum is larger than we originally calculated, unfortunately. Despite high costs, it seems to be the most reasonable in terms of money and time saving in the circumstances we are facing now.
Sincerely,
Natasha

28 August 2006
Hello, Natasha,
Thank you for putting the fees together. Naturally, we will do whatever we need to do at this point to get our daughter home. I am terribly sympathetic for you and Vladimir to have to make this road trip! I appreciate your making this journey again. We had hoped it would not come to this!
I will make certain to have the money wired tomorrow to your account.
Sincerely,
Shelley

2 September 2006
Hello, Shelley,
I'm leaving for Kyiv tomorrow morning, staying overnight at my friends' in Kyiv, and at 4 a.m. Monday morning we are leaving for Poltava to pick up Anastasia's pre-adoption birth certificate, and then to Rustov.
This is a short letter just to mainly remind you of the original court decree accompanied by translation, which Charles took to the US. Please, bring it with you back to Ukraine. It is for the embassy, and you will definitely need it at the embassy. It will be returned to you.

Shelley, your fingerprints are still valid? Besides, since you are traveling to Ukraine without Charles, do you think they might need a similar paper; acknowledgment of Anya's medical condition, from Charles?

I hope everything goes quickly and smoothly for us in Russia and Poltava and for you during the preparations and flight to Ukraine!

See you in a week in Kyiv!

Natasha

2 September 2006

Hello, Natasha,

I have the court decree and will bring it with me. Our fingerprints and all embassy paperwork on American side are valid 18 months in U.S. I do have the notarized medical form for Charles.

Please e-mail me in Russia, if you have a moment at an Internet café, and let me know all is well. Call me if you need anything.

See you soon in Kyiv. Safe travels!

Shelley

The final days before my departure were both exciting and chaotic. I had everything organized and in check. I had no work to contend with except helping my mother with the planning of Katia's birthday party and, coincidentally, Anastasia's reunion party in my absence. Katia had longed for her sister to come home for months. I remember when she asked Grandpa for his birthday wish. That day in late May, Katia, and all of us, wished Anastasia would return for her birthday. Then suddenly, while Katia, Mom and I are hunched over the kitchen table tying giant pink chiffon bows and paper maché fairy's with tissue papered wings, all hell broke loose.

"Mama, I want all my friends to come to my birthday party."

"Yes, we already sent out your invitations, and almost everyone will be here!"

"Yeah, but don't I get to decide who comes to my birthday party?"

"Of course. Did you get into an argument with one of your friends who you don't want to come now? It would be better to fix things than be mean."

"No, I want to not invite Anastasia!"

"What? What do you mean? She is your sister; she was your birthday wish!"

"I know, but I don't want her here anymore."

"Katia, is this like when Julia Grace was born and you didn't want to share Grammy? Do you not want to share Grammy or the rest of us?"

"No, Mama, I just don't want her to meet my friends and go to my school. Anya is a stupid Russian, and she can't even speak English, like me. Do you knoooooow how embarrassing that will be?"

"Katia Katerina Schadowsky, don't you ever talk about your sister that way! How could you? You go to your room. I can't even look at you right now!"

Katia cried and ran to her room, and Grammy followed. I couldn't believe the words that had spewed from Katia's mouth. I did not raise a child of mine to act on intolerance. I knew the situation would be hard, and I had been concerned about changes that might occur as a result of their separation, and about how their relationship might be changed. I had constantly imagined what things would have been like had Anya arrived with Katia in April. I couldn't face that day's situation until Charles got home.

"Mama, I'm sorry."

"Katia, I just don't understand how you could say that about your sister?"

"I'm sorry, Mama. I love Anya, but I can't help how I feel."

254

RETURN **19**

$\mathscr{S}$ ometimes we find ourselves in the most unexpected places. I never dreamed a year ago that I would be returning to Kyiv, fighting for my family, fighting for so many moments lost and battles waged over the past months. I know I have been tested and forces more powerful than myself have tried me. However, it was only on my return to Ukraine that I could find some sense and justice for Anastasia. My 11-year-old daughter has endured political segregation and has been cast out from every country she has known and has been denied entry into the country she rightfully belongs to—America, in the arms of her parents. I recognize that our tests are only to prove that we deserve the things we seek.

7 September 2006
Hello, Shelley,

We just got to the nearest Internet club to inform you we have the birth certificate, if by miracle. I hope Dimitri brought you the news yesterday, if only to explain our difficulties.

By some reason, the local birth certificate office still didn't want to issue it, because it didn't return to Ukraine by mail. We had to meet the lady in Bokovskaya and talk her into bringing some kind of special paper empowering her to issue the certificate from Rustov without a waiting period. She agreed to do it under the condition we were driving the representative of her office to the court and make sure we followed the letter of the law. We had to drive the whole way back to Rustov to get the paper, return to Bokovskaya to get the birth certificate, and rush to Rustov to get an apostille. Thus, we made two extra trips (back to Bokovskaya, again to Rustov – five hours each way).

In our final arrival to get the birth certificate, the woman was still in refusal to issue the certificate. Shelley, the woman refused our request, despite the court decree and the presence of the official from Rustov! In honesty, she said she would not cooperate with our request and shamed us for adopting a child to America. She claimed, "Everyone knows the Americans kill and eat Russian babies." The whole situation was just crazy.

I am sure you can understand, with everything at risk, Vladimir threatened the lady with his hand to her neck and we retrieved the birth certificate from the file cabinet ourselves. Our court decree allows us to notarize the document. Under the circumstance, it was important for us to return across the border to Ukraine most expediently.

We were in such a hurry driving through Russia, we drove off the highway and almost rolled over, luckily it was a near miss and are both doing well. I still don't understand how we escaped such a wreck. We had damaged the discs of the wheel. The policeman said we are lucky—yes, the Russian policeman! I thought we would be arrested just then!

Unfortunately, there were extra expenditures, but we were sure, in our situation, you will understand as it was most sensible to obtain the "precious certificate."

When we get a passport, hopefully Saturday, I am heading to Zhytomyr and picking up Anastasia. By Sunday afternoon, we can return to Kyiv and meet you at the airport.

Sincerely,

Natasha

In the final days before my return, Natasha and Vladimir risked their lives to complete the journey back to Russia. I am still in shock at the severity of risks they undertook to obtain Anastasia's freedom, however I am not surprised in the slightest that I have heard no word from Dimitri, and neither has Scott. Still, I sit here among piles of clothing surrounding my suitcase with no tears, no surprise. I feel nothing but empathy for Natasha and Vladimir. I know too well the lengths to which Russia would go to keep our family apart.

I would embark on my return journey tomorrow! It was all so elusive, as if I had willed it to happen during the previous months. I had purchased tickets, I would travel and somehow it would just have to work out. Tonight I finished packing my bags knowing I would make the trip as a wholeheartedly different person.

I was wakened by the Saturday sun, and was driven by both its radiance and my ambition for this day. The airport bustled with excitement. I was ignorant of lines and delays. I thought only of Anastasia as I stood in a line of people disappointed by a canceled flight to Cleveland. None of that could change my mood. Luckily, I was moved ahead of the line because of my international flight and the inability to e-ticket. The other continental passengers held up the line for fear of technology.

As the gate approached, Papa held Katia to a stop. "This is it!" he said with a smile.

Her happiness turned to a frown. I dared to shed a tear, though not wanting to frighten her with my expression. A child who had lost so much from her experience in Ukraine should not be separated from her mother! I leaned down to hug her and kissed her forehead.

"Mama loves you, Katia. I will be home in just a few days with Anastasia, and we will celebrate your birthday!"

"MmmmHmmm." She attempted a smile and wiped her tears.

"Be safe. I love you!" Charles said as he saw tears well within my eyes. He kissed me and wished me luck.

"I love you, too. I promise you, I won't come back without her," I whispered. I turned and moved into the crowd, cupping my head in my hands to hide my tears from Katia.

I did not look back as I forged through security and on to my gate. I approached the counter, carefree, knowing my daughter was ready and waiting at the other end—somewhere.

"I am sorry, Mrs. Schadowsky, but we no longer have any available seats."

"Excuse me, I arrived two hours early? These tickets were purchased a month ago. There must be a mistake!"

"I apologize, Miss, however the flight is overbooked. Seating is first come, first served on check-in. We will need to reschedule you for another flight, and we'll be happy to offer you a $50 voucher on any future American Airlines flight."

"No! That is not acceptable, I have two layovers to Ukraine, and I have be at the U.S. embassy on Monday to complete my daughter's adoption!"

"I can't make any promises—let me see what I can do?"

I waited impatiently as the flight attendant called over the loud speaker for volunteers to take the evening flight to Chicago. Graciously, a young man stepped up to the counter. He was on his cell phone with his girlfriend at home in the windy city. He said he loved her and would see her late that night. He stepped forward and smiled back at me.

"Good luck!" He winked.

"She can have my seat, he said addressing the attendant.

"Thank you!" I replied in tearful appreciation.

With one simple gesture of kindness, I left Phoenix and watched the sky envelop us.

9 September, 2006

There are no words to describe the past six months that have led me back on this road. I find myself alone this time but in a familiar place at Chicago O'Hare, in passing to Ukraine. I take the journey with an open mind despite the events that have led to this day. My return has been a hard road and has involved many tears. Even in most recent days since Anastasia's court decree, both N and V have traveled the long road back to Rustov, Russia, by car and were still denied her precious birth certificate. They drove back and forth through Russia to cooperate with the most ludacris requests, and in the end they simply refused to accept no for an answer. In an act of true dedication and justice, the birth certificate was driven personally, by hand, from N and V. They have survived the road to Poltava after a blowout and potential rollover. As I sit and write, they will hope to acquire Anastasia's new Ukrainian passport in her true Schadowsky surname, which she was given over six months ago. Tomorrow, I will meet them with my daughter Anya, whom I will see for the first time in six months since we were forced to abandon her.

As with every part of this journey, my trip thus far has been a challenge, however, I have come to expect this and find tiny smiles along the way. The bravery of my two daughters through this ordeal has taught me how. American Airlines in Phoenix tried hard to bump me from my plane, which would have made me miss all my consecutive layovers en route to Ukraine. The only thing I can say is I promised my husband, my dear Katia, my mother and the world—I will not return without my sweet Anastasia. So, try as they might, I have emerged from this ordeal a different and stronger person. People can strip me of my job and my money, even try for my home, but they can't take my pride and I will never sacrifice my family.

With that said, American Airlines had no chance against this mother, and subsequently they called for volunteers to take a later flight. For this, I thank a young Chicago man who gave up his seat for me! TSA has strip-searched my carry-on at every port, and I continue to smile at their smugness and tell them all to have a nice day.

I am sad to leave Katia behind. I have become so attached to our daily routine and her adorable brilliance in my life. It took everything to hold back the tears and leave her, and Charles, so that I could return to Ukraine and finally get to know the daughter I left behind so many months before. I have never forgiven myself for leaving early while Charles stayed that extra month. I spent only five days with Anastasia not knowing our fate. Charles is lucky for that month and those moments, which he cherishes, and I now know I am lucky for these moments I am taking to correct my mistakes and find redemption in Anya's forgiveness.

So, here I go for the long haul to London as I pass from day to night, I am unwavering in the challenges that lay ahead because of the bravery of an 11-year-old girl standing at an airport in Kyiv.

Love,
Shelley

After a mad dash through Chicago and an unending leg overseas, I finally landed in London. I prepared for my last, short leg to Anya. London was a frenzied carnival, nothing like I had remembered from past layovers. Breathless to be on the same continent, I ignored the crowds of angry passengers. My layover began innocently with a two and a half hour time for breathing room as I entered an invisibly ending line to terminal one. I watched, as anxious passengers, one after another missed flights. I too began to worry. After nearly two hours, I reached the bus to terminal one, and I remained hopeful of making my connecting flight.

Upon a winding arrival to terminal one, the bus crowded into line with the dozens of other buses to disembark. In a glass foyer, escalators moved to the upper level. A woman carrying a walkie-talkie manned entry to the elevators and commanded us like cattle—handfuls at a time. I was in panic mode as the pacing officials made clear their rule of no priorities. I panicked by the time I was able to enter the escalator.

At the top, I began to sense all was not right with my journey, when faced with zigzags of roped lines. Impatient and determined, I reached my threshold for waiting and approached a terminal assistant. "My flight leaves in a half hour, can you help?" I begged.

"You'll have to proceed to customs first and recheck one of your carry-on's," she said smugly, pointing to a sign. "Only one carry-on is allowed through London!"

"You're not serious, that is not what you have posted on the Internet!" I argued.

"You need to go through customs and re-entry Miss." She said, with a rude wave of her finger.

I ran to the red line for customs, which coincidentally had no line. Maybe I would have a chance! I ran through the corridors and down the elevators to Airline Check-in, Section E, as directed by the stamping authority. After fighting for a place in the line of complainers, I pleaded for my flight. The lady picked up the phone to the gate after agreeing to check on the status. Hoping the disfunctionality of the airport had carried over to the arrival and departure gates, I had to believe I would be on that plane.

"Your plane is in final boarding. You will not make it in eight minutes. We will have to rebook your flight." Curiously, the woman smiled as she spoke.

"No, you don't understand! You can't rebook my flight. I have to be in Ukraine, my daughter is waiting!" I could feel my breath stagger out of my body and dwindle to nothing.

"Let me see what is available—hmmm, our next available seat is on Tuesday."

"Tuesday! Are you kidding me, Tuesday?" I began hyperventilating.

The woman rushed from around the counter and urged me to sit on the floor.

"I cannot wait until Tuesday. I have to be at the U.S. Embassy Monday—tomorrow, to complete my daughter's adoption. She has been waiting for six months!" I heaved and sobbed.

"I am sorry, Miss."

"No, I will be there tomorrow!" I stood up and yelled in her face, "I don't think you understand—I will be on that fucking plane today!" I could not hold back my rage any longer.

The attendant ran to the phone and people crowded around me while I sat screaming on the floor of London Heathrow. It wasn't long before I was surrounded by security.

"I will be in Ukraine tonight, do you understand me? Does anybody here understand me?" I began screaming louder.

In the midst of my nervous breakdown, security approached closer and grasped my arms, the arms of a crazy woman. I was detained in a small office on the lower level of terminal one. A man dressed in a suit and complacent in his stature, approached me in an attempt to calm my anxiety.

"What is the problem?"

"You—you're the damn problem. I have spent, I don't know how many hours, patiently waiting for a stupid bus to go from Terminal four to Terminal one and now my flight is gone—it's fucking gone!"

"I'm sorry you missed your flight, but we need you to calm down."

"My daughter is waiting for me in Ukraine, she has been waiting six months for me to come for her!" I waved my adoption papers from one of my two carry-on's in his smug face.

"I have to be at the embassy to complete our adoption tomorrow—not Tuesday."

"Miss, I am sorry you missed your flight, but there is nothing we can do. I will make sure there is not another route before then."

"Excuse me! I missed my flight? Did I hear that correctly—I missed my damn flight, because I was delayed by your incompetent terminal buses and security system? I missed my flight? Are you crazy! I had a three-hour layover!" My voice shook from screaming, and tears began falling like a barrage of bullets.

"Miss, you will calm down or we will be forced to take you into custody.

"I promised my family I would not come home without my daughter, so arrest me! Does that make you people happy?"

In my madness, Security remained prepared.

Seated in his chair opposite me, the Heathrow manager was calm as he spoke. "Let me try to help you and your daughter. Okay?"

"Yes, please. What can you do?"

"Wait here while I review the flight schedules. Okay? Do you fancy a water?"

"Yes, please."

"I can get you through a layover in Moscow and arrive in Kyiv tomorrow morning."

"I have to be at the embassy in the morning. This is impossible!" I wept.

"Okay, okay. Wait here, please." He returned after an hour of waiting.

"Here is a ticket on Lufthansa. You can arrive in Kyiv at 10 p.m. tonight. This is the only flight out today. British Airways has covered the fare for your ticket. Are you all right now?"

"Yes. Can I call my lawyer in Ukraine and tell her, so that my daughter knows I am arriving late. I don't have any pounds on me."

"Allo"

"Hello, Natasha, it's Shelley. I am in London. There has been a problem with my flight, I won't get into the details now, but I will now arrive on Lufthansa at 10:04 p.m. tonight. You can just send Vladimir if Anastasia is sleeping."

"Yes, Shelley, that is fine. We will all be there to meet you. See you soon—Poka!"

Wiping the tears from my eyes, I retrieved my tickets, my water and a complimentary food and beverage coupon from the manager and collected my bags. Too broken up to eat, I curled up in a restaurant booth upstairs and prepared to endure the four-hour layover. I watched the crowds of people, like me, as they gathered in massive groups at check-in for rebooking, and I wondered how long I would be standing among them if I had not tried to get arrested. They obviously could not buy each and every one of them a ticket on a more competent airline. I was one of the lucky ones. Eventually, I would convince my feet to walk and forge through security that was seemingly less hostile, and shorter. I was forced to surrender another bag to the airlines, leaving me with one carry-on, which, by requirement, had to be the size of a laptop bag or smaller. I packed only the bare necessities. I had my adoption papers, laptop, charger, 15 pairs of underwear, medicine and a T-shirt to sleep in. With two hours remaining and no stomach for food, I spent my 20-pound coupon on beer and some bread, to calm my frayed nerves. Then I wrote home, before heading to the Lufthansa gate.

10 September 2006

Hey, guys,

I am sitting in London waiting for another flight out on Lufthansa. I won't get into details, but I was not arrested and I will be with Anastasia around 10 p.m. tonight. I miss you and promise not to come home without our baby. My promise is proving challenging.

Love you and miss you more than you know! Please give Katia a kiss for me!

Shell

Munich was like walking into a spa. It was surreal after the madness of Heathrow. No one was in sight—nobody. As I got on a shuttle to the next terminal, a young man entered behind me. That terminal, too, was empty. We followed the wayward signs. Favorably broken out into several languages with English being one of them. After walking in a circle, we repeatedly passed an elevator marked "Do not Enter," with a slanted arrow that directed us back to the foyer. After a short time, an older British man in a business suit had joined in our game of running in circles. We prepared to question a sleeping guard. Yes, he was actually sleeping! He appeared to be about 90. We had no choice but to overlook his nap. He pointed back to the hallway, which we had first entered, opposite the direction of the sign, and up an escalator. We assumed, rather than replacing the sign, his job was to direct people lost as a result of the erring sign.

As we approached yet another security terminal, the guard looked at me strangely as I unpacked my laptop and set it on the conveyer. After an assortment of German, for which I had not prepared myself for on that trip, I reached deep into my brain.

"Sprekenzie Englaize bitte?"—Speak English, please?

"Ya, Can you open your bag, please for me?"

Did he just say "please?"—interesting!

"What is in the bag?"

"Paperwork, a laptop, batteries, charger, undergarments and medicine."

"Yes, you may go. Thank you!"

"Ya, Veilen Dank!"—Yes, thank you very much—I always did like the Germans, although I find their security measures a little hospitable and odd.

I had an adequate layover, and decided I would check into my gate anyway, just to verify that my transfer through British Airways was actually valid. The man at the ticketing counter was generous in his confirmation.

"Ya, dieser ist gut."

"Ummmm, das ist gut, sprekenzie Englaize bitte?—Ummmm, this is good? In English, please—I asked.

"Ya, This ticket is good, you are ready for your flight."

"Danka!"—Thank you!—A sigh of relief passed my lips.

"Sorry, you have no idea what British Airways has put me through. Their security is horrendous at Heathrow. I was only allowed this one little bag. I can't believe people actually fly in and out of there."

"You ever try to fly into your country?"

"Of course, I've traveled in and out of the U.S. many times. I've never had a problem."

"No, because you are citizen. Your country is impossible to travel in security now. They allow no carry-on's for foreigners."

"I am sorry, I did not know that."

"Can I ask you something, why does everyone support your President George Bush?"

"Well actually, if you followed the elections, he only won by 51 percent. The rest of us don't care for him. We voted for the other guy." I smiled.

"Hmmm?"

"Please don't think we're all arrogant. Some of us are good people who don't believe in starting war and ruling the world!"

"Ha! Ist gut to know."

I enjoyed my conversation with the attendant and excused myself to exchange a small amount of currency into Euros to buy a brat for my dinner. The exchange rate was startling, having doubled in favor of the Euro since the last time I visited Germany, for vacation. I stepped into a café briefly, to write to Charles and Katia.

10 September 2006
My Love,
I am in Munich, I've been awake 27 hours now. I miss you both!
Shell

I found the crowd that began filling the gate. The crowd was an intriguing mix of cultures as Western Europe meets Eastern Europe. The last leg of my journeys had always offered an interesting set of characters, along with many languages. I listened to a tall blonde feverishly speak Ukrainian on her phone. She talked as though the words would escape her if she didn't say them fast enough—much like Natasha's speech.

We moved onto a bus, distinct with Ukrainian socialites. The men hovered near three beautiful women, and I became aware of competition for the attention of the tall blondes. I observed the game as it followed onto the plane, where the businessmen rearranged their seats accordingly. The babushkas and more homely mothers sat idly near the front.

The flight was like none I have ever experienced. Wine and vodka were offered free of charge on the night flight to Kyiv. It wasn't long before happy hour became an after-hours club. Laughter turned into flirting and even dancing and grinding in the back of the plane. Fortunately, I was situated in the middle, over the wing, wondering how I ended up club hopping on Aerosvit airlines, a Ukrainian partner of Lufthansa. The ladies parted upon arrival—one having entered a limo directly outside the plane.

The remainder of us shuffled onto a bus and headed for the passport authority and into the customs lobby. Though familiar with the process, I was totally unprepared to declare myself and my two carry-ons. I waited anxiously, rotating my head back and fourth between the empty carousel and the swinging doors leading to Anya.

I surrendered myself to the fact that my luggage probably would not join me that night, and I became aware of another passenger in the same predicament, as a woman complained of lost luggage. Following her lead, I file a complaint with the Lufthansa Agent, although, I was certain it remained in London at British Airways.

The Lufthansa agent assured me my luggage would be taken from my "missed flight" and rerouted. Clearly, it was certainly against the law for the luggage to fly without me! I was requested to fill out an extra customs form as punishment for not being in accompaniment of all my possessions.

"How long does it usually take for another flight to bring my bag in? *Tuesday?* I thought"

"Two to three days!"

"I'm curious, how many bags have been lost from connecting British Airways flights?" I asked.

"Nearly all of lost bags are from British Airways. There are about 93 today."

"Great!" Yes, my sarcasm was quite thick.

"You can call Lufthansa at this number and check after 3 p.m. tomorrow. We should know more by then."

"Thank you for flying Lufthansa."

Tired and eager to see my daughter, I felt I had fought the good fight to get there. For the time, missing luggage presented a minor problem. I headed for the drab gray doors, dragging my body and hoping to find my Anya waiting.

LOST & FOUND 20

My tears fell and I wept like thunder as the doors from the customs lobby at Kyiv Borispol Airport swung open and I saw Anya perched at the entrance. She ran to me. I was afraid, not knowing if she would recognize me after the six long months and the changes that affect us in stress. I was different on the inside, and I felt aged on the outside, unlike the carefree blonde American who laughed with her before. She knew her Mama and saw through the stress that had ravaged me. Cautiously, she threw her tiny arms around me. I held her tightly and gasped for breath in my outcry of joy. Our reunion had come at great sacrifice and was more deserved than any reunion I had ever known.

"I love you, my baby," I said, managing to get the words out between sobs. "I promise I will never leave you again, Anastasia! I've missed you so much. Mama loves you!" My voice was shaky.

Anya did not understand the words, but knew only love. Her eyes remained fixed upon me, a stranger in some respects. Anya's eyes were unmistakably bright, unlike those of an orphan. An orphan would never know this deep of love. Our understanding was beyond language barriers. More importantly, I was mama, I was here and I was not leaving without her.

I held my daughter closely as we walked into the crisp night air. Finally, I had a moment to make formalities with my comrades, Natasha and Vlad, who had stuck by us through hell, with their devout faith.

"You look wonderful! How are you?" I asked Natasha, as Vladimir gracioucly towed my remaining luggage behind us.

"I am well," she said. "It is good you. Everything will be fine now!"

I took a moment to look at Anastasia and note how she had blossomed since I last saw her. Vlad tossed the bags into the back and the car pulled onto the highway.

"Well, how are you?" I asked Vladimir, as Natasha translated. I laughed. "So, you're still pretending not to speak English!"

He smiled into the mirror and replied to Natasha in Ukrainian.

"Same shit, new day, good."

Together, we laughed.

The car filled with the clamor of Ukrainian voices in the background, a fond recollection for me. I twirled Anastasia's hair as we headed for our apartment, where we would spend the week.

Vladimir, the same as I remembered him, mumbled to Natasha upon our arrival as I picked up my bags.

"Let Vlad do his duty," Natasha said. "You know it makes him feel like a gentlemen." He was hovering behind me.

I stepped back and let Vlad take the two small carry-ons that had arrived with me in Kyiv.

The apartment stairwell was decrepit, with unfinished concrete and littered with cigarette buts and shattered vodka bottles. The smell of urine, all too familiar in Ukrainian housing, was distinct. But

I was thankful to be there again. Our apartment nice, I found, as we passed through the steel and wood doors to a five-room maze. The spaces were not at all open, like at home. Anastasia was playfully eager to show me around the home she had shared with Papa months before. I had never been there, but I felt at home with the knowledge that Charles had cared for my girls there in my absence.

"Papa's!" Anastasia showed me to my room. I felt that, to her, it would always be Papa's room.

It was hours before we went to sleep. Like a group of school girls returning from summer camp, we stayed up until after four in the morning. I was surprised at how open Natasha had become with me. Before, she had always been distant. I supposed that raising our daughter crossed more boundaries than anyone in her profession ever would have imagined. I liked her openness, although it was mostly girl talk and probably due to the absence of Charles. I missed Charles and Katia.

I recognized that my time here was for Anastasia—for Anastasia and me. And I looked forward to our week together. She certainly deserved those moments in which I would devote all my attention to her.

After Anastasia excused herself to go to bed, Natasha was eager to share every memory and conversation she had with Anastasia, and I was there to listen. She was the woman who had every piece of intimate knowledge about my daughter. She knew her habits—both good and bad—and her likes and dislikes. Most importantly, she had built a trust that had allowed Anastasia to open the key to her past and much of the trauma to which she had been subjected. It was obvious to both of us that there was much more beneath each story, and knowing would give us insight into how to best help her forgive, trust, have faith in people and find happiness. It would take at least a year to establish a bond and break the language barrier, and for her to explain her frustrations with enough vocabulary to satisfy an array of emotions. It was much easier for Natasha, speaking in her native language. As the words trailed on I forgot the chaos of the day and none of it really mattered any longer after a heartwarming girl's night with my daughter in Kyiv. As I lay in "Papa's" bed late that night, I felt close to Charles and missed him so much. The room was comforting for me.

11 September 2006

Sweetheart,

How are you doing? We are fine and doing well here. Anastasia is beautiful and so much more alive than I remember. I couldn't believe how much I missed her until I saw her face and wrapped my arms around her. She was happy to see me, and she is happy to be going home, but nervous at the same time, I wish you could be here!

We are having a nice time. Natasha, Anya and I stayed up late talking about our daughter, just getting to know more about her and her past. Natasha is very excited to share all this information with me before I leave. Sadly, it is a bit easier without you, because it is like a four-day slumber party for the girls and N is so much lighter with me and open. This is good in the final days.

Anyway, I arrived safely, however, my baggage did not! I am still having a warm fuzzy feeling for British Airways! The luggage was lost in London and never arrived in Munich. As of today, they still cannot find it and tell us it could be two to three days, and possibly after I am gone! So, I have no clothes except fifteen pairs of underwear and one sleep shirt.

I miss you so much. I slept in the hard bed you had slept in here in Kyiv, and all I could do was think of you, I guess trying to feel your presence. Anastasia calls it Papa's room; now it is mine, so I suppose we are sharing it.

Love,

Me

With Anastasia in my sights, I slept for what seemed like years. I hadn't found resolve, and spent most nights sleepless and fighting my consciousness for having left her behind. Last night was a surrender I had only dreamed I would find someday. When I woke, it was late afternoon and the sun was sprinkled across the bed from the ornate white lace curtains that draped the windows of every home in Eastern Europe. I had never really seen the sun shine on Ukraine, and it was about time!

I crawled into my clothes, or possibly they crawled onto me. They were so worn, they could walk—another familiar feeling. I stepped out into the corridors of the apartment looking for Anya, following the noises as she lay in front of the television engrossed in music videos. We were still on one-word speaking terms, and Natasha is nowhere to be found.

"Preveyet!" I smiled as Anya sprang from the couch with an abundance of words in Ukrainian, then disappeared. I lingered on her words as her sweet voice drifted into the kitchen.

"Allo, good afternoon!" Natasha called out as the door slammed and latched behind her. "How did you sleep?" she continued.

I let out a huge sigh. "Wonderful!"

"Wonderful! We did not want to wake you when Vladimir arrived early this morning for Anastasia's medical appointment."

"What appointment? I asked. You didn't mention an appointment last night."

"Well, of course, Vladimir made the appointment first thing this morning, but everything went well. There were some minor issues. We will have to return tomorrow. But, do not worry. We did not notice the notation on her medical records that Anya has been exposed to tuberculosis. This is quite normal here. I assure you, she does not have TB. Anya's records show her testing negative, but we will have to return for an X-ray tomorrow to confirm for the U.S. Embassy records. This will show us her lungs are clear since we do not have time to take the traditional skin test." Natasha was casual in her conversation.

I asked more about the TB exposure, completely blindsided. I felt anxious, but somehow unrattled, knowing that was the least of the problems we had endured. We knew her health status upon entry to the United States would now be lowered to a level B, and I had a power of attorney on Charles' medical acknowledgment.

I was sorry to have missed the appointment, although I was certain I would not have been coherent with only three hours of sleep in three days. I would ask the doctor in detail the following day.

Natasha and Anastasia made a trip to the notary while I took a shower and cleaned up. I was greeted by silence when I emerged from my room, and I took a moment to look around the apartment in the light of day. I stood alone, but I could hear laughter, and I could see the girls as they smiled and danced around the rooms; and I could see them reading their book of Ukrainian nursery rhymes, *1000 Kazooks* and Katia holding her doll. Memories Charles had brought home in the photos I had studied endlessly. Everything was strangely familiar and felt comfortable and safe. I knew I belonged there as I sat on the girls' bed and imagined Katia in the room with her sister—the two together. Regardless of the fact that the family had been divided in two, I was there to make amends. The clashing of metal latches, one after another, stole me from my solitude as Natasha and Anastasia returned.

"Are you hungry?" Natasha asked.

"Ravished!" I exclaimed

"Okay, good," she said. "We can go to the exchange, have lunch and go to the market as well. It is a beautiful day!"

As we stepped into the courtyard of the apartments, the view was familiar. The girls had fought with Charles to go down to the park and swing, but it was too cold out, he had said. The snow had melted by the time they had left the previous April. It was spring then, and they played in the park with childhood enthusiasm.

Anastasia ran toward the swings. I cringed and grasped for her. The mother in me panicked. Katia had never left my side.

Natasha sensed my anxiety.

"In America, a child can't just run off!" I said in concern.

Natasha looked from Anastasia to me. "I will talk to her. Anastasia wanders off a lot! I will need to explain this is something she cannot do in America, that it is not safe."

I was confused as I looked at my surroundings. *Is it safe here? I read about human trafficking in Ukraine all the time. How can wandering be safe here?* I looked around at strewn glass from broken vodka bottles, cigarette butts and a pathway of littered syringes. I felt sick at the idea of this playground as some kind of freedom. I hated the fact that it was still Anastasia's luxurious reality; though it had become Katia's forgotten past.

It was a beautiful Indian summer day in Kyiv as we walked across the street to the marketplace. The bank was crowded as we stood in a long line of people heading home at day's end. Two men were laughing and talking loudly until the teller shouted at them. Natasha laughed at the reprimand for their having had a lewd conversation in a professional establishment. As I approached the barrier of glass and small sliding metal tray, I struggled for words, which, surprisingly, rolled off my tongue.

"Dobry den, pietsot hryvna's, pojalsta."—Good day, five hundred hryvna's, please.

"Spaceeba," I replied, handing the woman a crisp One-hundred dollar bill in exchange. I smiled in a very un-Ukrainian manner.

Anastasia cocked her head in confusion. "Mama balakate Ruskee?"—Mama speaks Russian?—She asked Natasha.

"Da!" Natasha laughed loudly, knowing, I spoke very little Russian.

We had a choice of McDonald's or a decent looking bar and grill. I knew Charles and the girls had favored Micky D's on many occasions, however, I opted for a nice sit-down venue. Although I had remained cautious of the Ukrainian food that had wreaked havoc on my system the previous winter, I had little choice but to make the best of the situation, noting the obvious—I was in Ukraine. Natasha had not changed a bit as she scoured the restaurant and took notice of a large group of men smoking and drinking inside. She opted for the patio tables outside. I always preferred outside back home, anyway. The patio had never been an option for me in Ukraine before in the below freezing temperatures of my last visit.

Natasha took a moment to go over the menu with me. The selections were scary and odd, but I went with the ham and cheese and asked her to have the waitress put bread on it and make it a sandwich, just to be creative. I sat mimicking my hands together like a sandwich. Anastasia wanted hot chicken soup, her favorite, although soup seemed strange on an 80-degree day. Natasha told her to ask Mama if it was okay. She explained, now that Mama was there she needed to ask Mama for things, not her. Natasha was delighted to pass the buck. Anastasia looked down at the menu and refused to speak, embarrassed by her English. I waited a moment.

"Yes, Anastasia, chicken soup is okay," I said, in English.

Natasha was polite and thorough as she placed our order with the waitress. The waitress followed her with a series of "nyet's", in a blunt manner, followed by a stabbing at the menu. It was a situation I had become accustomed to.

"What's the matter?" I asked.

"They don't serve bottled water here and they don't make sandwiches."

"Hmmm? Well, how can I order a serving of bread?"

Natasha translated to our pouty and increasingly belligerent waitress.

She stabbed the menu again.

"You can order the olive tray and it comes with four slices of bread."

"Okay, I will have the ham and cheese and one olive tray, pojalsta."

Natasha announced that she would walk to the market and get bottled water. I tried to talk with Anastasia; clearly, though, it was difficult for her, as, she covered her face in shyness.

"Are you happy to go to America?" I asked

"Yeees," she quietly replied.

"Katia and Papa can't wait to see you. We missed you so much!" She smiled and broke into laughter as I placed my arm in something questionable on the table—something wonderful, like meat jelly!

When the waitress returned, I mimed wiping the table with a washcloth and pointed at my arm and the thick blob. The waitress was confused. Anastasia caught on and translated, asking her to wash the table.

When Natasha returned with water and sticky buns from the bakery, the waitress was hovering over our table. She began belting out "nyets" and other emphatic words in Ukrainian, I was certain, by her tone and the "nyets," that her words were not friendly ones! The waitress stormed off, and Natasha burst into laughter.

"I am being reprimanded," she began, "since there is no food or drink allowed from another establishment." Natasha added that the woman would allow the bottled water, since I was a foreigner. "But," Natasha said, "I must place my rolls out of sight immediately!"

I laughed, too, I was at a loss for words. It was just too funny!

Questionably, I looked at my olive plate. The olives looked wonderful, but the bread was about three inches thick. I was determined to have a sandwich, and I began to cut my bread lengthwise, down the middle, with a plastic butter knife intended for spreading lard on my bread and olives. The waitress watched inquisitively as I repeatedly stabbed the knife through the bread, making a gigantic mess of crumbs. In the end, I placed two mutilated slices on either side of my ham and cheese and ate my sandwich, pushing the lard aside in a very un-Ukrainian fashion. I ate a couple of olives with my pinky fingers and smiled as Natasha ate her rolls, throwing all caution to the wind. The waitress looked on in horror.

Eventually, the waitress warmed up to us, and she returned with an offering from the men inside. The gentleman had purchased a glass of vodka for Natasha, which, as usual, she politely declined. She was later offered another by a new group of patrons. Anastasia giggled as, on their way past, Natasha rolled her eyes. Apparently the two had become accustomed to being gawked at, flirted with and offered drinks. The waitress warned the next group that she wouldn't accept.

Later, the waitress asked Natasha if she could step inside for a moment. We laughed, figuring she would be reprimanded again for the sticky buns. However, she returned amused at the waitress's interest in how she had learned English so well? She was certain that men were drawn to Natasha because of her linguistics. However, it was obvious to everyone that it was the blonde hair, blue eyes, self-confidence, laughter and, well, a size- 0 body doesn't hurt either. We chalked it up to a good afternoon and tipped the waitress out of pity. I shuddered as I watched Natasha pull out her calculator and tally the bill.

"I think we are beyond this now! You have raised my daughter for six months, and this is the least I can do this week." She smiled and accepted my gratuity.

We headed to the market for the week's groceries, giddy in the afternoon. I instantly remembered Charles and my first day in

Ukraine at the market. Time stood still in the amusement of the "sex you up" song while babushkas felt their produce. I wished Charles were here to share these moments. I remembered to weigh the produce in the produce section and get a sticker, having causing a commotion the previous time when I arrived at the cashier, who had no scales. The produce lady snapped at Anastasia after she set bananas on the scale. She was upset, and I asked Natasha what had happened?

"Children are not allowed to handle the food! She scolded her."

I proceeded to walk to the scale with our produce, and, glaring at the rude woman, I had Anastasia place each item individually on the contraption.

I learned from Natasha what my daughter liked and did not like. I had a particular interest in her newfound liking for sweets, cookies, cakes and ice cream sundaes, like the one she had begged Natasha for at lunch, which I allowed. I found myself giving into Anya's every whim, thinking of all the things I had not been able to give her. I just could not deny her at that time—not during our week! *Everything will change when we get home.* However, in Ukraine I maintained my prepackaged, preservative-rich philosophy.

After checking out at the food section, we had to place our items in a locker to go upstairs. The upstairs had all the department store-style boutiques, where I could purchase toiletries to replace those I had placed in my checked luggage because of the no-liquid policy concerning carry-on's.

Surprisingly, a week's worth of groceries had cost us the equivalent of $18. However, makeup was imported and cost more than U.S. prices. So, I made due with a low- maintenance routine, using Anastasia's fruity toothpaste, Natasha's blonde shampoo with peroxide. Although I am blonde, I wasn't looking for a Ukrainian white-blonde makeover on my trip. I ended up choosing only lipgloss and body lotion since my whole body was thirsty from the dehydrating trip, and it cost only twice as much as our groceries!

We headed home with the bags from our locker and gallons of bottled water, and called it a day. Anastasia was bright-eyed at the full array of groceries as we unpacked, and she immediately asked Natasha for a banana as a bedtime snack. Again, Natasha reminded Anastasia that her mommy was with her, and she must ask me, in English. Anastasia crossed her arms, put down the banana and walked away, rather than challenge herself with English vocabulary that she had come to loathe throughout months of tutoring. I felt bad for her, in the situation in which she had been placed. She had not chosen to be there, nor had she chosen to be an American.

"Yes, Anastasia, you may have a ba-na-na." I spoke slowly and clearly, and I handed her a banana.

I sympathized for Anastasia during the transition and the struggle with the attachment she maintained with Natasha. The rational side of me understood how natural her dependence was, however, the mother in me felt jealous and envious of the bond they shared. I chose to remain sensible, knowing that in a week's time Anastasia would once again lose her sense of security and all attachments, in leaving to embark on her new life with her new mother in America.

Natasha and I made the best of our nights, in continued talks of Anastasia. I had come to depend on anything Natasha knew of our daughters' past. We knew their languages would transition and their memories would fade over time, and Anya held the key to the past. Most of the things Natasha had to share were hard to hear, but that was in the past, and I was confident in the ability of the girls to live a happy life with us. We had already witnessed Katia's metamorphosis into a carefree American girl.

Natasha talked as if the burden of knowledge was too heavy on her for too long. Her words were fast and anxious, as if there was not sufficient time to get every word out of her mind and through her lips. She felt the need for me to know all that she had known, and she could not let me leave without every piece of the puzzle that she had discovered.

It was abundantly clear from the beginning that Anastasia had a harder life than her sister, with more tainted details. She had, after all, been the eldest. She had raised Katia, Maryana and Mikola. She was also the only stepchild in the house. Until that trip, I had only known the obvious pieces of her troubled history, the parts which had been documented. The last trip, however, provided a significant opportunity, which most adoptive parents are never given.

As a result of the months she spent with Natasha, we were able to understand how far Anya had come in expressing her emotions, and we recognized her newly found ability to trust others with her pain. The more I learned, the more increasingly proud I became of my daughter. It was my wish, though, that I might speak to her in my language and hear her story in her voice, but I would have to wait for those words. I felt that the telling of her past could be healing, and it might help those who were not given the opportunity to escape.

While Anastasia escaped to her music videos as a pastime, Natasha made phone calls and caught up on paperwork, and I took a moment to connect to Charles and Katia back home. Anastasia was fascinated with the computer and the Internet, so we wrote to Papa and Katia together. It was a welcome moment. When we were finished, I took time to show Anastasia and Natasha what I did for a living, since graphic design and marketing had not yet become a commodity in the former Soviet Union, nor in most of Europe. Both seemed confused, but convinced that I made things look pretty.

Anastasia hugged me tightly and spoke to me in English. "Goodnight, Mama."

As she had remained quiet thus far, hearing her speak was music to my ears.

11 September, 2006, Kyiv-bound Reunion

I have finally arrived and have my sweet Anastasia in my arms. It almost seems impossible to believe. It has been such an emotionally trying journey to get here, and I could not refrain from tears of happiness in her arms. I still can't take my eyes off her, and it makes her nervous. Nonetheless, she is doing well and looks healthy, happy and well adjusted to life outside the orphanage—no different from any other little girl. She is nervous to come to America now that I am here and everything is really happening. I cannot wait for everyone to meet Anya.

My trip back turned into a chaotic mess at London Heathrow. I cannot even begin to tell you the levels of incompetence on behalf of the British. Regardless, I missed my plane after over three hours in lines, and British Airways had to purchase a ticket for me on Lufthansa after nearly arresting me, just so I could make my embassy appointment rather that stay at the airport until their next flight out on Tuesday. Unfortunately my bags did not accompany me on my flight.

The reward was worth it, as the doors opened to the beautiful smiling face of my sweet Anastasia. I wasn't sure she would even recognize me. The stress of the last six months had taken a toll on me. Anya welcomed me with open arms in the middle of the night.

Natasha took Anastasia to her medical appointment in an effort not to wake me. I had been awake for over 40 hours before turning in the night before. I was upset I missed the medical appointment, but Anya is still more comfortable around N in these situations for now. The Doctor found her sealed record indicated that she had latent tuberculosis exposure, called PPD, as a child. They will need to perform tests and an X-ray to confirm there is no tuberculosis in her system. However, the doctor must still classify her as class "B" health because of the childhood illness. Next, we will need to obtain her visa at the U.S. embassy and approval of all documents, which we have. I am just relieved Anya is healthy and we will be home soon.

To sum it all up, we are having a successful adoption process this time around. The trip has been a little more entertaining. I still have no luggage and I am told it could arrive after I leave. So I am wearing the same clothes everyday. However, I was smart enough to switch all my undergarments into my carry-on with my laptop and medications when I was reduced to one laptop-sized bag.

Mostly, we are having a wonderful time. Although I miss Charles and Katia very much, our time here is precious and well deserved for Anya and me. We stay up late laughing and talking like at a slumber party. Natasha and I have had time to share all the little things about Anya that are so precious, it would take me a while to learn with the language barrier. I have learned much about her likes and dislikes and also secrets into her past that she has opened up to Natasha and her mother about over the last six months. I love you all, especially you, Charles and Katia.

Love,

S & A

Vlad arrived after breakfast the next morning. Although I had slept well most of the night, I awoke early that morning with a terrible stomachache. I was not surprised, one meal of Ukrainian food had already taken me down. Immediately, I took my Cipro from the doctor at the first rumble of my stomach and drank nearly a gallon of water. I managed to eat some breakfast later that morning and felt well enough to make Anya's follow-up medical appointment. The American Medical Center was located not far from Independence Square and was very clean, compared to most offices in the city. We sat for quite awhile and talked among ourselves while Vlad read his newspaper. Anastasia and Natasha began giggling and tickling each other, and drove Vladimir nearly insane before he reprimanded both, like children. I realized then that Natasha had not played the role of a mother, but that of a friend and older role model, who is young and carefree in spirit. She and Anastasia listened to the same teenage pop music and watched the same music videos. When Natasha was my age, she was single and enjoyed going to clubs and hanging out with her girlfriends. She was just a girl at heart, whom Anastasia looked up to.

"Schadovsky," the doctor called.

I was keenly aware that they still did not allow the use of the "w" in Eastern Europe. By the end of the last trip I had begun pronouncing my own name wrong, just to speed up the translation process. Our name read and was pronounced there as Schadovsky. Anastasia and I, are the Schadovsky's. The doctor began by reviewing the visit of the previous day, and asked me if I understood her condition—her having been exposed to TB.

"Yes," I said, "however, her X-ray confirmed she does not have the disease."

"She still must see a specialist immediately upon her arrival in America to determine if she requires preventative treatment. Do you understand?" The Doctor became very serious in her explanation.

"Yes, I understand."

"I need to be sure you understand the severity and potential risks of her exposure?"

284

"I will take her to a specialist as soon as we are in America. I assure you we have excellent medical insurance and treatment availability." I spoke very slowly since she kept repeating herself.

After further review, the embassy doctor advised that Anya be seen by an osteopathic specialist, to be certain she did not have scoliosis.

"Scoliosis is a very common problem in Ukraine." She stared at me, waiting for a response.

"Yes, I will have her evaluated for scoliosis, too." I nodded affirmatively as I spoke.

Leaving the building, I was profoundly convinced the woman was a bit neurotic. I was more than happy to see a specialist in America despite her record of negative skin tests and a clean chest X-ray, and I would, of course, have her fully evaluated, just as we had for Katia.

As for the dire concern of scoliosis, I remained shocked that my daughter could stand, or walk for that matter, given the severity of her alleged spine-crippling condition. Her attempts to make me believe Anastasia was in desperate need of medical care lead me to believe the embassy doctor was somehow in cahoots with the red-haired man at the consular office. He had also tried to convince me my children were severely medically challenged, and that I just was not yet aware!

We waited patiently a few more minutes for our precious signed, sealed and stamped envelope, which I could not tamper with until our arrival in customs on U.S. soil. Unfortunately ours contained a large X-ray which, by law, could not leave my person and had to travel in my carry-on, which in London must become smaller than the size of a laptop. *Could the situation become any more complicated?* I marveled at the enormous X-ray, contemplating childhood origami techniques, while Anastasia wore a matching look of puzzlement, not having understood a word during the entire English-speaking appointment.

Relieved to have accomplished one task of political obligations for my week's itinerary, we went out for a late lunch at a contemporary Ukrainian cafeteria-style venue. I enjoyed the food selections that way, mostly because I could see exactly what I would be eating beforehand and keep it very simple. Anastasia remained picky and insisted on ordering her usually large decadent cake—just cake. It had become apparent that ice cream and cake were Anastasia's main daily food group since I had last seen my daughter 20 pounds lighter. I felt bad for Anya. Natasha had called several times during the previous six months telling of Anastasia's shrinking clothes and correlating self-confidence. I knew her eating habits would have to be dealt with at home, as that was certainly not the place for such emotions.

As we sat down for our meal, Anastasia immediately began to pout because she had forgotten to choose a drink. Natasha again told Anastasia to tell me what she would like to drink, in English. Anya perched her lip and crossed her arms for the long haul.

"Ne Znaiyou!"—I don't know!—She said assertively, in a snide end-of-conversation tone.

"You don't know what you want to drink?" I asked.

Anya glared at me and put her sunglasses over her eyes, refusing to talk to anyone. I felt certain the preteen years would be exceptionally entertaining in our bilingual household. I took my usual approach, just as I had done with all Katia's tantrums, and ignored her public drama. I continued in my conversation with Natasha in English about music. After a time, I got up, purchased bottled water and set it in front of Anastasia, who was sulking, arms crossed and lip still in full pout. Natasha was shocked and waited for a full-fledged tantrum. She explained that Anastasia did not care for water, preferring sweet sodas or juices. I shrugged in amusement.

"If she chooses not to make a decision, then I will make one for her, and I prefer water. It is better for her! Please tell her to drink her water." I asked for translation, and Natasha was nervous as she began.

"I think there is too much estrogen for his liking today!" I commented, as Vlad had exited the premises.

We peered out at him as he stood in front encircled by cigarette smoke. There, he kept watch over his precious car, which was parked on the sidewalk at the front steps of the restaurant. I could not complain about front-door service with Vlad as our driver!

Caught up in our laughter, a miracle happened as arms unfolded and Anastasia decided to add her two cents, while sipping water. It was the first of many dramas I would have to deal with, but apparently I had learned how to push her buttons.

After lunch, Natasha and Vlad were quick to change their minds about a stroll around the center of Kyiv when we received an important call. They quickly drove us across town and left us in our apartment for some down time. Naturally, Anastasia made a B-line to the television for her fix of music videos. I reminded myself of how different things would be when we arrived home as I hear that wicked-witch cartoon laugh in my head. Oh, the fights that will be battled to modify her preteen laziness. In the meantime, I made an effort to spend the time with her and suffer through the Indian-Turkish rap beats. After reaching my threshold, I shouted and signaled for her to turn down the volume somewhat! Naturally, she was annoyed, however. I had begun making telephone calls to the baggage claims of "It's-not-our-fault Airlines" in the U.K.

"Allo, British Airways. How may I be of service?"

"Hello, I am calling again to see if you have found baggage?"

"What is your baggage claim number."

"I don't have one for British Airways, my last flight was on Lufthansa."

"Ah, then you will need to call Lufthansa to find your missing baggage."

"Yes, I have. Lufthansa, never received my baggage on any of their planes, it was last documented on the British Airways flight I missed in London."

"Well, the baggage would most certainly have been removed from that flight, since you were not on it."

"Yes, I understand. However it never made it out of London Heathrow or the British Airways baggage system. British Airways lost my bag, not Lufthansa."

"Madam, I do not show any record of your baggage. Please call Lufthansa."

"Sir! You lost my bag, I need you to find it!"

"Madam, *I* did not lose your bag."

"Yes, I know *you* did not personally lose my bag, but you are a representative for British Airways, yes?"

"Yes madam, but *I* still did not lose your bag."

"Okay, British Airways, the company that *you* represent, lost my bag! Can we find it?"

"Madam, *I* did not lose your bag and *I* do not have your bag!"

"Clearly, the British take absolutely no responsibility for their actions or pride in the companies they work for. Can I just get the number to the British Airways office at Kyiv Borispol Airport, or even the main office in London—please?"

"Sorry, I cannot help you. Please call Lufthansa."

"Sir, get therapy!"

I took the handset and slammed it on the telephone at least twenty times, for impact! I just needed to be sure Mr. Deniability was aware I was hanging up on him and all his arrogance!

"ASSSSSSSSSHOLE! I screamed at the top of my lungs.

Anya ran from the sofa, terrified of me.

In the queen's English, aka high English, the words "customer service" stand for deniability. They have many different meanings for words, sort of like the way "loo" and "restroom" are synonymous, as are "lift" and "elevator," "deniability" and "customer service." The words flow from their mouths, but the meanings are completely different.

I tried deep breathing and continued my effort to find my baggage. I began with another misplaced, routine call to Lufthansa. I received a cordial apology, followed by an explanation of bad news, yet polite and apologetic.

How dare I place the blame on the infamous British Airways. I had once again bantered the snobbish attendant at 1-800-lost-baggage, although the attendant would not provide the phone number to the main office in London or the closet branch office at Kyiv Borispol Airport. It felt only natural to do some good old-fashioned research – I did have internet after all. With confusing country codes and unlisted Internet contact numbers, I continued to search on my little ibook at Internet speeds compatible with the ancient, high pitched "errr-aaang-errr-heeeeeeee" sounds, and finally came up with a London Customer Service number, with country code.

At this point, "blah, blah, blah" was all I hear from one end of the phone in response to my wardrobe-less time in Ukraine. My daughter was watching music videos again, a Turkish man singing in Ukrainian and being rubbed with oil by nearly naked women (who had apparently lost their luggage, too). I was screaming repeatedly for Borispol's number in one agenda and trying to decipher the word for "off" in Cyrillic on the remote control, to salvage my daughter's virgin eyes, as she stormed off. This American mother in Ukraine was at wit's end. I knew I was on the other side of the world, but somehow my world had turned upside down!

I had finally hailed a number from the Brits that was a Kyiv code and was not on my current hit list. I took a moment to collect myself, when Natasha returned home after her business with Vlad. Anastasia lay in her bed face down, and I sat across the apartment cupping my hands in my palms. Natasha dared not tread those waters and cautioned to ask, as I shook my head. I picked up the phone and dialed the new set of numbers on my list.

"Allo, British Airways, Kyiv Borispol." It was a miracle!

"Po-Americanskee?"—Do you speak English?"—I asked. The phone banged around before another young man spoke.

"You speak English, yes?"

"Yes! I am looking for my baggage that was lost when I flew in on the September 9."

"You have claim number?" He immediately began with the formalities.

"No, I flew in on my last flights from London to Munich and Munich to Kyiv on Lufthansa. However Lufthansa says my bags never made onto their planes. They were lost in London. It was supposed to be pulled from an earlier British Airways flight I was supposed to be on, and missed."

"You not on British Airways flight, your bags not allowed on plane. They be removed," He explained.

"Yes, yes, I get it! We all know, it is illegal for the bag to travel without me. I still need to find the bag. Can you please just check your lost and found?"

"What your original flight number and baggage identification number." I gave him the information.

"Please hold I check storage."

I waited on hold briefly.

"Allo?" a woman called out.

"Yes, Hello."

"You have missing bag, yes?"

"Yes!"

"Please show me how bag look?"

"My bag is silver with silver zippers and a large pouch in front and a small pouch on top, with a red label on it."

"Yes, okay, this your bag. You want it?"

"Yes! Please keep it there and I will come pick it up. DO NOT let it leave you sight—please!"

"Da, da, good-bye."

I was not sure how I would make the 45-minute drive to Borispol, but I was relieved. The young man returned to the phone and asked again if I would pick up the bag, and when.

"Exactly how long has my bag been there?" I asked.

"This bag is arrived September 9 at 10:30 a.m."

"But, it was illegal for my bag to come in on my original flight without me!" I shrugged, wanting to scream.

My bag had been sitting in British "Deniability" Airways storage at the Kyiv Borispol airport the entire time. The bag arrived before I did! My bag was just a few feet away from me as I waited in the airport to unite with my daughter—filling out lost baggage forms. I could feel the steam brewing between my ears, but kept to myself and breathed a sigh of relief. He explained that I would need to follow instructions to the lost and found and bring my passport and customs declaration to enter.

"Okay, just don't let it out of your sight."

"Yes, is sit here. Good-bye."

"They have my bag, they have it!" I felt so relieved as I shouted to Natasha.

"Wow, where is it?" She smiled at my relief.

"British Airways! They have had it in the airport storage since my original flight, before I arrived!" I rolled my eyes.

"I will need Vladimir to take us to the airport, or we'll need to get a driver."

As I spoke, Natasha's phone rang.

"Lufthansa has just found your bag in the computer and will deliver your bag this evening by courier." She smiled at the irony.

Not only had Lufthansa not lost my bags, but they would personally deliver them at no charge. British Airways, on the other hand, who swore not to let it out of their sight, only gave directions on how to re-enter the airport 45 minutes away, through customs. Did I mention, they let my bag go (which I am okay with, as clearly it was in better hands now). Nonetheless, I had learned my lesson and I had now saved $60 in fuel fees to Vlad. And I would have nice attire for our embassy appointment the following day. Most importantly, I would return to the United States with my bags, I hoped. But then, we were flying back through London!

Biding our time between the arrival of my long-lost guest and the dog day afternoon, we took Natasha up on her invitation for a stroll to the market for copies of recent paperwork updates to our now towering file. Ukrainian markets fascinated me. The faces were expressionless and characters were silhouetted by the colorful electric lights of the market. I realized how different Anya looked, as my daughter stood near my side. Except for, well—at that moment. I panicked! I could not see her as we waited by the copy machine.

"Natasha, where's Anastasia?" I shouted.

"Oh, she will be fine. She probably wandered up to the music store."

Wandered? I ran up the stairs after her. Do they not understand an 11-year-old girl wandering in a foreign country equates to sudden heart failure in America. She immediately crossed my eyes coming down the stairs, and I called out her name. Anastasia smiled back naively. Summoning myself back from the white light, we returned to Natasha at the copy stand to find her impatience wavering.

The line of patrons had grown and dwindled. The babushka in front of her was waving an iron fist in the air. I could only guess she was unhappy with the service when she too stormed off. Natasha tepidly tapped her heeled boots on the floor and rubbed the face of her cell phone, from which she had worn the color over time. I distinctly remembered her habit from the long nights we waited for Vladimir's calls the previous spring, during our prolonged and desperate final hours until court in Poltava. Natasha explained it was normal for that market. The copy attendant was always absent from her station. She had caused Natasha to miss courier trains and many late notaries. I asked why she had never called the number on the counter to complain.

"She would certainly be fired, and that is something we take seriously in this country. A job is someone's livelihood!" Her voice shook as she explained.

"Natasha, there are many woman who take their job very seriously—just like you! Why should a lazy and inconsiderate woman hold this job and be paid a precious salary when there are women living on the street forced to sell themselves and lose their families? Some of those women would do anything to have a respectable job like this and actually work hard to service their customers!"

Natasha pondered for a moment and started dialing the number after a long pause. As soon as she pressed the talk button the copy attendant appeared, like a genie from a bottle. Although she could not hear our conversation in English, she had been watching. When I found Anastasia earlier, I had recognized her at a makeup booth around the corner on the stairwell corridor visiting with another attendant. She could see through the glass, but not be seen.

After our more than 30-minute wait, the copy attendant was rude as she glared at us and snatched the pile of papers from

Natasha's neatly organized pile. I could not understand their words, but the tone was unmistakably harsh. Natasha proceeded to complain about the girl on the walk home, as we passed a woman and her son holding a tin can for food. Natasha looked at Anastasia and me, reached for her phone pressed redial.

"Thank you. That is the most liberating thing I have ever done." She said to me.

"What did they say?" I asked.

"The woman, who owns several copy centers around Kyiv, says she has had the least revenue from this location and thought that this was simply a bad location, and that maybe she should close it? I explained to her that I've rented this apartment very often for years and I always have the same problems with her copy attendant. I explained that it has affected my business negatively, as well. She apologized and thanked me repeatedly. She said she would never have known, if I had not called. I also told her there were probably nearly eight others that walked away while I continued to wait."

"That's wonderful! I'm so proud. Someone more deserving will now have a good job and you won't miss your deadlines anymore."

"I did feel a little bad, but I think about my assistants that help me when I am in another region on adoption and I would be devastated if they did not do their absolute best. It is my reputation and adoptive families that are on the line. I am certain I would want to know!" Natasha was silent for a moment at the forces she had shifted.

As we arrived home, we talked more about why it had been so hard for her to do. She had a hard time shaking the fact that someone would lose a job as a result of her words. I did understand; unemployment and poverty were so prevalent in

Ukraine, however, that does not make a bad seed in the system justifiable.

"Unemployment will lower when businesses see more success. If the owner of the copy business had seen more profit from this market over the last few years instead of paying this useless attendant, with no sales, she may have afforded to buy more machines and placed them in other markets, hiring a few more attendants, therefore, lowering the unemployment." That is how we are told to see things in America.

"Honestly, I have just never looked at it like that," she said. "Free enterprise is so new here, we just accept our roles are in society. We have never been allowed the freedom to complain or make a difference until now, so we continue to just accept things as they are. This is so liberating!"

"I would not be sitting here with Anastasia and you today, Natasha," I said, "had I not challenged everyone—the governments, foreign policies, the airlines! Challenge everything, Natasha!"

"Your daughter will do just fine in America," she said with a laugh. "Anya is built for challenges. She surprises me some days with her audacity, I tell you! She will certainly speak her mind to anyone, and I would have to stop her. Shelley, when we were in Crimea, she expressed to my best friend that she was fat!" She laughed again.

Natasha began telling me about their journeys in Ukraine. I realized I was much more accepting at the time of my daughter's opportunities—perhaps because I was there—there to take her home. Maybe it was because I had found a true understanding of Natasha; that we were two women from different worlds faced with unexpected circumstances, that were certainly extraordinary and sometimes much too deep for our hearts to handle. But, at that time, we understood our differences and appreciated that we did our best.

The phone had chimed several times during our conversation as the Lufthansa driver weaved his way to the lost banks of Kyiv. Apparently we were a little remote in the city suburbs, but he was getting closer. It was dusk before he announced his arrival on the drive. Natasha and I run down to meet him so that we could identify the missing bag from the lot of deliveries. The van was full, which surprised me, given time of night. The sparkle of silver caught my eye. I am relieved to have my personal belongings back by my side. Being in a foreign country with none of your belongings was awful. It felt better than Christmas as I ran up the stairs with the enthusiasm of a child.

"I am going to put a fresh pair of sweats on!" I shouted.

I sat in my room and opened my bag. The smell of the laundry detergent reminded me of Charles, as I thought of the fragrance of his clothes. *Everything is here! Airport security is not wandering around in my American brand clothing.* Yay! I had packed gifts for Natasha and her mother that I would not have been able to give her. It felt wonderful to slip on my velour sweats and soft clean socks, I felt renewed as I join Natasha in her room.

"It's all there," I said. She was pleased.

Another day tucked itself under the horizon and gave way to the moon. The conversations shifted, as the sound of glass shards on pavement indicated the onset of night. Our vodka-swigging neighbors had lit their fires and had begun to party. Voices cried out in drunken rage, and it was impossible to sleep, so we stopped trying. The reality stabbed at my heart, as I knew that each shard on the pavement held a memory for my sweet Anastasia. She winced at the noises and retreated again to the TV. Natasha and I curled up in blankets along her bed and prepared for another night of downloading information from one heart to another across languages and worlds, as our time there grew short. Natasha expressed fear that Anastasia's past was much more lurid than she was willing to relate.

"She screams out in the night," Natasha said. "I have tried to wake her and she began striking me with such rage and fear. She is always restless but the screams come and go."

"Katia, too, is restless," I began, "and she kicks in her sleep. She tosses violently and throws herself from the bed. Katia tells me she can't sleep without Anastasia to protect her because her father is going to come for them and kill them. I asked Katia about her dreams. Her father fought with her mother and hit her. He hit her all the time. 'He held a knife to my throat and said he would kill me," Katia said. "Anastasia saved me. Anastasia stabbed him in the butt with a kitchen knife, and we ran. We ran out of the house at night and hid until morning.' She tells me the story often. 'Mom, he will find me in America and kill me.' She cries in sweat and tears.

"I always console her. 'Katusha, I promise you are safe. Papa and I will protect you.'

"I would cry after putting Katia back to sleep after her nightmares. I could not imagine what it was like for them here, and we always knew Anastasia sheltered Katia from much of the abuse."

"Yes, she did," Natasha said. "Anastasia says they would be beat up at night. Katia's father would bring men over and sell her mother, so to speak. He would beat the children if they woke up. Anastasia, made sure all the kids kept quiet, and if anyone made a noise she would take the blame."

I tried to hold back tears, preparing myself for the truth, but my heart ached for my Anya.

"Did they ever…?" I trembled to ask.

"No! Anastasia was never assaulted by any of the men. Such acts are unheard of in Ukraine. It is not like America." She was certain in her belief.

I had heard that before but remained only convinced that such acts are just not openly talked about in a country with such newly defined freedoms and stringent media. It is only in America that we even publicize trafficking problems. I was certain these things happened here too. Natasha is blind to the realities of such a closed political society. I held onto the hope that they were strong enough, or too young or maybe just lucky, and I vowed to wait and see what the future might tell. I knew the girls' lives would continue to unfold in a tale of past horrors. I was left devastated, but felt empowered to carry them to a safe place. We left the past to fall asleep and get rest for our adventure at the U.S. Embassy the following day.

13 September 2006, Lost and Found

Today has been a day of gathering information and documents, and was filled, in between, with moments of reuniting. I am learning so much about Anya that I was never given the time to know. Somehow those moments seem stolen from me. I wish I had never lost them.

Anya is still very much attached to N, but that is something that I had expected, and I know their relationship will forever change them both. I hope they remain friends for a lifetime, I know, despite all our challenges, Natasha and I will forever remain close friends. I try to remain neutral in this time of change that my daughter is forced through, with yet another identity struggle— having been passed through so many guardianships in her short life. I know I will have my time to mother her for the rest of our lives. In the meantime, for these few remaining days, she often uses N as a crutch and asks her permission for a piece of cake or to watch the TV, and N will tell her, "Your Mama is here, ask her, in English." Anya is quick to shy away, and I understand, but the moment we set flight there will be no N, no crutch, no Ukrainian to look to, and we will learn our way just as Katia has done—with brilliance.

We had a short lunch outside Independence Square, and I have met my first match of moodiness and discipline with Anastasia over a bottle of water. I remembered everything Mom has taught me, which has worked so wonderfully with Katia. I did not cater to her tantrum. I simply ignored it, and she gave in.

I finally received my luggage from Lufthansa, although they got it from British Airways storage, and it has been sitting in the Kyiv airport since my original flight. I was finally able to change my clothes for the first time in four days and put on a fresh face for our embassy appointment tomorrow.

We will meet with the U.S. embassy with all of our forms at 8 a.m., An appointment that is a dollar short and six months past due.

All in all, we are taking the steps to correct the things in the past that were lost and are finding our way home.

Love,

S & A

REDEMPTION **21**

he winding streets back to the U.S. Consular Offices retraced the fate of Anastasia's moratorium, as it was so preciously held in their impetuous hands and so easily dismissed to the wind. Vladimir's car pulled up to the familiar crowd of desperate hope, which I knew all too well. Most of these people's hopes would end in abandon waiting to enter America—a day that will never come. Vladimir and Natasha offered again to walk us to the door.

"We will be okay. I got it this time." I grasped Anastasia's hand with my left and my passport with my right, and we waded through the crowd.

Although my compassion for the people was not any less real, my fury for the government before me that had abandoned us six months before drove me, by force, to the steel door. My face was stern as I waved my passport before the guard and pulled the heavy bullet-proof door open.

Inside, I began emptying my bag and pockets and presented my paperwork to the guard, who asked my name and called to confirm my appointment. I made note of the all too familiar changes posted on the walls—no liquids, no anything—like airport security, with metal detectors and security wands. A lot had changed since the previous spring, when I walked through without a care in the world, just a wave of my blue passport. With a nod we walked through the X-ray machine and were X-rayed again with the wand, before proceeding. We made the walk through the outdoor campus, Natasha and Vladimir waved once again through the wall of razor wire. I wondered who exactly was being protected when my 11-year-old-American daughter was segregated on the other side. Through each level of security, I held my daughter increasingly tighter, making sure she was one with me and my passport, as I watched groups separate and move, one by one, through bulletproof entryways. Finally, we arrived at the the long and daunting hallway to the visa office at the end. I had hoped not to meet the red-haired pessimist or the heartless military coward who looked into Charles' and Anastasia's eyes as he stamped "Denied" on her visa in April.

The room was empty as I pressed the bell and asked for Olga. A young brunette approached and spoke through her microphone in Ukrainian.

"Dobry den. Kak, mogoo ya pomochi vam?"

"Hmmm…? English, please." I spoke firmly. I was in the U.S. Embassy consular office, after all.

"Yes, you 8:30 appointment?"

"Yes, Schadovsky."

"Paper please."

"May I speak with Olga? I do not have our papers. They were left her in April by my husband when my daughters were—

separated. Anastasia was denied a visa after our adoption last spring. However, we do have the papers you requested, now."

"You paper here?"

"Yes! Olga, please?" My patience was too thin for this government, this embassy, and this consular office, in this country after everything we had been through!

"Please be seated."

"Thank You."

Anastasia and I sat in a blue room, in blue chairs and watched the chairs fill up along the wall of gold curtains. I thought of the fact that when I was safe at home, Charles and Anya sat there together, with hope, waiting for hours. It was in those blue chairs that Anya read her mother's death certificate, innocently placed on the top of Charles' paperwork. He had no idea what document read when the officer handed him the files. Natasha had been quick to translate Anya's tears and that she had discovered that her birth mother was dead. Nobody had bothered to sit and talk to her about it, the orphanage, Natash—or us at least our excuse was a lack of vocabulary. We were all waiting for a better time, not there, in those blue chairs, in that cold, blue room.

One person after another approached me with questions, in Ukrainian.

"Ne Znaiyou."—I don't know—I responded repeatedly.

I tried to imagine their stories, their suffering, the pain, and how long it must have taken for them to just get into this building and up here to wait in this little blue room.

"Mrs. Schadovsky?"

"Yes."

I returned to the front window, where a tall blonde with long hair stood—It was Olga. Olga opened a folder containing all our paperwork, fingerprints that had been so carefully notarized back home long before we knew our girls, before we knew this country, or knew of the fight that would lead me here today.

"Yes, I remember you Mrs. Schadovsky, and it looks like we have everything we need. You have your daughter's birth certificate we were told on the phone?"

"Yes, here it is." My hand shook while the very thought of letting that priceless document leave my body terrified me.

"Wonderful, thank you." Olga carelessly tossed it in the folder with the other documents.

"I also have my husband's notarized medical acknowledgment."

"That will be great." she flipped through the papers and handed me the outdated files, denied temporary visas, expired applications and a stack of faxes from Senator McCain's office that, allegedly, they had never received!

"Have a seat." With those words, Olga disappeared with our file.

We waited and watched the pleas of others taking their turn at the revolving window. A young red-haired woman sat next to us after speaking with another officer. She rolled her eyes and began hurling her frustrations toward me.

"Ne govoreet po-uukrainskee moya mama."—My mama does not speak Ukrainian— Anastasia replied to silence the woman.

The young lady smiled and kept talking to Anastasia and me in a mix of English and Ukrainian, as she pointed to her visa. She said she worked in America and she had to fly back to Ukraine to renew her visa, I think. I nodded and only wished I could apologize for my country. I wondered what it must be like to walk in her shoes, or in the shoes of any of them, for that matter. I did feel grateful to be an American, but there would always be a part of me that could not forgive what they had done to my Anya. There was an injustice there, and my daughter had paid. After nearly 45 minutes, we were called to a processing window around the corner.

"Mrs. Schadovsky?"

"Yes."

"We will have the visa ready at 3 p.m. We take applications in the morning and then it takes a few hours to prepare the actual visa. You may return then. Thank you." The blonde woman stated as though no emotions were involved, no sacrifice, nothing.

"Thank you," I replied.

I walked with Anastasia along the wall of chairs on the golden curtains, and a thin, gaunt man tugged at my sweater.

"Did you get one?" He asked.

"Yes, but I am an American. And it took six months to get my daughter's visa through adoption." The glimmer in his eyes faded, as if I had just swiped the last golden ticket.

I could not offer him encouragement. I felt no hope for him— not through a country that had betrayed its own. I felt ashamed walking through security. *Would I ever find pride again in a country I was raised to be so proud of?*

It had been hours since we passed the razor wire and the crowds had dwindled at the front door as we collected our belongings from the security entrance. We walked outside looking for Vladimir's black Rada and saw them waving from the windows.

"So, how did it go?"

"It went as well as could be expected. We'll need to return at 3 p.m. to pick up the visa."

"Okay, well, Vladimir and I have another appointment, so we will drop you at the apartment and return at 2 p.m."

"That is fine. We will find something to eat for lunch at the apartment."

The afternoon was quiet as Anya and I spent our last day there, I was anxious for Anastasia's visa, and I missed Katia and Charles more than ever. We needed our time together in Ukraine, but I felt ready to make the journey home. Anastasia and I made a nice lunch together. Natasha called shortly before 2 o'clock to tell us she had been delayed and Vladimir would come for us as planned. She will meet us as soon as possible.

Anya and I went to the playground for fresh air and sunshine, while waiting for Vladimir's arrival. Much like a toddler, Anastasia loved the wood swings. I realized there had been few such joys for her and that she found such simple pleasures in the little things. I couldn't imagine an 11-year-old American child finding such peace and enthusiasm in a wooden swing. A part of me was hopeful that Anya would never forget this part of her, which was pure and special. Another part of me held hope that she would move on from that place.

I took photos of Anastasia swinging and of our apartment—the apartment where Charles and the girls lived, where Anastasia and I lived and where so many other adoptive families will pass through. The photos tell the tale of the sorrowful nights—the bottle shards that pierced our ears and the syringes that were left along the edge of the walkway.

Vlad's horn blared through the entrance tunnel. He hadn't noticed us in the playground, and he sounded the horn repeatedly. Anastasia jumped from the swing and ran to the car. In Natasha's absence I sat in the front of Vladimir's racecar. I feared for my life, as I could see everything so much clearer from that perspective. Clearly, Vladimir had an aversion to red lights, yellow lines, white lines, stop signs, yield signs and sidewalks. However, I had never seen a serious accident there, and only heard of one on the news. It seemed odd, with no speed limits and no snow. I would probably see half a dozen accidents during my commute home from the airport in Arizona! I still could not convince myself of my safety, and I dealt with my fear by closing my eyes. I was thankful when we stopped. Vladimir smiled as we arrive at the consular's office, at ten minutes to three. I supposed he was proud of his racing stats from the other end of the city. I smiled at him with a hint of sarcasm, and with fear.

As we approached the steel door, I noted the absence of crowds—not a single person was in sight. Perhaps because they only take appointments in the morning. Anastasia and I entered, with no guard outside, and I began the routine of unpacking my bag for the guard in security. He looked at my passport.

"Nyet!"

"English, please!" I felt my face grow warm, and I was certain it was turning red.

"You no on the list. You no come through!"

"Excuse me, we have an appointment at 3 o'clock to pick up my daughter's visa."

"Nyet, you no on the list. I no let you in!" He waves his hand in a gesture for us to leave.

"Listen, I am sure you remember us from this morning. We were instructed to return at three to pick up her visa. There is obviously a mistake with the list."

"No mistake! You no understand, you no on the list. You go now!" He pounded his fist against the clipboard.

I took a deep breath. "No, you don't understand! I am here to pick up my daughter's visa. We are leaving for America tomorrow, and I am not leaving here without her! Therefore, I am not leaving here today without that visa!"

"You leave now!"

"I am not leaving without my daughter. I will not leave without that visa!"

The arrogant Ukrainian guard shouted into the phone and immediately five or six U.S. Marines ran in! Anastasia looked up at me in fear as they stood in full uniform—guns drawn.

With a rush of adrenaline, I leaped in front of Anya in a panic of anger.

307

"I am an American! This is my embassy!" I shouted.

For the first time, I felt ashamed of America and of what those men stood for. My grandfather, my husband, my brother were all soldiers! Was this how we trained our men to treat American citizens—at gunpoint? I was in shock. And I was terrified!

As he bellowed in Ukrainian, I did not understand what the guard said to the Marines.

"You go now!" He repeated to me.

"I am a U.S. Citizen and I will not leave here without my daughter. You will have to arrest me!"

He stared at me.

"Arrest me, but I will not go." I stood firmly in front of Anya.

Another Marine grabbed my arm and shoved me through a steel door, as I pulled Anya by the arm close beside me. He pointed to a gray phone on the wall outside.

"Dial the visa section at 2444," he said, "and maybe they will help you." The door then slammed, as all my papers dropped from his hand to the pavement.

Glaring at the guards in the window, I picked up the phone and dialed #2444. The phone rang repeatedly, with no answer. Then I got a message in Ukrainian. I hung up and dialed #2444 again and again. Vladimir arrived at my side, having watched us from across the courtyard of razor wire, and he asked Anastasia what was going on. She was in tears as Vladimir stepped inside to talk to the guard. I tried to tell Vlad that the message was in Ukrainian and I couldn't understand.

"It for message," Vlad said, confirming the voicemail message.

Vladimir became restless and called Natasha, waving his arms around as I continued to dial #2444. Natasha left everything at Independence Square and headed immediately for the consular office. She tried on her phone to get a hold of Olga at her personal extension. Vladimir and Natasha worked their phones, and I continued to dial #2444 over and over.

"Okay!" Vladimir said as he hung up his cell.

I didn't understand but kept calling #2444, and finally got an answer.

"Allo?"

"Hello! This is Shelley Schadowsky. I am here to pick up my daughter's visa, and security held us at gunpoint. They will not let us through because I am not on the list! Please, find Olga. I need help!" I was in tears as I begged.

"Yes. Yes, Shelley, this is Olga, I will call down, Bye!"

Vladimir nodded. "Okay?"

"Da!" I still can't breathe.

I grabbed the steel door and slammed my passport onto the counter. The Ukrainian guard was just hanging up the phone, apparently with Olga. He took my items and nodded. I glared at the arrogant, pretentious bastard, with a look that could seer hatred to his core. And I forged through, without looking back.

I feared that Anastasia had become terrified of America, and understandably so, considering the circumstances. The halls were empty and the waiting room was silent. I could only assume we were the only ones invited back at 3 o'clock that day for a U.S. visa. Considering the negligence in not having placed our name on the list, it was my guess that it was rare for anyone to return for a 3 o'clock appointment to secure an American visa. I pressed the bell, for what I hoped was the last time, and a boisterous brunette approached.

"Mrs. Schadowsky?" Clearly she was American, as my name was actually pronounced with a "w."

"Yes, I am Mrs. Schadowsky."

"Meet me at Window 4." Around the corner, she stood before us, smiling.

"Congratulations! I've heard your story, from the embassy in Poland; I guess it has been quite a hard time for your family. For what it's worth, I am sorry for that," She said in a consoling manner.

For the first time in six months, I didn't feel anyone had expressed any sympathy. I held back my tears. If only she knew!

"Well, here is your visa!" She was bubbly and outgoing, not like anyone in that country, Obviously, she was not from around there.

"Thank you!" I said.

"I don't know how to say congratulations in Ukrainian, I am just filling in from the embassy in Poland. I can say it in Polish!"

She leaned down to Anastasia: "Gratulacje!"

"Lena, how do you say congratulations in Ukrainian?"

"Pozdorovlenya." I responded to her question, with one of the few words I knew.

"Poz-dor-ov-len-e-ya, Anastasia!" She handed Anya her visa and me her medical packet.

"You must not open the sealed envelope," she said in a strict manner. "It is to be given to U.S. customs on your first U.S. destination."

"That is home." I said.

"Where is home?" She asked.

"Arizona. We fly directly from London to Phoenix, where our family and her sister are waiting." I choked.

"I am really happy for you. Good luck! She said good-bye, and her eyes welled up.

I placed Anya's passport with a U.S. visa in my secure pocket and headed for anywhere but there. I was just as spiteful on our last turn through security as I clutched Anastasia's hand and resisted the urge to fly over the counter and strangle the despicable guard. Vladimir was anxiously waiting for us outside.

"Yes?" he asked.

"Yes!"

I removed the visa from my pocket, and he smiled larger than any Ukrainian I had seen and gave Anastasia a big hug. I gave Anastasia her visa and took a photo to text home to Papa, Katia and everyone else who had given their soul in blood and tears for that moment, knowing full well we had witnessed a miracle. A sudden pounding and shouting came from all directions, and a security guard came running after us waving his hands.

What have I done now? I am photographing my daughter on the street, not them or the consular office.

We leaped into the car with the guard shaking his fist and running after us as Vladimir speeds off.

"Fucking Americans!" Excuse my English, Vlad says.

We drove to Independence Square to meet Natasha, who was stuck in traffic. Anastasia ran to her waving her visa. Natasha congratulated her and smothered her with hugs.

"How did it go?"

"Don't ask."

"Not good, I hear!"

"Nothing out of the ordinary. I threatened embassy officials, was held at gunpoint and almost get arrested, well, twice! There was the whole camera incident, and all!"

"Well, okay, we have the visa. That is good news!" Natasha tried to rationalize the severity of the situation

"Yes, this is good."

Anastasia burst out with a long story about the afternoon—one I could only guess involved the conclusion that her new mother is completely crazy and she is terrified of all Americans.

Natasha had been waiting with her best friend, who was up from Crimea. She was another tall blonde—very tall and very pregnant. I understood why Anastasia had unknowingly called her fat several months before. Oxana said nothing except to give Anastasia a hug and exchange formalities from their summer together. I could only imagine what she must have thought of me, given the differences between Natasha and me concerning the parenting of Anya.

"This must be Oxana," I said, not having been introduced. "I had no idea Oxana was in town."

"Yes, this is my best friend from Crimea!"

"Hello."

"Allo." She replied simply.

"We are going to sit and eat something in Independence Square. if that is okay?"

"Sure."

"Oxana has some business to do here."

We all moved toward the underground mall. To celebrate Anastasia's visa, I had hoped for the nice little restaurant where we had visited with Nathalie on our second day there. However, Oxana and Natasha headed toward the food court. The food was horrible, but Anastasia enjoyed pizza and cake. I had noodles in butter. Natasha was completely different around Oxana and spoke hardly a word to us. I had not heard one word from Oxana except "Allo" an hour before.

"Do you speak English, too?" I finally asked.

"Yes."

"Yes, Oxana offers the same services I do and does her own translations, too. She is the one who got me into the business and taught me everything." Natasha laughed at my silly question.

"Oxana, I have heard a lot about you," I said. "And the photos of the Crimea were beautiful. I am sure Anastasia had a wonderful time!" I complimented, but apparently I was only one trying to make nice.

"Yes, we took very good care of your little girl!" Natasha said.

"Too good!" Oxana added.

Okay the making nice session of this afternoon's itinerary is over. With a glare, I indicated my disapproval of Oxana's behavior. Oxana took cue, excused herself and attend to her business.

We took a walk around the underground malls and let Anastasia toss coins into the fountain from above. The afternoon improved as we saw the sights of Kyiv and wandered the gardens above the mall. It really was a beautiful day, filled with miracles. We stopped at an art show on the opposite side of the mall and the paintings amazed Anastasia. She wanted to become an artist—a fashion designer. We climbed to the walkway over the road above the square. It was beautiful to see the city from that vantage point. With its bustle and flow, it appeared similar to any other urban city. It was nothing like our time in Poltava. It's easier to overlook the flaws from a distance, I suppose.

"We must go now."

"Where are we going?"

"We will meet Oxana and share a ride out of town with her. It will save expenses."

"Where is Vladimir?"

"He is with his fiancée this evening. We will need to get a takci." We walked all the way down to the city center.

"Vladimir has a fiancée?"

"MmmmHmmm!" Natasha giggled.

Anastasia spotted an ice cream cart. "Anastasia would like some ice cream."

"I suppose, but she better not get used to these things at home. The girls are only allowed sweets on special occasions; otherwise, we don't eat sugar." I made the house rules pretty clear.

As Natasha translated our house rules to Anastasia, her eyes widened in shock and she began pouting.

"Anastasia says she likes sweets."

"I know, but our society is so prone to diabetes and heart disease because of refined sugars, I will not feed them these things!"

We stepped away from the sidewalk and arrived at the ice cream cart.

"What would you like?"

"Ne Znaiyou?"

"Okay, then we certainly don't need any ice cream." I walked away and there stood Oxana.

We crossed several streets over the next half-hour trying to catch a takci, with no luck. Unfortunately, it was rush hour in Kyiv, and while there were a million takci's, they were all full. The girls stood waving their arms in the air as several cars approached offering us a ride. Finally a man and his wife in a Mercedes stopped, and Natasha asked how much for a ride.

"Natasha, lets just wait for a takci." I rationalized.

"This will be fine, it is normal here, and many people give rides to cut fuel costs." Natasha tried to make the idea of hitch-hiking appear acceptable. "We'll be fine, I do this all the time."

I was shocked, that the ever-cautious Natasha would resort to hitch-hiking.

I agreed, and, with Anya close to me, we entered the Mercedes. Anastasia had to lay across us. Natasha spoke in English so that the couple would not understand our conversations.

"Do you think they are wondering which one of us is the mother?"

"I think they're wondering which of us is worth more—dead or alive?"

Natasha laughed. "No, you're so funny."

"Are we at least headed in the general direction of home, or into some desolate warehouse district?"

"This is the correct way!" She laughed again. Oxana didn't say a word.

Natasha and Anastasia played like children fiddling around. I started singing to an '80s song that I had not heard on the radio there yet. They played a lot of English music, but not *Come on Eileen*. The driver turned the radio up for me, which was a nice gesture— that, or he couldn't stand my nervous singing. Finally, we arrived safely, for only 12 hyrvnas, or less than $3 for a 30-minute drive in rush-hour traffic. Not bad, but I didn't think I would risk it again. I was ready to get back to reality.

I wondered why Oxana was still with us, but somehow was not surprised, and I anticipated a scheme in which she would be staying in my apartment free of charge while in Kyiv on "business."

"Oxana and I still need to do some business before she goes to stay at her uncle's."

"Sure. I will help Anastasia sort through her things and get our bags packed and separated for the airport security and our overnight in London. It'll be tricky."

Natasha translated to Anastasia to take all her belongings and spread them out on the bed, including her things in the bathroom. I looked over my daughter's things, everything she owned, literally– every possession. As I looked at all the little toys, dolls, games and clothes that Katia and I had put together in special care packages just for her, I remembered that Katia and I had packed it with few words, when she too, knew very little English. Now, here I was re-packing it with Anastasia, at square one again, speaking barely any English. I missed Katia and wondered how they would do together again.

"Malenkai." I tried to explain when Anastasia became confused as I began separating her piles.

This is too small, or the soccer ball will not fit in our luggage. She would have to run and get Natasha for translation.

"Please explain to Anastasia that we are not taking any of her toys or soccer balls because we have so many at home, and we will leave them for the kids you sponsor in Zhytomyr. I want her to keep anything that she got here with you or from Italy that is sentimental. I also need her to sort out her clothes and tell me if they are too small. We will donate those, too." Natasha translated and Anastasia quickly nodded her head in acceptance.

Anya eagerly filled one of her duffle bags with soccer balls Frisbees and toys and began piling all the clothes that had become to small, most of which were to small from the first trip there since we did not know which ages we would be adopting. The clothes ended up being between Anastasia and Katia's sizes, but worked out in the interim. She would hold each item up and say, "Malenkai." I tried to move some of her tank tops that she had acquired over the summer that I clearly thought were "Malenkai" as crop tops on an 11-year-old with a growth spurt and an ice cream fetish. She would shrug and put them in the duffle bag. Fortunately most of the capri's and summer clothes we mailed still fit and we folded them neatly into the suitcase Charles had left behind.

It was a tough night to go through so much with such a language barrier, but we managed to bond too. Anastasia came across all her drawing books. There must have been dozens of them. She pulled out a red cloth-bound book with embellishments and pointed out all the fashion drawings she had made. They were brilliant and she was so proud. Anya had filled the entire 120-page book with original fashion illustrations, in addition to construction booklets and loose-leaf paper. She had so much talent in her sweet mind. All I could do was hug her and smile. I could not find the words to tell her how beautiful they were. She grabbed them and tossed them in her suitcase before I reached in and collected all her notebooks and pages and tucked them neatly in my carry-on next to my laptop and her medical records. They were priceless and would not leave our side. After finishing, we chose her clothes for the airport and a change of underwear to put in her carry-on for London, with her toothbrush and Papa's ipod shuffle. We zipped the bags, and she presented Natasha with her first donation to needy orphans. My Anya was no longer in need.

With that said, I invited Natasha in my room to give her the gifts I had brought for her and for her mother. Although they would never be enough to say thank you for raising my daughter for six months, it was the best we could do. I was then unemployed and we were in unimaginable debt. And, well, they had traveled half way around the world to get there and sit in lost in found. I had two beautiful frames with starfish and a poem, *The Star Thrower*, that had inspired me long ago to sponsor Ukrainian orphans. There was one in English for Natasha and one in Ukrainian for her mother.

The Star Thrower

A couple was walking on the beach, taking in the ocean air and a beautiful cloudless day when they came upon a stretch of beach that was just littered with literally thousands of starfish that had washed up on the beach during a storm the night before. They couldn't believe how many were lying helplessly on the beach starting to dry out and die in the sun. As they walked, they ran into a little boy who was picking up starfish, one by one, and tossing them back into the ocean. They stopped and asked him what he was doing.

"Rescuing starfish," he replied.

"There are thousands of them," they said. "You can't possibly save them all. You're not going to make any difference."

Undaunted, he picked up another starfish and tossed it into the ocean.

"I made a difference to that one." he said.

By L. Eiseley

"This is the most thoughtful gift I have ever received. Thank you. My mum will love this, too. She will miss our Anastasia so much. She says to tell you!" Natasha began to cry.

"Tell her thank you, I wish I could have met her. She is lucky to have a daughter like you!"

"You sing music to my Mum's ears, she always says."

Natasha called for Oxana.

"Wait, that is not all."

"What? This is too much!"

"Never, I have brought a very special gift for your Mishka." I pulled out a dark brown suede laptop with leather straps. It had silver details, and a sterling silver "H" on the front leather strap, which is an "N" in Cyrillic letters for Natasha.

"It's beautiful. It is a purse?"

"No, It is a laptop bag for when you are traveling for work."

"Wow! We don't make such things here. I mean, wow, it is beautiful!" She ran into her room and put her floor length suede coat with fur lining on and pranced back and forth in front of the mirror.

"I cannot believe this. It is beautiful! Oh, but will it fit?" she asked, heading back for her laptop.

"Yes, it is the widescreen size."

"You're kidding. I cannot believe they have such things in America. Thank you so much. It is beautiful, thank you. Mishka loves it!"

Oxana watched as Natasha paraded in front of the mirror, and she continued to glare at me.

"Wait, I have one more thing, I brought a leather makeup box for your travels."

Natasha's eye shadow was forever getting broken in her bags.

"This is too much!"

"No! There will never be enough—I only wish I could do more!" I began to cry.

"Thank you for raising my Anastasia, and don't ever forget how priceless the work you do is. I pointed to a silver starfish on the zipper of her laptop bag. This one is for Anastasia." Natasha and I hugged in tears.

I smiled. "Now, take your things so I can pack my bags. They're in the way."

13 September 2006, American Girl

It is official, Today Anastasia was finally granted her visa. But don't worry, we only risked our life a few times to get the precious visa! I will write another letter to the department of state and wait for yet another apology for how poorly we have been treated. Nonetheless, a visa and a deliriously proud American girl—photo attached (Another long story, but V is a fabulous get-away driver!).

We spent the afternoon around Independence Square and the underground mall. Upon returning home, we prepared Anastasia's suitcase for the strict airline security and donated many of her things to the local orphanage in Zhytomyr, where N volunteers. I am not sure how much Anya realizes why we are parting with her things, but she is a generous girl. We kept all her sentimental items and her beautiful drawing books. She is definitely an artist.

With that accomplished, we are all but set to leave tomorrow afternoon and will spend a day's layover in London. Although it is not my favorite place right now, I am looking forward to making the best of it and hope Anastasia and I have one last girls' night, before uniting with the entire family in Phoenix on Katia's birthday! We can't wait to see everyone—miss you all so much.

Love,

S & A

I had finished packing and wrote my final good-byes back home from Kyiv, when Natasha approached me in the living room.

"I understand that this is your apartment, however, it is getting late and I was hoping it would be all right for Oxana to stay the night. She could share my room, if that's okay?"

"Of course, however, I will need a moment with you to finalize the currency amounts I owe you and Vladimir before I go to bed."

"Certainly, I will get my notes now."

I separated my Euros, coins and hyrvnas and broke it down to very little foreign change, other than mementos, and placed Vladimir's in a black envelope with "spaceeba" written on the front. I set out a pair of sweats and a large T-shirt for Oxana. I am at least a hospitable American!

I had said my good-byes and the ladies left to the market for a toothbrush for Oxana, while I curled up next to Anastasia and said goodnight on our last night in Kyiv. She fell asleep as I took one last walk around the apartment in the silent darkness. I was unsure if I would ever return, but Ukraine is a part of my family now and a part of me. I relinquished the demons the country had caged within me, had one last Slavutich beer and fell into a deep sleep.

REUNION 22

J took the opportunity to sleep in, since our flight was not until 3 o'clock. Natasha and Oxana were nowhere to be seen, and my sweats and T-shirt were neatly folded and left in the foyer for me. It was nearly ten before Natasha arrived, as I ate rye bread with raisins and a banana to tide me over until dinner in London.

"I was worried about you," I said. Where were have you been?"

"I had to pick up a gift I ordered for Anastasia." She handed her a CD of her favorite musician, *Arash*.

The Turkish music had become all too familiar, having heard it nonstop on the air waves, TV and in the car. I had actually grown to like *Arash* in a comforting and familiar way. Maybe it was just the hum of Anastasia and Natasha happily singing along to his songs. Anastasia was so excited, she screamed and ran through the apartment.

"I have something for Charles and yourself, too! You cannot leave Ukraine without our best vodka." It is small, so you can fit it into your luggage.

"Thank you!" I smiled, knowing I will never drink it.

"These are famous Ukrainian truffles, you will love them, and please give Katia a gift for her birthday tomorrow!" Natasha handed me a beautiful necklace and earring set.

"Thank you so much. It is very thoughtful!" You would think after all our time here we would have more mementos from Ukraine."

Natasha laughed. "You have your daughters; that is the important thing."

"Yes, I have my daughter now!"

To be on the safe side, Vladimir arrived promptly at 11 o'clock. Just as he stepped in the door, I finished placing the vodka in my suitcase.

"You will need this!" He said, and smiled coyly.

Like a gentleman, he carried all of the luggage down four flights of stairs. Any other way would have been an insult. I looked at the rotting stairwell one final time and walked around the rusty metal wheelchair ramps angled at 45 degrees. I felt grateful for the life we were headed back to.

In the car, I admitted to Vlad that I wouldn't miss his driving! "Are you happy to finally send us back to America, Vlad?"

He reached for the cross that dangled from his rearview mirror and made the sign of the cross on his head and over his heart.

"You're not on the plane yet." Natasha said.

Yes, many events leading to our adoption could be construed as bad luck, but I chose to see our journey as a series of unfortunate obstacles, on a path to miracles.

Kyiv Borispol moved into view through the trees, and soon we were at the airport. Vladimir left us for front door check-in.

"Vladimir will bring the bags in," Natasha said. "Let us find check-in and flight information."

Everything appeared in order as we arrived at the gate of no return. My bittersweet passing so long ago in March was something I had tried very hard not to forget. I had kept my promise, and Anastasia was by my side, I will not walk through this gate, or any other, without her hand in mine.

Vladimir arrived to assist us with the baggage.

"Well, this is it. Thank you for everything!" In tears, I reached over and hugged Natasha.

Natasha held back tears. "You take care. You are a lucky family!"

Vlad whispered to Natasha.

"Oh, yes, Vladimir needs his payment."

"Yes, I know. I am holding it as a bribe!" I opened my hand, which held a black envelope.

"Please tell him, he cannot have it unless we both get a good-bye hug."

I was certain bribery would work. I would not settle for another handshake. Vlad smiled and obliged, with a hug for me and a giant one for Miss Anastasia.

"Thank you Vlad!"

Natasha reached for my hand as we were pushed through the gate. "We will wait over here until you go up the escalator, when we can't see you."

"Okay!"

Anastasia held on for her life in the frenzy of the crowd. For the first time, she had let go of Natasha and was completely handed over to me. As we waited in line at the ticketing counter, we both kept looking back at our Ukrainian family. Natasha was smiling and waving in silliness and Vlad, well, he was still doing the cross thing about his upper body. I felt sure I wouldn't miss us.

Our tickets were issued and our bags were checked all the way through to Phoenix, and we headed off for our overnight in London. We stepped away from the counter and apart from the crowd. Anastasia looked up at me as I blew a kiss to our dear friends and waved our boarding passes, with a giddiness I had not felt in months. They disappear into cherished memories as distanced up the escalator. I didn't know if I would ever see them again, but I knew I would hold them close to my heart forever.

Upon our entry into customs, our last Ukrainian obstacle, I carried an agenda. I measured each agent for his or her commitment to corruption and I looked for laugh lines, defining true character, or for an expression of empathy that might result from having children of their own. With all options weighed, I chose the longer line, which was attended by a younger woman with thick brunette hair and a seemingly pleasant demeanor, and, cautiously, we waited. On our approach, I smiled casually with a look of exhaustion after my long week of chaos. I hoped for something to go right!

"Strasveetya."—Hello. I said and handed the young woman our documents, pointing directly to Anastasia's newly appointed U.S. Visa.

Then a barrage of Ukrainian questions erupted—an entire mouthful! And then ...

"Nyet, nyet."

"Americanskee, poljasta!"—I am American. English, please?

The woman rolled her eyes; nay, she hurled them from her cheekbones to her forehead and stepped from behind the gray booth. She leaned down to Anastasia and repeated her questions. As we stood in customs, I patiently waited for my 11-year old daughter to converse our way to safety. I had no idea what was being said except, "Moya mama!" It was a good declaration, however.—My Mama.

The agent, quite frustrated at that point, began talking to other people throughout the customs lobby. Finally, she returned with a very young woman who spoke English.

"She needs to review your adoption decree from the court and the child's birth certificate in your name. Okay?"

"Yes, thank you." I pulled the documents and set them on top of the folder containing all our papers. I gave the agent the entire folder, in the event she might want to search for anything further.

The customs agent demanded that her newly assigned translator remain with us.

The young woman was in volunteering her service and was very pleasant. She congratulated us on our adoption.

"Where are you traveling to?" I asked.

"I attend university in Paris," She said with great pride.

The agent talked with Anastasia considerably. Anastasia was always nervous around government figures, which I found understandable considering her excommunication from every government she had known. The agent then conferred with our "volunteer" translator again.

"Her supervisor insists on speaking with the judge in Poltava to validate the adoption decree. The agents consider the documents unusual, since they are dated back to March."

I tried to explain, but the agent turned her back and walked away toward her supervisor in a glass booth. They waved our papers about in the booth and talked on the telephone for nearly half an hour. Worried that the judge in Poltava might be on holiday, I was ready to call Natasha for help, when the agent returned. Within a few minutes, she questioned our translator, who had been brought up from the back of the line.

"Thank you, good luck!" she said, waving us on.

"Okay." Having waved us forward, she then returned all our paperwork in shambles and, fortunately, placed two stamps on both of our passports.

Despite Charles' consoling words that customs was a simple walk through, somehow, I new Anastasia's would be challenging. I rearranged what was a perfectly organized folder of adoption paperwork as we sat waiting to enter through security and into the boarding area.

Anastasia and I began our silent communication, using hand gestures and facial expressions. I yearned for the day she would speak in the words I could understand. With a fond memory of those moments with Katia, I knew it would come. Anastasia watched me carefully as I moved, curious concerning my American habits, which were strange to her. I offended her as I dropped an airborne tablet into her half-full bottle of water. Orange bubbles began to fizz.

"Sook, horoshow! It's good. It's juice now." I spoke the best I could, in both languages, and she cocked her head.

"Okay?"

She waited, watching the fizz, before giving it a try. "Yes."

After we had finished our "juice," our flight number approached the top of the list on the digital monitor.

"Toilet?" I pointed to the restrooms.

She shook her head no.

"Yes!" I said.

I certainly would not leave her alone, and I couldn't explain, "It would be best to go now than on the plane." She got the hint that she would have to follow me.

We moved into line for security. I saw no posters of banned items, indicating everything a human being would need to survive, nor were there any trash bins filled with makeup and water bottles. No signs to remove shoes, laptops, cell phones—everything. I found it very odd for an Eastern European destination coming into London. I reached in my bag to remove my laptop, when the security guard grabbed my arm and shouted "nyet" at me. Anastasia quickly pushed my laptop back in the bag and lay it on the conveyer, as she interpreted his words. With no bins and no fancy machines, it certainly didn't feel secure for flight, but where does one draw the line between there and the London chaos we would enter?

Walking into the boarding area felt like being in a large oxygen tank, I had suddenly become weightless. I knew the second Anya was on the plane and lifted into the brilliant blue skies, there was no turning back to Ukraine, and there was no turning back on her. There could be challenges in London or with immigration at home, but I knew Anya would never be stuck back here. Any problem they chose to find, from that gate forward, would have to be resolved on U.S. soil. I had never wanted to be in the air, with no land and no country beneath, more than at that moment. As the British Airway's ticket agent spoke her three words, I felt Anya's freedom was finally calling.

"Prepare for departure."

I gave Anastasia a motion sickness pill Natasha had given to me, advising they had worked best on their many train trips around Ukraine. We were settled in our seats and I was relieved for the short three-hour flight to London and the opportunity for Anastasia to have a good night's sleep before our 11-hour flight to Phoenix the following day. I dreaded the journey, but the reward was worth the miles. Anastasia did well and enjoyed listening to Papa's ipod shuffle, I had filled it with pop songs from America that Katia liked. Occasionally, she gave me a strange look and shoved her earpiece into my ear, inquisitively. Eventually, my sweet girl leaned back and relaxed, with her hand upon mine, until our arrival at Heathrow.

Heathrow is a whole new beast and not one I was pleased to return to. Upon arrival, I was a bit surprised to not see posters of myself along the corridors, with "wanted" stamped across my forehead, considering my last rendezvous. I would have to see what my passport might register at the customs gate.

Ah, customs again, with only a few thousand people in the lines. I wasn't sure how to define Anya and myself. At that point, we certainly weren't visitors and we weren't transfers exactly, as our flight was leaving in exactly 26 hours. I decided "transfers" would be easier, and it had a shorter line.

Anastasia was fatigued. We stood in the labyrinth, waiting, most likely for another meltdown from her crazy American mother. She leaned against me with a certain amount of anxiety as she watched others, like her, with red Ukrainian, red Russian and red Chinese passports. Some red passports made the cut and some of the bearers were being sent to other lines or to little glass offices. All the maroon British and blue American passports were quickly stamped and sent on their way. It must have seemed selectively cruel through the eyes of an 11-year old to single out people and cultures by color-coding.

"Next," beckoned the attendant, after nearly two hours in line. "How are you today?" asked a young agent who stood before her podium.

"Wonderful. How are you?"

"Nice. Thanks for asking." She smiled and looked over our color clashing passports curiously, but kindly and without judgment.

"How are you related?"

"This is my daughter, Anastasia. She was adopted with her sister in March and has waited six months to come to America."

"I am sorry to hear that. That is tragic!"

"We are only staying in a hotel for the night because of our extended layover. We were told it shouldn't be a problem?"

"I will need your hotel agenda, to get supervisory approval. Please be seated." She smiled sympathetically as she walked into a booth. Pointing toward us from above, she kept us hopeful, with a quick nod. Smiling upon her return.

"I can offer you a visitation visa for one year, but your daughter can stay only 24 hours, if that's all right."

"Yes! That is wonderful. No offense to the queen, but we just want to go home."

"Okay, you must wait. Your plane does not leave for twenty-four-and-a-half hours. Please have a seat and I will call you when the time comes."

Anastasia and I sat on a long wooden bench filled with other visitors and watched for the clock to turn to 6 p.m. local time.

"Mrs. Schadowsky?" The agent's supervisor called as the minute hand reached twelve.

"Yes."

"You and your daughter may enter now. You do understand, although, your visitation is for one year. Your daughter must leave on your scheduled flight at 6 a.m.

"Yes, thank you!"

"Good luck!"

With that, the second bout of luck in one day, I had discovered we were finally finding our way home.

I stopped at an ATM, hoping it would not decline me, I was unsure if my hotel had been paid in full by my parents when we made the reservations with their visa card, or if it was just being held. I had hoped I could afford enough for the hotel and a meal, having given all but $20 to Natasha and Vlad. To travel across the world on my last trip, I had $50 and no child to care for. I was beginning to doubt our ability to care for our children, having lost our entire savings, mortgaging the house and selling everything—nothing like we had planned! Charles and I had started out two years before financially carefree. So much had changed. The world had given up on us. I was terrified as the machine sucked in the card and I punched in 200 Lira, just to feel safe. The ATM machine was slower than a 56k modem. Ahhh—redemption shot out with an array of colorful bills with the queen's moniker.

Too relieved to care, we visited every newsstand and market in the terminal before finding a tube of toothpaste for the night, I had just hoped soap and shampoo were essentials at the hotel as we strayed off in search of our hotel shuttle, or any shuttle entrance. After three trips up the lift, we finally inquired. We were instructed to go through the doors marked "Do not Enter," and past "Lost Luggage." There we stood in an underground tunnel with numbered maps and a raging scent of tar and petrol, which made Anastasia nauseas. We took breaks inside and finally went back to a market for water and a snack bar to settle her stomach. Upon our return was an obnoxious ticketing agent.

"Tickets! Got your tickets?"

"Excuse me, do we need tickets for the shuttle?"

"Yes dear, 4 Lira each. The shuttle isn't free!" He laughed.

It was the equivalent of $10 each for a ride around the corner. I was beginning to appreciate American hospitality, again! I asked if there were children's rates before handing off my money.

"Only for children under 12, Miss."

"My daughter is 11."

"We'll need to see her identification, then." I smirked and presented her Ukrainian passport. I felt he was jealous because he was shorter than she.

After nearly an hour of waiting, we were on the road through the English countryside. It was very beautiful and lush with trees. It looked honest to its movie portrayals as we drove through cute little villages. I would have enjoyed looking, around, but Anastasia was tired and hungry. Our hotel was nice and very clean. Fortunately, we were paid in full, and I took note of the cozy restaurant in the lobby. I just hoped they had something Anastasia would eat.

First, we settled into our room and dropped off our luggage. Our room was small and charming, and it was stocked with amenities such as soap, shampoo and conditioner — the threatening items forbidden by airport security. Another perk, Wi-fi! I was thankful I had decided to pack my bulky UK adaptors.

I wrote a quick e-mail to Charles and Katia—our last journal entry before arriving in their arms. Anastasia sighed with each key I typed, so I made it quick, and we stepped downstairs for dinner in London.

14 September 2006, London Bridge

We have safely arrived in London and were actually treated respectfully at passport inspections. We have settled into our hotel and will go down to the bistro for fish and chips, or something—in a little while. It is such a relief that we have made it here and are far enough away from any former soviet country that feels the need to lay claim to our daughter!

Anastasia is doing well. She is tired, but has been mostly curious. She didn't have any problem with motion sickness, just a little nerves at take-off. I couldn't explain to her how to pop her ears for landing. She just looked at me like I was crazy, as I tried to show her yawning and blowing her nose—plugged. Eventually, it worked. We listened to our ipod shuffles for the three-hour trip, and she understands, from the in-flight magazine, there will be movies and video games for our 11-hour flight tomorrow, so she is very excited.

Cheerio,

S & A

"Spaghetti!" I exclaimed.

"Da!" Anya drew a quick smile. Spaghetti was one word we both understood, and her love of Italian food, stemming from her trips to Italy, was a shoo-in.

After a week of fried Ukrainian food, I veered away from meat, and opted for the pomodoro and the bolognese for Anastasia. We fiddled patiently with our silverware and our drinks, smiling back and forth when words did not come. The waiter finally emerged with a bolognese and a carbonara plate. I had to say something, as my stomach began to speak for me, with a grumble.

"Excuse me, I ordered the pasta pomodoro, please?"

"No, I have written here a pasta carbonara!"

"I am certain that is not what I ordered, as I don't eat cream." My stomach grumbled more.

"Miss, the carbonara is what you ordered."

"No, I would never order carbonara."

"Certainly you misunderstood what you were ordering."

"Most certainly not, as I don't eat carbonara."

He set the plate in front of me.

"Sir, I cannot eat a cream sauce. I have lactose intolerance."

"What do you expect me to do with your order?"

I distinctly recalled my luggage escapades, and I felt a splitting headache coming on. And I recalled the meaning of "customer service," or lack thereof.

"I am not sure what you will do with the incorrect order, however, I will wait for my pasta pomodoro in the meantime."

"We don't have pasta pomodoro this evening."

"Okay, then I will have spaghetti with tomatoes. Thank you."

In that Bolognese was made from pomodoro sauce with meat, how could they not have any? Interesting! The waiter finally dismissed himself, with the carbonara plate, and fortunately for him, I did not have an opportunity to place it on his distinctly pressed white shirt, tie and apron. Anastasia was long finished eating before I had my plain, cold pasta.

Hotel, $160; dinner tab, $72 (without the carbonara); the first night out with my daughter, priceless.

We returned to our room. Another day had departed, and I could count the hours before we would be were back where we belonged, in Katia and Papa's arms. Anastasia snuggled under my arm and watched "What a Girl Wants." If we couldn't see London, we might as well watch it. Anya drifted off at the end, and I locked up and set the alarm clock for morning.

"Thwap." I wakened as a small arm whacked me across the face.

Not a good sleeper, I had always felt fortunate that Charles sleeps silently and still. I had not expected repeated abuse throughout the night. I had started to understand what Natasha was talking about. I moved each limb carefully, trying not to wake her, in fear of a full beating. Each time she tossed a leg over me, she would land with a thud on top of me. I had been beaten thoroughly by morning, as I watched the clock. I dreaded my 11-hour flight in sleeplessness.

"Hi, Mama!" Anastasia perked as sun rays peeked through the shades.

"Hi, sweetheart," I mumbled, drying my hair from the jolt of a cold shower."

We hurried for the morning shuttle, well prepared for the security catastrophe I was certain we would encounter.

I promised Anastasia breakfast as soon as we arrived at our terminal, fearful of missing another flight and being delayed there again. I wouldn't dare risk it! We arrived four-hours early and breezed through security in about 20 minutes. Naturally, our bags were packed perfectly, our liquids and toothpaste having been discarded after brushing our teeth. With four hours before us, we had a small breakfast and meandered through the incredible shopping extravaganza at Heathrow. On my previous London layover, I had been to lucid to window shop.

Anastasia had her eye on a bedazzled "I love London" T-shirt. I thought to myself, *you must be kidding me.* The hot pink letters would always scream at me, "Detour in hell!" I felt that one day she would understand, but obviously not that day. She found a cute shirt with a cartoon emblem in Katia's size, and she smiled as she held it next to the choice for herself. I looked at the two shirts on the counter, side by side, and imagined the bodies that would define them, one day standing side by side again. I gave in, knowing I would never be invited back to that country again!

With a few more moments before lunch, and to avoid the airplane food, we settled in for some real Italian food across from our gate, where we watched the passengers in rows of seats.

As we checked in for boarding, the flight attendant was moved by Anastasia's journey. She escorted us onto the plane first. Anastasia found the massive plane overwhelming , but not nearly as shocking at the 300-pound man who tried to sit next to her. Her innate fear of men was expected, however, one on top of her was terrifying. Fortunately, he was confused, and he reseated himself, with some assistance from the flight attendant. Anastasia looked at me with big-eyes and wiped her brow in relief. Carefully surveying everyone who walked toward us, we began to feel we had won the lottery, as the overhead bins began closing and the flight attendants prepared for take-off. Suddenly, a tall, slender man took the aisle seat beside Anya.

"Do either of you prefer the aisle seat?"

"No, we're fine, thanks!"

"Perfect, it gives me room for my legs. But if you want to switch, let me know, It's going to be a long haul."

"We'll be fine."

He looked at Anastasia's ipod shuffle. "What are you listening to?" he asked. "Are you listening to something good?"

I smiled. "She doesn't speak English. We are headed home after an adoption."

"Wow, that is awesome. Where is she from?"

"Ukraine." For a long time, we discussed the chaos, the moratorium and the metamorphosis that found us traveling half way across the world on that day.

I found him to be kind. His many attempts to socialize with my preteen diva were quickly diverted, even with the introduction of his video playing ipod. His story was no less miraculous than ours. He was on his last leg of his journey home from Iraq, to see his wife. I understood their time apart all too well.

We talked a lot about America, I felt anxious at the pride I had lost in my country. There were so many things our government had done wrong. I apologized to the soldier for my negativity and applauded his service. He told me he understood how I felt and consoled my loss of pride.

He excused himself from our conversation to said goodnight with a bite of rum, and a Tylenol and Klonopin cocktail. Anastasia slept too.

I watched as the plane flew across time overseas and shifted into night. I had always marveled at international travel and the nights that seemed to escape time. It made me think of what time had done to our family. I wondered again, how our daughters would reunite from two separate worlds—one American, and one lost and holding onto the Ukraine she coveted as being everything she had known.

Grateful for a long rest, Anastasia awoke in time for supper and a much-needed bathroom break. Unfortunately, Mr. Iraq had no intention of waking up in the near future after his special cocktail. After several attempts at nudging, which turned into shoving and shy of punching, we buzzed the attendant for more forceful action, which proved to be to no avail. She helped Anastasia climb over the man, standing on his legs with her butt in his face. I, on the other hand, would just have to hold it and refrain from drinking anymore water until sleeping beauty awoke. I envied his sleep, as my body grew weary and my eyelids burned. The exhaustion began working its way to the bones as I lay awake staring out into the infinite night.

When dinnertime arrived, I could not find the strength to eat. I huddled in the corner until I noticed the aisle seat was empty. We were pleased with the opportunity to use the restroom and stretch our legs. I was certain that would revive me, and it would be the last stretch until reaching home. Afterward, I curled back into my seat, taking a moment to question Mr. Iraq regarding his ability to sleep, with a 100-pound child standing on him. He laughed and apologized.

"Maybe we will have you all over for a barbeque in Anthem. My wife would love to meet your daughters." He handed me a napkin with his wife's name and telephone number.

"We live only a few miles south," I said.

Somehow I could feel the Phoenix night air as the plane approached the runway. There was a distinct smell of cactus blossoms after a dusty rain. I felt tears, one after another, well up in my eye as I realized I would finally have my family together for the first time. The September heat engulfed the exit ramp as we shed our jackets. We walked listlessly into another customs maze. Once again, I questioned how to define us, Anya and I. We were Americans, it occurred to me. We were standing on American soil. My sweet Anastasia is forever an American! We moved into the citizen line with hundreds of other passengers.

My body felt in flames. As I stood among the crowd, I fought to keep my eyes open and I wiped perspiration from my forehead.

My hand slid across my hair, which was soaking wet. Anastasia was doing fine, so I was certain it was more than the weather ravaging my worn body. I braced myself between each metal post and alternated leaning on Anya, I could barely stand or walk as the drug-sniffing beagle weaved around us and through the lobby. When we finally reached the customs booth, I cleared the perspiration from my face and presented our passports. The lady asked us to follow her to the immigration office.

"All adoptions will be processed here. It looks like you'll be helped shortly. Have a seat, please."

Anastasia and I sat patiently as I fought to keep my frail body upright. I knew I could not show any weakness. I could not risk exposing an illness. Anya was home. She had the courage to come that far, and I would not have us placed in quarantine. I talked myself into keeping my head upright and holding on for a few more minutes.

A British woman in front of us fought concerning her tainted passport of immigrating from country to country for only as long as her visa lasted. Finally, the officer moved her aside to help us. I stood, hunched over Anya, acting as though I was holding her, not holding on. I was aware of perspiration dripping from my hair, as if I had just stepped in from the rain. I pretended nothing of it and smiled in a boisterous manner at the immigration officer. He reviewed Anastasia's sealed medical records and stamped them, along with her U.S. visa, which read "Permanent Resident." It was September 15, 2006—Katia's birthday. We had fought so righteously for that one little stamp, my heart sank for all the glory it had bestowed. Why had it been so sacred? Why had it separated two sisters, a family? I closed the passport, knowing I would never find answers to those questions.

Our baggage was waiting for us beside the carousel, as the flight had been processed hours before. The customs and immigration lobby was silent as the night grew late. The signs pointed home. The walk seemed unending, though not nearly as long as the journey. We reached the elevator that led to freedom. Anastasia clutched my arm with a sweaty palm. Although she could not speak the language, it was my hope that one day she would tell her story to the world of her mother's return to Ukraine for her and how she became an American on her sister's 9th birthday, six months and two days after their separation. Together, Anya and I had found each other, and we had found redemption, through the courage and perseverance, for her freedom.

The elevators opened to the familiar corridor of Phoenix Sky Harbor's arrival gate. Katia's beautiful "Welcome Home" sign marked the end of our journey. In a glimpse, I saw my dear Katia flying down the corridor as the security guard propped up the side ropes, encouraging her entry.

With her arms open like the wings of an angel, Katia ran toward us. "Nastiya, Nastiya," she cried out in a flood of emotion.

I have never witnessed a love so pure or as justified as my daughters experienced that day. And they had never known such tears of joy. For the first time since we left Ukraine, Anya let go of me and swung her little sister into her arms, showering her in tears.

I fell to my hands and knees in a fever of perspiration and tears as I reached the threshold. There stood my family—everyone. I looked up to Charles and my mother as they reached to pull me up. I could finally let go.

"Are you okay?"

"Everything is okay now. I promised you I wouldn't come home without my Anya!"

Those were the last words I spoke as I collapsed into Charles' arms with a fever of 104.9 degrees with the Russian flu. It would take my ravaged body weeks to return to its soaring spirit.